Laurie Cabot's Book of Spells & Enchantments

by Laurie Cabot

with

Penny Cabot &

Christopher Penczak

**COPPER
CAULDRON**
PUBLISHING

Credits

Cover: Derek Yesman and Daydream Designs
Editing: Tina Whittle
Copy Editing: Lisa Curley, Virginia Villarreal
Photos: Rory McCracken and Terra Nova Creative
Layout & Publishing: Steve Kenson

Acknowledgements: Special thanks to Jean Renard, Susan Cohen, Jean Mills, Tom Cowan, and everyone in the Cabot-Kent Hermetic Temple.

Any Spell in this Majick book
Shall not come to be if it is not correct and for the good of All.
The eyes of the God and Goddess shall be upon
all that I do with my majickal workings.
So Shall It Be!

ISBN 978-1-940755-03-8, First Printing, Printed in the U.S.A.

Disclaimer

This book and all spells, rituals, formulas, and advice in it are not substitutes for professional medical advice. Please confer with a medical professional before using any herbs, remedies, or teas in any manner. Unless specifically indicated, formulas are not intended to be consumed or ingested. The publisher and author are not responsible for the use of this material.

Table of Contents

Foreword

When Laurie and I first spoke about this book, she had recently closed the Official Witch Shop in the famous Salem, Massachusetts, area of Pickering Wharf. Like many schoolchildren growing up in New England, I took field trips and family vacations to the historic museums and sites involving the infamous Witchcraft trials of Salem. It was not until I was a late teen, however, that my eyes were opened to the reality of the busy Witchcraft shops in Salem, making Witchcraft a real, living tradition and not a closed chapter of history or something out of a horror movie or book. I was enchanted by Crow Haven Corner, at the time a shop run by Laurie's daughter, Jody Cabot, and it was there in the back room where I was first introduced to Laurie and started taking classes with her that would utterly change my life.

While ultimately the rituals, classes and celebrations were more important, the shop was a gateway to me. It literally and figuratively opened the door to a majickal world. I loved the little packets of herbs and incense, the assortment of stones, curiosities and statues. I got quite an education simply asking whoever was behind the counter what all these things were and how they were used.

Things changed, and Laurie moved from Crow Haven. She had been associated with a number of stores, included Pyramid Books, the first incarnation of Nu Aeon, and the shop Enchanted. She also opened her own shops, one prior to Crow Haven, which was the first in Salem and one of the earliest occult stores in America, and one later on the wharf—The Cat, the Crow and the Crown. Eventually she opened the Official Witch Shop. Running a shop that is more like a community education and religious resource center is hard work, and eventually the time came for her to close her doors. I feared that much of the special majick that made up her shops would be gone and forgotten.

While interested in a wide variety of topics and community work, Laurie's main joy is helping people by sharing majick. My visits to her apartment would occur while she was working on new spell designs, crafting items, or researching new ingredients. We'd talk life and majick while she worked away with a great joy. It was that majickal joy I wanted to see in a book, documenting and sharing her work in the many shops she had created and taught at. So on a Beltane evening, while discussing the state of publishing, I suggested that she release a spell book because she loved sharing the majick. She agreed, but asked for my help in organizing it, along with her daughter Penny, and thus the seeds of the book you hold now in your hands were planted.

Our goal throughout the book has been to gather the majick she has used through her history together with all the new things she is working on, and in her voice, share the teachings she has to offer. My job has been scribe and supplementation, adding connecting bits of wisdom to her oral teachings when we would get together. It has been my joy and privilege to share this time with her and to be able to share the fruits of our labor with you now. Open this book and you open the door to a world of majick and enchantment, just like taking the first steps into a wonderland where mystery awaits you!

Blessed be,
Christopher Penczak

Introduction

"Enchantment" is a word I like to use, enchantment and conjuring. When I hear the word "enchantment," I immediately see in my mind a Walt Disney movie where owls talk, Alice speaks to a caterpillar, and an alligator plays a trumpet. They are all surrounded by sparkling stars and are living in a mystical faraway place with singing flowers. They evoke a strong sense of the mysterious. "Enchantment" and "conjuring" are words that Witches can use and should use. For the layperson, they may seem untouchable, but they aren't. Majick is not out of reach for anyone. The world is full of enchantment, and anyone can conjure it. I have dedicated my life to sharing this world of enchantment with those who seek it.

What is needed in the world is majick. Some religions exclude it. Science excludes it, even though to Witches, majick is really a science. And most cultures have hidden their majick so you can't see it. You can't find it. Yet the world needs majick now more than ever. Every person is capable of some feats of majick, because majick means changing, and such change includes changing the world and the environment, lives and emotions, health and general well-being. Majick is simply change.

My dream was to open a store. I didn't dream of opening it up in Salem, Massachusetts, the now famous destination for those seeking majick which is also infamous for its Witch trails. I dreamed of opening a Witch shop in Boston, but I ended up in Salem, Massachusetts, and I think that worked out better. It balanced some of the past history there. Specifically I dreamed of opening a Witch shop where people could be taught that majick is real, where they could learn what to use and how to use it. Everyone behind the counter would be a living Witch who could help people with their problems, teach them how to do their own majick, and understand how not to do harm with majick while still accomplishing their goals. There would be visible Witches, several of us in the shop, dressed in our traditional robes. People could come to us and ask us for help. Most Witches were in hiding. There were none in Salem. They were not visible or accessible. I figured if we had a shop, it would make us accessible to almost anyone. All you would have to do is come to the shop to learn.

People think majick is more mysterious than it is. It is very scientific. There are structures and principles. It is very practical, and practical majick is what we need today. We need things we can figure out, that actually work. Sharing my majick doesn't mean it lessens my power. No one can take away your personal power unless you allow it. If you have protection, no one can harm you, so you don't worry about people harming you, though you can certainly harm yourself; your stars, your astrology, can be crossed. But sharing the blessings of spells and enchantment is a wonderful thing.

Most people who are not Witches have major superstitions about spells and rituals. They think anyone can do a spell or place a curse on them. Or they feel they have a long-standing curse or that a family member has placed a major curse on them. Most people do not have the knowledge for a true curse. And most spells do not last for years. Spells can always be broken. There is always a solution to curses real and imagined.

When the typical person comes into the shop, they come in with their superstitions and worries about the dark side of majick, and we need to teach them how to neutralize the dark side of majick, how to use it for good and for protection, and how to feel comfortable around anyone who does majick of any kind. We need to teach them about the blessings of spells, and how majick can be used by anyone.

You don't have to be a Witch to borrow majick. Some think you do, but I say absolutely not. Anyone can use majick. We teach the science and art of Witchcraft separate from religion, so you can be a scientific Witch. You can be an artful Witch too. And you do not have to practice the religion at all. There are three separate phases of Witchcraft in our tradition. You can retain your own practices and beliefs, but seek practical majick for your life. Who knows where it will lead you?

After forty-two years, I have closed the doors to my store in Salem, Massachusetts. With a store, I was limited to those who could make it into the store. With this book, I want to share all the work of the Witch shops I have run, continuing my mission to share this world of enchantment and the life of the Witch.

While so many of the spells we do are done immediately, as needed, without taking the time to write them down exactly as they were spoken in a moment of inspiration, the spells in this book have been written down. They work. These are the spells, formulas, and teachings that I used in my own shop. I shared them with my clients when people came to get a psychic reading. I shared them with my students to teach them how to do learn to make their own majick. They are based upon the science of Witchcraft, upon the solid principles of majick. They work because their construction is sound. People continue to come back to the shop and back to me, because they know my majick is reliable, and it is these proven spells and the principles that created them that I want to share with you. Some spells are from our family Book of Shadows.

Unlike the store, this book can go anywhere in the world, into everybody's library. Anyone can learn what they would have learned if they'd walked into the store, and even more. There, they might have gotten the answer to one question, but this book is going to teach them about the "how to" for every spell. I never thought Witches would be writing "how to" books, but here we are. The world has changed so much. In the past I'm sure people never thought Witches were going to open up shops.

When I walked on the streets of Salem, with the cobblestones peeking out from beneath the asphalt, I loved the cool breeze coming from Salem Harbor as it lifted the edge of my cape. You see the historic houses and the harbor, and your mind goes automatically to the age of the Witch trials, and you feel that you are a part of our history as you are strolling through Salem. As I walked down the street in my robes, I made a vow that I would not take off the robes so we would have a visible Witch. So that everyone who has a misunderstanding about Witches and what happened to Witches could have the education and know that we are real. They need the connectedness, and it's a value to them to cohabit with Witches as we have always been the caretakers of our cultures. Our communities need us, and the world needs our majick. It is good to be visible now. It is good to be walking the streets where people were once so zealous and prejudiced, where they once killed people for believing they were Witches. Now we are here to help our neighbors, our communities, and the world, to be a visible part of life.

Not everybody can always run around in capes and robes, so this book can go to people who don't have a visible Witch in their community, because they can't find us in their community still. You see, feel, and hear the enchantment wherever you go, in whatever you do. Let this book open the door for you into a world of majick, spells, and enchantment.

Chapter One: Spells & Enchantments

Whenever people think of Witches, they think of spells. The idea of the Witch casting a spell to get what they need and want paints a mystical picture and is a part of our culture. We can find it in our mythology and folklore, and in popular books, movies and television shows. Many people want to learn how to do their own spells, but often think that they can't because they are not powerful enough, because they are not Witches. Yet anyone can weave a spell if they put their mind to it.

A spell is what other religions would call a prayer. Witches think of prayer—and spells—differently from most people. We know our own very being and our own power can manifest the result that we are "praying" or spelling for. We don't necessarily have to kneel down to a deity, or beg to be granted something. Witches recognize the ultimate deity is the Universal Mind, what people have called the Tao, the Force, God/Goddess, the First Cause, and many other names. It is the ultimate power in the universe, no matter how we see it or what we name it. We know that we are a part of it. In one of my favorite books on Hermetic Philosophy, *The Kybalion*, it is called the Divine Mind, or the All. All things exist within the Divine Mind. By understanding that you are a part of the All, you can affect change through majick.

Ordinary people do spells more often than they think. New Year's Eve is a great example of majick at work. Most people don't realize that New Year's resolutions are a type of spell. On New Year's Eve, people go out. They dress up in their best and most glamorous clothes. They have a great dinner with champagne and other drinks. They put themselves in a state of fun, of luxury, and project for the future of the next year. They want to have a "good" year filled with good fortune, good food, and good times. Their resolution for the year is a spell. It's not just a simple resolution because of the ritual around it. If you put yourself in a certain state of mind through your dress, actions, and setting, and then set your intention, you really are doing majick. Every year people are casting spells without knowing it.

If you find that you are spending New Year's Eve with a beer and Chinese food in front of the television, you should probably change that custom or you may be doing the same thing next year. Go out to a play or to a show. Dress up. Do something magnificent and then make your resolution. You'll have a better year. Witches do the same thing on our highest holy day, Samhain, celebrated as Halloween by most people. For us, it is our New Year's Eve. The Celtic people started the year on this day, with the waning season, as the light grew darker. We continue their traditions, consider it the spiritual new year. Cabot Witches dress up as something they want to invoke and become for the next year. The act of dressing up on this special night helps us cast that spell with our New Year's resolutions.

Along with casting spells, a Witch is also considered enchanting. Enchantment is a necessary component to the practice of majick. It is one of those delicious words filled with a sense of fantasy and wonder. It helps you to emote and create the setting and vision of yourself as being majickal and powerful. Enchantment is the romance of majick. Romance is not always love between two people; it's also filling your life with things you love. Decorate your home with things that enhance your personality and character. Create an enchanted room or enchant your entire home. When you start using these items that you love, and do your majick in such a setting, you create a vision of your majick at work. You create a vision of yourself as powerful and majickal. You truly sense it and feel it work. Enchantments create an atmosphere of majick. For example, I have a doll hanging on my wall and an antique Victorian dresser and gold frame mirror.

Not only is your environment enchanting, your own self is an object of enchantment. You might wear make-up, robes, or even a top hat to set the mood of your majick. Right now I have my nails painted blue for the enchantment and prosperity of Jupiter. It's the planet that rules good fortune and successful businesses. How you dress yourself alters your consciousness and perspective, helping the majick. Make sure you have many mirrors in your home to reflect your self-image.

Enchantment is beyond physical objects and decorations. Enchantment is the use of words of action and beauty. You can create a picture of your majick with your words, as well as "visualizing" a spell. The use of words to bring your intention to life is an important act of majick. It's like writing a book. The words help you see it happen by creating a scene. It's an important aspect to spell work.

Like any other skill, you can develop your sense of enchantment. Words create beauty, and enchantment creates a mystical beauty, but not everyone has this ability right away. You can experiment. Play with the sounds and words that bring out your own majickal self. Read up on some folklore and fairytales. Look at the dialogue in the scripts of a play. Read through the poetry that is most evocative for you. Why do you like it? What stories and authors are most enchanting to you? The more you study and practice, the more your skills to create with your words will grow.

Through this book I will share my own secrets of spells and enchantment, using the ideas, tools, pictures and words I find enchanting, and successful, in my majick. Spells are a method to focus your intention, and Witches have studied the science and art of effective spell casting to effectively focus our intentions. Through experimentation and practice, you'll be able to use majick to transform your own life, whether you identify as a Witch or not, but as the journey continues, you just might find there is a little Witch in you.

THE RUDIMENTS OF A SPELL

While in Witchcraft we tend to speak in a religious way, for Witchcraft is a religion, the underlying science behind spellcasting is the science of light energy. The romantic words of Witchcraft do not teach you what light does, even though such romance sets the mood of enchantment. Sometimes you have to learn in a more stripped-down and less romantic way to understand the science. Mystery is important in the religion of majick, but mystery can be overrated. People need to be clear. Things need to be pragmatic to have value, at least in the initial science of Witchcraft. Once you learn the rudiments of a spell, you can then use the art of Witchcraft, the enchanting romantic language, to cast your spell. But you must always know the underlying power behind all majick.

This underlying power is what many Witches refer to as the Universal Mind. We can personalize it and call it Goddess and/or God, and many of us do, but it is also perceived as an impersonal divine intelligence, the impetus of creation. It is the sum total of everything seen and unseen. And Witches know that the Universal Mind is light. The energy of the universe creates everything in the world we experience through light. Light, both the visible spectrum of the rainbow and the unseen wavelengths of energy we consider psychic light, are the medium through which the universe is created and sustained, and the medium through which we can communicate our needs, desires, and intentions to the Universal Mind.

Our own thoughts, words, and mind are also light because they are part of this Universal Mind. We use our thoughts and words to project out into the Universal Mind. We do so through light energy, through our inner visions of the psychic, or third, eye, and through the energy around and through the body known as the aura. Our thoughts, words, and mental outlook affect the inner visions of our psychic eye and the aura. From our own thought energy, our intentions are projected into the energy of the Universal Mind. These intentions come to be in the universe, in one manner or another depending on how clear your energy and intentions are. Those with clear focus manifest what they want. Those who without clear intentions, like most people in the world, have a wide range of unclear and muddled manifestations in their life.

The rudiments of a successful spell are:

★ **End Result:** You must decide what the end result is that you want or need. What should be created?

★ **Clear Vision:** You must see it clearly in your mind's eye. Imagine yourself being there. Watch it exist on the psychic level, so it can manifest on the physical level.

★ **Tools:** Set about using the appropriate tools of majick, ones that contain the appropriate energy to project your intentions.

Together, these three things can be called a spell. They are also called a "projection" as in "I am projecting for my desire." Projection is a modern terminology more comfortable for people who find the concept of spells too archaic or romantic, but they are essentially the same. Sometimes when someone refers to "projecting," they might not be using physical tools, but the more ephemeral tools of enchantment.

The end result of the spell is the ultimate outcome that you want. In this *Book of Spells and Enchantments*, we have divided the spellcasting chapters into several popular general intentions, such as love and romance, prosperity, protection, healing, home, travel, and empowerment. Yet such general intentions are not usually enough. You must focus on the end result of what you want, unless you are satisfied with a general intention. What do you want exactly, and are you sure?

Sometimes we ask for something because it's the means to an end, and we should focus on the end itself, the result. Few people really want money, but they want to do the things that money provides. What do you want to do with the money? If you want a vacation, do a spell for a vacation. If you want a new car, do a spell for the new car you want. Letting go of any fixation on the money helps you truly manifest your desire.

To help focus that end result, visualize yourself with the end result when doing your spell. Don't worry about the way it will manifest. Hold the intention that it be "for the highest good" or "harming none" but don't feel like you have to figure out all the details. The Universal Mind is far wiser than we are, and can work things out in ways we can't imagine. If you feel you can't visualize, try to make the spell as visual as you can. Draw a picture or cut one out of a magazine. Put your face in the picture to show that you want it to manifest for you. Visualization skill can grow with time and practice.

I knew a man in Salem who got a job out in California. He had to sell his house in Salem and buy a new one in California. Three months went by and nothing was happening on either end. He was having an awful time trying to get things to change for his move. He met a Rosicrucian who told him not to worry about the details, to just imagine himself in California, in a new house, with his kids in a California school. Imagine it all set and joyful. Don't worry about the how, said the Rosicrucian, just focus on what you want. Then let it go. Go take some time to relax and don't worry about it. Go for a dip in the pool.

He followed this advice. Immediately he got a call from his new company. They set him up with a broker who found a house for him in California and paid for the move. His house back in Salem still took three more months to sell, but it all worked out without any problems once he let go of trying to control the "how" and focused on exactly what he wanted.

Tools for your spell can include various substances found in nature, such as herbs, roots, resins, stones, metals, and animal fur. They are often made into potions, which can be water or oil based. Such potions are anointed upon yourself as you cast the spell, or upon other objects involved in the spell. Stones and other objects, such as jewelry, can be made into charms. Several objects can be placed in a small colored cloth bag, often known as a mojo bag, and carried with you until the spell manifests fully. Tools also include written words that are burned or carried in a small bag and colored candles that are burned.

The tools of enchantment are also considered tools for your majick, and often used with, and without, other tools. Hand movements, gestures, and eye movements all move energy. Certain spells require certain movements, such as hailing to the Moon or Sun, or touching the ground. Some traditions of majick have classic poses and gestures to move energy.

Most spells should be spoken out loud in a strong and commanding voice. Sound and light cannot not be separated. While seemingly internal, your thoughts have a sound, a vibration to them. There are many sounds we can't hear and many forms of energy we cannot see, but they are still very real and affect our spells. When you coordinate a proper voice with your inner vision, you often don't need any other tools.

Words are particularly powerful in majick, because your words are the manifestation of your thoughts. Your whole life is created by your thoughts, no matter if you understand that fact or not. Deliberate thinking—using clear sets of concepts, words and images—is essential to spellcasting. Think your majick by reciting the intention in your mind. Speak it out loud so that not only you hear it, but you have uttered it into the physical world. These are words of power. The Universal Mind will interpret it, usually manifesting the easiest possible outcome in harmony with your words. Sometimes your words won't match your intentions, so make sure you mean what you say. If you can clearly communicate to the

Universal Mind, the Universal Mind has total information and intelligence and can find words to work your majick and make things happen. We don't know all the ways things can manifest, but the Universal Mind does.

I wanted to go to England. I had wanted to visit for a while, but had no idea how that would be possible with my bills and commitments at home. No sooner did I express that intention and cast my spell than a chemical company from the United Kingdom called me up. They wanted to hire me to do psychic consultations on the people they were about to hire. They paid for me to come out. I lived in their house in the midlands, complete with a French chef and indoor pool. While the work only took me three days, I was invited to stay for three months. I appeared on the BBC (British Broadcasting Company) and many other talk shows in the United Kingdom. I met one of the loves of my life. I didn't make any money from this job, but they paid all my bills back in America and gave me cash to go shopping in London. I got to perform majick and rituals in the countryside, surrounded by the scent of heather. It was an amazing experience, and I had a great time, all because I projected for an extended vacation in England.

Completely separate from the vacation spell was a projection for a Rolex watch. I wanted to feel successful and have a sign of that success. A month later when I returned, I got a package from my hosts at the chemical company. They sent me a Rolex watch as a thank-you gift. Two spells fulfilled in one situation, thanks to the Universal Mind's wisdom. I never would have thought of a chemical company fulfilling these two wishes.

Music is another form of tool, be it song and chant, instruments you play yourself, or recorded music that sets a mood. Music lends an emotional power. Emotions can help us project the intention. The stronger the emotions regarding a spell, the stronger it can be projected, and music helps set a clear emotional mood. Think about how many movies cue your own emotions through theme songs and soundtracks. The music at the romantic points is very different from the music during angry confrontational points of the story. The music helps punctuate your experience of the movie, and as in majick, can help enhance the experience of the movie. Our lives should have background music.

Sometimes spells work best in a group setting, when the majick is shared. Other times they work best in a solitary setting. Group workings have to be done by those of the same "ilk" or those who consider each other family. They have to be confident enough in their relationships to allow everyone to have what they wish, without subconsciously stopping each other's thoughts. If there is underlying conflict, it is best to do your spells alone. But when you do find people of a "like mind" and shared purpose, you can have amazing results. The sparks fly and the majick is successful.

WISHING, THINKING AND CASTING A SPELL

While majick might seem simple, there are some serious differences between wishing a spell to come true, thinking about a spell, and actually casting a spell, and many people confuse the three. By understanding the difference, you can decide how much energy you want to put into a spell, and what you can expect out of your time and effort.

To wish for a spell is to simply hope that an intention comes true. Sometimes this is enough, but usually it's not. Very little energy goes into a wish. If you ritualize the wish, then more energy goes into it, and if you perform your wish in a traditional wishing ritual, then you have a build-up of power from past wishes, which could make it more successful. Wishing upon a star—or at a fountain or well—is a traditional ritual that lends some power to your wish. But people wish for things all the time, and most of the people who don't have energy and focus usually never see their wishes fulfilled.

Thinking about a spell is just that, thinking about your intention. Depending on your level of focus and concentration, that can be good or bad. Many people are very clear with their intentions, and when they think about them, their mind is focused like a laser beam. Others are more vague. Some people obsess about their intentions and never let their majick go to manifest. Once you are clear, you need to let it go, rather than obsess on the details. Focusing on the end result is important. Otherwise your thoughts will entrap you in a psychic soup.

Casting a spell uses the science and art of majick. To a Witch, this is the most effective way. It simply works the best. You craft your spell using the correspondences of majick. You choose the appropriate spell tools – the herbs, stones, candles, and colors. You pick the most appropriate time to do the spell. You use your enchantments to set the mood for yourself and to enchant others. You use ritual to enter into a sacred space between the worlds, where your intention is best received by the Universal Mind.

ENTRAPMENT

Entrapment in majick is when we are not clear. I wish I could have instant success in all my spells and projections, but sometimes we all get muddled. When we get muddled, we say we become entrapped. Our culture doesn't operate on the principle of first projecting for the ultimate result. Everything we do is detail oriented. When we don't think towards the end goal of our intention, we get muddled by the details and become entrapped by them. While Witches don't believe in the Christian concept of the Devil, there is some wisdom to the saying "The Devil is in the details."

The Universal Mind creates everything we experience. It has an intelligence that guides creation. We create through interacting with it, whether we know it or not. Most people don't know it, and even those who do are not always clear in their intentions because we are not raised with this way of looking at the world. If we truly understand the nature of creation, we would not be so muddled in our own thinking. We would be very careful in how we project what we need and want. We would be more careful in our thoughts and words. If we think or speak something, and do not neutralize it, then it is now out to the Universal Mind and can manifest. If those thoughts or words are muddled, or harmful, then our manifestation will be confused within the Universal Mind, or can cause harm to others or ourselves.

Witches who think, say, or do something that they do not want to manifest as a part of their majick will neutralize it. To neutralize it, simply think, "I neutralize that" right after the unwanted thought. If you say something you wish to neutralize, speak "I neutralize that" right after speaking it. If you envision something you don't want to create, in your mind's eye, imagine a white "X" over it, canceling it, and think or say, "I neutralize that." Then replace that thought, word or image with what you truly want to create.

KARMA

Karma is technically a borrowed term as it is used by Witches today, but it is a very important and valid term. Karma is a term from the Hindu traditions and technically translates to "action," referring to the results, or consequences, of your actions. Many erroneously believe that karma is about having to pay dues for something bad you've done in a past life, but karma is really about working on your own life and evolution. Karma is the response you have to the cosmic energies you have acquired when you came to this place and time. It does have to do with events from past lives, including the things you have learned before and things still left to learn or experience. While many think of karma as a punishment, it does not have to be bad. Karma simply is.

Karma is a form of majick, isn't it? It's a part of the reincarnation cycle and the ascension to a higher mind. Through the experience and balance of karma, we can move from one state of being in the universe to another, moving beyond where we are now to the Divine Mind. If the Divine Mind is "the All," then to become one with the All, we must experience it all. Karma is the mechanism by which we experience and learn and accomplish this great work. We have all played or will play all the roles there are to play. We have all been thieves and the one who has been robbed. We have all been murderers and the murdered. We've all be leaders, and we've all been led. We have to play all these roles to understand the lesson each one brings. We believe those who are involved in more subtle and esoteric information have an understanding and experience of some of the more primal roles, but there is so much to learn as we move towards union with the Divine Mind. But in this life, we each have a role to play.

Karma is simply understanding our place in life as we come into it, and the process by which we grow and change. Karma is not personal. We might want to fulfill our personal desires, but karma is not about that at all. Karma helps us pay attention to our own lessons, our role in the universe in this lifetime.

In astrology, the planet Saturn rules our understanding of karma. Saturn's cycle takes twenty-nine and a half years; that is called your Saturn Return, as Saturn returns to where it was when you were born at twenty-nine and a half. Between the ages of twenty-seven to thirty, we are reevaluating the lessons of our first thirty years on the planet. If you don't learn and integrate them, you'll find yourself repeating them in a similar place when you are sixty years old. It's like getting hit in the head again by the same two-by-four. But if you do, the lessons at sixty are more subtle, more refined, and you have a greater chance at wisdom.

UNLIKELY WITCHES AND MAGICIANS

There are people all around you using majick all the time. They are the unlikely Witches and Magicians. They do not identify as such, and might not use the familiar romantic trappings of majick, yet they use the tools of enchantment regardless. Just like most of us do at New Year's Eve, they set the stage to create a majickal otherworldly self. Show me someone successful in life, and most likely, you are looking at an unlikely magician. Musicians, artists, and business people all project their intentions clearly to the Universal Mind. They know what they want, and they imagine themselves attaining it. They are clear in their goals. Be it the outfit they put on to sing on stage or the business suit donned before a power lunch, they evoke a confidence in themselves that translates to enchantment.

Take the time to think about the use of such skills and your own success. I bet even if you have never done a spell before in your life, you've done some sort of majick nonetheless. Now with a greater understanding of the science and art of spellcasting, you can be even more clear and successful.

Chapter Two: Majick and Ritual

Technology is the machine that puts the principles of science into useful practice, from the wheel to the computer. If Witchcraft is a science, then ritual is the technology that makes it run. While most would think ritual is superstitious and archaic, Witches know that every part of a ritual serves a purpose. While some of it is dressed in the romance of enchantment, all of it has a function. Just like all cars have an engine, wheels, and steering wheel, yet can look different based upon the style, color, model and make, each ritual, at least in Witchcraft, has fundamental similarities, though the style of it can differ. This difference of style accounts for the art of Witchcraft. Rituals and tools are not just props. Each act and tool has its own power.

You might have noticed that I usually spell majick in an unusual way. For a time the more traditional way of spelling "magic" was for slight-of-hand illusions, like those performed by Harry Houdini. Infamous magician Aleister Crowley favored the use of a "k" at the end of it, using the word "magick," a Victorian-era spelling that resulted from his obsession with the number eleven (K is the eleventh letter of the alphabet.) Numerologically, the word "majick" is the number two (4+1+1+9+3+2= 20, 2+0= 2). Two is the power of polarity, where things come apart and then come back together. It is the Yin and Yang of the Chinese Taoists, the balance of the Principle of Polarity. It is the male and female, God and Goddess, in Witchcraft. Some of the career choices of those whose life path number is a two include healers, teachers, counselors, or creative paths such as musicians, designers, or architects. Others will seek to be diplomats or advisors. Majick has this theme embedded in it. It is a creative force that can be used for healing and teaching us. This helps us communicate as a counselor or advisor. Majick embodies all of these things. Cabot Witches spell majick in this way now to remember that.

Majick and ritual require tools, and not just the tools of spellcraft. There are some basic tools that will serve you no matter what type of spell you are doing.

The first of these tools is the knowledge of alpha, a particular brainwave state that helps you access your psychic abilities and majick better.

ALPHA

Though alpha is a key to majick, it is simply a brainwave state that everyone enters into several times during the day. The only difference between Witches and everyone else is that we know how to use alpha at will, to empower our majick.

Our brainwaves are measured in cycles per second, or hertz. Four main brainwave states exist, known as:

Beta	24 – 14 cps	Normal Waking Consciousness
Alpha	14 – 7 cps	Relaxation, Dream, Psychic Awareness
Theta	7 – 3 cps	Deeper Visionary States
Delta	3 – 0 cps	No Thought, Pure Consciousness

We each end up cycling through all four states when we sleep. Many do not consciously realize they are in an alpha state. Alpha is a between-state where we can rest, clear, heal, retain information, be creative and experience psychic information, and project our majickal intentions. The way we receive information while in alpha is similar to how we receive information in a dream.

To get into alpha, I have created the Crystal Countdown, based upon the science of brainwaves and the properties of light. This countdown accesses the crystal rainbow of light in your aura. This light carries information, and using this technique will help the full spectrum of light enter your pineal gland, the gland associated with your third eye, the seat of psychic vision. It will stimulate your psychic ability and help you receive information.

To perform the Crystal Countdown, close your eyes and relax your body. Imagine the screen of your mind in front of you, between your eyebrows, where the "third eye" would be. Do not try to see with your physical eyes, but your mind's eye, seeing as you would in a daydream. Visualize each color and number on the screen of your mind as you count down to a deeper state.

THE CRYSTAL COUNTDOWN

Sit quietly in a chair and close your eyes. Take a deep breath and relax. Relax all the muscles around your eyes and eyelids. Relax your jaw. Feel the warmth on the top of your head and feel warmth over your forehead down your face and shoulders, down your spine, over your arms and fingertips. Feel the warmth down your thighs and your shins, over and under your feet. Relax.

Now you will go into alpha level. We will use the Crystal Countdown. Look up at the screen of your mind's eye, with your eyes closed, and relax. You are using your brain and not the muscles in your eyes. Look at the screen of your mind.

See the number seven, and see the color red.
See the number six, and see the color orange.
See the number five, and see the color yellow.

Number four is green, see the color green.
Number three is blue, see the color blue.
Number two is indigo, see the midnight sky.
Number one is orchid, see the orchid.

You are now in alpha level.

I will now count from ten to one, at which time you will be in a more perfect level.

Ten, nine, eight, seven, six, five, four, three, two, one.

You are now at your innermost level where everything you do will be accurate and correct, and this is so.

Perform your majick or psychic work at alpha and when done, count up.

To count up, erase your screen with your hand. Give yourself health clearance by placing your hand above your head, and with a sweeping motion, bringing it down in front of your body. At your solar plexus, push the hand out and away from the body. Count from 1 to 10 without colors. Count from 1 to 7 without colors. Open your eyes.

A useful technique is to program your Instant Alpha Trigger. When in alpha, cross your index and middle figure and declare: "Whenever I cross my index and middle fingers, it will be a trigger for Instant Alpha." I use it for:

★ getting parking spaces
★ relaxation, better health, and blood pressure reduction
★ better reading comprehension and retention
★ remembering important information from lectures or conversations
★ better recall while taking tests
★ removal of bad habits and development of correct behavior

★ anything my mind creates as a use

Afterward, say:

"I ask this be correct and for the good of all."

Now when you do spells and rituals, you can perform your Instant Alpha Trigger while casting the spell, or count down into a lighter alpha state where you can still light candles and speak majick words.

ALTAR TOOLS

The tools of Witchcraft are the parts, the pieces involved in the technology of ritual. We use the tools because they can focus particular types of energy and help us create space. While a Witch can do majick without tools, they can make things easier and clearer. Just as someone doesn't need a car to travel a hundred miles, having the tool of "wheels" attached to car, bike or another device does make it easier than walking.

The following tools are the most important for general spell casting:

Altar – The altar itself is necessary for spells. What surface will you use for your workspace? It could be the kitchen table, counter, coffee table, or bureau – any flat surface with enough room. Some Witches have an altar specifically just for their majick. I used my bureau for years, though for larger rituals, it was more comfortable to set up on the kitchen or dining room tables.

Altar Cloth – Place a piece of fabric on top of your altar surface, beneath your tools. Cotton is ideal as a natural fabric, and it cuts easily without the need to be hemmed. Don't bother to hem most of your altar cloths. If you are a working Witch, they will soon be covered in wax and need to be replaced. The altar cloth color can be coordinated with the color of the planet associated with your ritual. For an all-purpose altar cloth, choose black. Black is the culmination of all colors and draws in all universal colors.

Wand – A majick wand is usually a length of wood that has been charged to create the sacred space of the majick circle. It can help focus your energy. While wands come in all sorts of sizes and styles, you don't need a long huge wand to be effective. The type of wood can affect the majick of the wand. Many Witches prefer apple wood because it is the sacred wood of Witches. The apple has a pentacle of seeds in the middle of it. Apples and pomegranates are sacred symbols of the Goddess. When you work with them, you are attuned to the Goddess' energy. Other sacred woods include oak, willow, ash, and hawthorn. Modern wands are often crafted from crystals, glass, metal tubing, and clay. All of these substances have their own properties and majick, but traditionally a wand is made from wood.

Thurible – A thurible is an incense burner, a vessel in which to burn charcoal and sprinkle loose grain incense made from herbs, resins, and woods. Most homemade incense will require a thurible or similar tool. Thuribles can be made from any dish or bowl. Put a few pebbles at the bottom and then sand. The stones and sand will absorb and diffuse the heat of the charcoal. If you use enough stones and sand, you could even make a thurible out of a decorative crystal bowl, though traditionally they are brass bowls, or now, small iron cauldrons. To prevent marking your altar top or counter, find a heat resistant substance, such a disc of marble available at most kitchen shops, or a trivet, which will also help diffuse the heat at the bottom. Don't burn your altar top. Small discs of charcoal available at Witch supply shops are then lit and placed upon the sand, and then incense is sprinkled upon them to make smoke. Stick incense can also be stuck upright into the sand, with the vessel catching the falling ashes. In spellcraft, the incense is usually matched to the intention of the spell.

Athame – An athame is a ritual knife, traditionally double-edged with a dark handle. Today, modern Witches use a variety of athames, including those made from crystals and gemstones. A small sharp athame is needed for carving candles.

Candle Holder – Many spells require the burning of candles. A good set of multiple candle holders is needed for spellwork. Brass candle holders are the best, but pewter is also good. Both are good conductors of majickal energy. Avoid glass, as glass candle holders will often crack with the extra heat and energy of the majick.

Candles – A variety of colored candles are useful for most spellcraft. The flickering light is the element of creation.

Matches – Traditionally matches, not lighters, are used in majick. Lighters have too many unknown variables, from the chemistry of the lighter fluid to the plastic of the casing. Plastic is a petroleum product, ruled by Neptune, the planet of illusions and deception. It's best not to have such energy in your circle unless it's been cleansed and charged. Matches with no writing upon them are ideal for majick.

Paper – Paper, or fancier parchment, is necessary for spells that require a spell to be written. The only time I'll tell you not to "go green" is with spell papers. Don't use recycled paper for spells, as they have the previous energy and intention from their writing. Make sure there is no watermark or writing upon your spell paper, nothing that will interfere with your majick. Use fresh, new paper. Paper colors and inks, like altar cloths, can be coordinated to the color associated with the intention of the spell.

Potions – Bottles, for the potions you create, are necessary for long-term serious spellcraft. Potions are used to anoint candles and objects, as well as yourself, for majickal effect.

Other tools are more religious in orientation, for specific types of rituals. They include:

Chalice – A chalice is a vessel for water, used for sacramental drinks and for pouring out libation offerings to the Earth, gods, and ancient ones. It is usually placed in the West of the altar and can be made from silver, glass, or crystal.

Peyton – A peyton, or paten, is traditionally a ritual dish to hold sacred cakes for sacrament. In Witchcraft, it is usually a disc with a pentagram upon it, used as a focus for energy. Items can be placed upon the peyton to focus their majickal energies. You can cut out a paper peyton if you wish.

Bell – A bell can be charged to call to a specific energy or deity. Often the material the bell is made from will help determine the kind of energy or entity it can call.

Statues – Statues of specific deities you feel close to can be placed upon the altar.

Cleansing and Charging

All the tools must be cleansed and charged prior to use. To cleanse an item is to remove any unwanted, incorrect energy from the tool. The energy might come from previous owners, from the environment where it was found, or from past intentions. A tool can be cleansed by anointing it with protection potion, salt and water, or by passing it through sacred smoke such as storax or frankincense and myrrh. Energies can also be cleansed and neutralized through thought and intention alone, passing your hands over the item while you're in instant alpha, wiping away unwanted energies.

Items are charged by putting the energy of a specific intention into them. If you are using the tool or ingredient in a love spell, you are going to charge it for love. If you are doing money majick, you will charge it for money. General tools can be charged with a general intention for majick, not a specific intention. Thinking and speaking your intention when holding the object, while filling it with the energy of your intention, is sufficient to charge a cleansed object.

Tools can also be "fixed" with an intention placed upon it that the charge does not change or become altered over time by other people. Once you have charged an item, you can add the intention of fixing it at the end of the process.

SETTING UP THE ALTAR

The altar is set up to make the casting of your majick as simple and easy as possible. The altar faces the North , a direction of power associated with the Goddess. Generally items that are associated with elements are placed in the direction of the element, though for simple spell casting, having tools for all the elements is not always necessary. North is Earth, and a stone or bowl of salt can represent Earth. Fire is in the East, and a candle is usually a good representative of Fire. Air is in the South, and an incense thurible or a feather is an excellent symbol of Air. The West is for Water, and the chalice or bowl goes in the West. In the center are the working tools necessary for the spell, along with a black candle on the left, a white candle on the right, and a working candle for the ritual's intention in the center.

Cabot Altar (courtesy of Enchanted in Salem – Salem, MA)

SPIRITS IN MAJICK

Some spells require you to call upon spirits to help you in your majick. While spirits are not tools in the traditional sense, they are allies and partners in our majick. Spirits can be incredibly helpful because they can see things from a bigger perspective. It's like Alice in *Through the Looking Glass*. Spirits can see what we don't see. Their thinking is different from our own thinking and perceptions. Things we may not think of as being good or bad, they can know more about. Some might even be able to see into the future. While Witches and magicians can see into the future, we often don't see our own clearly, and various spirits can help warn us because they can see clearly. Some spirits, such as the Knockers (see **Chapter Four**), warn us of unseen danger. They are a type of faery that will bang on the door or wall to alert you to danger, or wake you up if you are asleep and there is harm, if you ask them to do so.

Many kinds of spirits can help us with our majick. These are but a few:

Faeries – Faeries come in all shapes and sizes. The word "faery" is a catch-all name for many different types of nature-based spirits dwelling in a dimension close to our own. They are the little people of Celtic myth. Witches of Celtic descent are said to have Faery blood within. As a little girl, I used to give food to the faeries when my family lived in California. I would make beds under the rose bushes. Though it was many years later when I saw the faeries, as a child, I knew and believed.

Elves – Elves are spirits connected intimately with nature. They dwell on another plane, like the faeries, but are taller and do not fly. They walk and talk like humans, and many could be mistaken for beautiful, majickal humans. Some believe that such elves can sometimes walk among us, walking between the worlds at will. They can live among us for a time, and you'd never know it.

Gnomes & Dwarves – Gnomes are nature spirits like faerie and elves, but appearing smaller, stockier and more concerned with the deep earth. They are considered spirits of good fortune and prosperity because of their ability to dig up the riches of the land, but must be respected to gain their friendship.

Dragons – Dragons are powerful spirits connected with the life force of the planet. They encircle the globe and can move deep underground or up into the air. Dragons are said to guard treasures, and exist in a dimension very close to ours, affecting our lives sometimes for good and sometimes for ill. Some see them as cosmic entities, beyond the Earth. You can call upon four dragons for the four directions when in a majick circle.

Animals – Animals are primordial powers associated with nature, the land, and the gods. Each animal has a special lesson and message for humans. Animal spirits can be called upon for the four directions to help you in your majick circle. A common combination of animals in the

Cabot tradition is to call the Stag in the north, Red Fox in the east, Crow in the South, and Salmon in the West.

Ancestors – Many spirits are actually your ancestors, but sometimes the ones you knew in life will be willing to help you after they cross over. Family members, friends, and loved ones can be connected with from the other side and help protect us as we perform our majick. It's even better if the loved one was a Witch in this life.

Ancient Witches – The Ancient Witches, also known as the Ancient Ones, are the Witches from the past who guide us here and now. If you are initiated into a Witchcraft tradition, they are your ancestors, but they stretch back all the way through time, to the first ancestors of Witchcraft. They can help support you and teach you in your majick.

Heroes & Deities – Many of the most powerful spirits are found in folklore and mythology. The heroes of our cultures and in Witchcraft, particularly the heroes of the Arthurian myth, are our ancient ancestors and can be called upon by name for aid. While some see the gods and goddess of ancient myth as personifications of powerful aspects of nature —such as the Earth, Moon and Sun—many are also our most ancient ancestors, revered for so long that they became our gods. Witches in the Cabot Tradition call upon the gods of the British Isles, including the gods of England, Ireland, Scotland and Wales, along with the earlier gods of ancient Gaul. Different heroes and deities have specialties, and it's good to call upon those to aid you with their specialty.

Spirits can be called on for help in the Majick Circle ritual or asked through simple poetic invocations for their aid. If you call them with an open heart and a clear intention to harm none, they will hear you and help when they can.

THE MAJICK CIRCLE OF THE CABOT TRADITION

The Majick Circle is a ritual to create sacred space, a temple between the worlds. When someone is between the worlds, they are more in tune with the creative powers of the Universal Mind and able to speak to the Universal Mind, gods, ancestors, and spirit guides more clearly. Their vibration is more in tune with these divine intelligences.

Other names for this type of sacred space include the Witch's Circle, as Witches are known for dancing in a circle and doing their majick in circles since ancient times. Others call it the Moon Circle, as the Full and New Moon ritual celebrations use the circle ritual. Much of our majick is "ruled" by the Moon. When you want to manifest something, you do your spells when the Moon is waxing. When you want to banish or diminish something, you do your spells when the Moon is waning. Astrological calendars usually mark the Moon's passage in four quarters, and these four quarters can be used specifically for certain types of majick.

First Quarter	Waxing	Crescent to Half	New beginnings, slow manifestations
Second Quarter	Waxing	Half to Full	Powerful and immediate manifestation
Third Quarter	Waning	Full to Half Dark	Slow release and diminishment
Fourth Quarter	Waning	Half Dark to All Dark	Immediate banishment and removal

The circle of the Witches and Magicians is not unlike the rituals of other traditions that honor the four directions, such as the Medicine Wheels and ceremonies of the North and South American Indians. The most simple ceremonies found in majickal cultures across the world honor the four directions.

While there is no one way to create sacred space, each tradition of Witchcraft and majick has its own style and technique. Ancient Witches and magicians most likely had their own unique formulas. You only have to look at medieval grimoires, books of majick, to see a variety of circles, often marked upon the ground. It was not until the modern times that people began to codify and formalize the Majick Circle. Witches in the Cabot Tradition have their own methods of creating the circle. Those who are High Priestesses and High Priests of the Cabot Tradition often cast the circle with the light of their sword, filled with the light of Excalibur passed to them during their initiation. Those learning the spellcraft of the second degree cast the circle with a wand. Here is a simple circle technique adapted from the Cabot Tradition.

THE MAJICK CIRCLE

Set up your altar with all necessary tools facing the North.

Anoint your wrists, brow, and back of the neck with protection potion. If you have not yet made a protection potion, use a mix of salt and water. This will help clear you of incorrect energies prior to the ritual, similar to other traditions that use sage to smudge before ritual.

Holding your wand and facing North, visualize a beam of light coming out of the tip of the wand, coming from your own focused energy. With this laser-like light, trace a perfect circle of light around you. With this first circle, say:

"I cast this circle to protect us from any and all positive and negative energies and forces that may come to do us harm."

Repeat this step, tracing a second circle of light over the first. Do this in silence.

Repeat this again, tracing a third circle of light over the second.

Bless the circle with the words:

"This circle is cast, so mote it be."

You will complete the third circle facing North. Bow to the North, acknowledging its power and the sacred circle, and tap the altar three times with your wand.

We empower the circle calling the four quarters and elements. The guardians of the elements in this ritual are the dragons of the directions, ancient primal powers that can aid us in our majick.

Other rituals call upon animals or elementals. For simple majick, hold out your left hand to invite energies into the circle, and your right hand to release. If you are doing more formal or religious ritual, you can hold up a peyton (also spelled paten), a ritual disc or dish with a pentacle upon it, to open to the energies of the four directions.

Hold up the outstretched fingers of your left hand, like a five-pointed star, face the North and say:

"Dragon of the North, Power of Earth, we welcome you to this circle. So mote it be."

Turn clockwise, face the East with the outstretched fingers of the left hand, and say:

"Dragon of the East, Powers of Fire, we welcome you to this circle. So mote it be."

Turn clockwise, face the South with the outstretched fingers of the left hand, and say:

"Dragon of the South, Powers of Air, we welcome you to this circle. So mote it be."

Turn or move clockwise, face the West with the outstretched fingers in the left hand, and say:

"Dragon of the West, Powers of Water, we welcome you to this circle. So mote it be."

Acknowledge Spirit when you return to the front of the altar by saying:

"And Spirit, always with us. So mote it be."

If you are using a peyton, place it back upon the center of the altar.

The blessing of the circle, often considered the sacrament or mystery, is based upon the Celtic concepts of the Otherworld and inspiration. It is not necessary for all spellcraft, but is a quite beautiful and empowering part of the ritual. While facing North at the altar, hold your arms up in a receptive position. Say:

"This is Tara (lift left hand), this is Avalon (lift right hand). I am Sovereign in this space. We are Sovereign in this space."

Hold your wand or athame with a triangular grasp in both hands. Raise it up and say:

"I draw into this circle and water all of the most correct and harmonious energies of the universe."

Keeping the grasp as it is, stir the water clockwise three times. Say:

"I bless these waters, the waters of life."

Touch your thumb to the water, then to your lips three times. Raise the cup and say:

"A libation to the Gods and the Ancient Ones. Iska Ba!"

Replace chalice in the West.

Anoint your black candle three times from the top down, saying:

"I anoint this candle with the energies of the Goddess."

Light the candle saying:

"I strike this candle with the light of the Goddess. So mote it be."

Anoint the white candle on the right side of the altar three times from top down, saying:

"I anoint this candle with the energies of the God."

Light the candle saying:

"I strike this candle with the light of the God. So mote it be."

Anoint and charge your working candle, referencing the attributes of work to be done. Different colored candles are coordinated with different intentions (see **Chapter Three**).

Perform your spells and enchantments at this time. Once the working is done, we thank the gods and ancient ones.

Release the quarters by starting in the North, holding up your right hand (or peyton) and saying:

"Dragon of the North, Power of Earth, thank you for joining us tonight. So mote it be."

Move counterclockwise to the west, hold up your right hand (or peyton) and say:

"Dragon of the West, Power of Water, thank you for joining us tonight. So mote it be."

Move counterclockwise to the south, holding up your right hand (or peyton) and say:

"Dragon of the South, Power of Air, thank you for joining us tonight. So mote it be."

Move counterclockwise to the east, holding up your right hand (or peyton) and say:

"Dragon of the East, Power of Fire, thank you for joining us tonight. So mote it be."

Release the circle by moving counterclockwise around the circle with the wand and saying:

"The circle is undone and not broken."

The majick circle can be cast inside or outside. Ideally you should be in a location where you won't be disturbed by anyone. Many Witches have a room dedicated to majick, to be their temple, but most of us do not have that luxury. If indoors, you should cleanse the space thoroughly with incense and use your Instant Alpha Trigger to neutralize any unwanted forces by envisioning an "X" through them. The circle can be imagined to be a perfect size, going through the walls if necessary, since most rooms don't accommodate a full circle. Be sure to neutralize anything within the walls that might inhibit your majick.

Outdoor circles can seem more powerful to many of us, as there is nothing separating us from the flow of power through nature. A place where the elements touch is best, such as a windswept hill or near a flowing stream in the woods. Any place that is sacred and majickal to you, that inspires you, is an excellent place to create your circle and perform your spells and celebration.

Chapter Three: The Majickal Apothecary

A good Witch keeps a well-stocked supply cabinet of all her ingredients. Witchcraft shops often carry the unusual, hard-to-find items that we might want to use in our majick, connecting us to our ancestors, for they used such unusual ingredients in their apothecaries. Rich resins, majickal woods, brilliant stones, and oils have long been a part of the majickal arts of the Witch. Yet our ancestors also used what was available to them. When I began my path, there were no Witch shops, so I had to use what I could find at the supermarket, in the spice rack, and outside in the fields and forests.

THE BLESSINGS OF NATURE

Majickal spells can call for special ingredients through the concept of correspondence. In *The Kybalion*—a book of Hermetic philosophy used by Witches in the Cabot Tradition to better understand the universe, majick and our relationship with the All—the Principle of Correspondence is: "As above, so below. As below, so above." It means that patterns repeat themselves, and the unseen energies of the heavens above can be found in nature below. Astrology—and astrological majick— is the science and art of understanding this correspondence in our lives and majickal paths.

Certain substances in nature reflect the psychic light, the vibration, of certain planets and stars. They are said to "correspond" with each other. Light exists in the aura of all things. Everything has a field of light energy, an aura, that carries its own information and intention. This light corresponds with the light of the heavens. If you want to harness the energy of the Sun for success or health, it can be helpful to hold something that also carries the light of the Sun strongly within its aura. If your spell includes a lot of things that correspond with the light of the Sun, you can have a strong presence of the Sun's energy for your intention.

Nature is particularly good at holding a pure light, a pure vibration. Humans are easily influenced by all of the planets and stars, and likewise, everything else is too, but herbs, woods, stones, metals, and animals have a very pure consciousness, a very pure aura, and are able to anchor specific vibrations from one or two different planets. We say that a majickal ingredient is "ruled" by a particular planet or sign.

In particular, these astrological energies in the world, in the "below" of our Principle of Correspondence, best resonate with the elements. Along with astrological correspondences, majickal ingredients also have elemental correspondences. The four elements of western majick are associated with the four directions and each embodies archetypal forces best described in the form of the element.

Water
Emotions, Love, Healing, Relationships, Family, Home, Nurturing, Flow, Psychic Ability

Fire
Will, Light, Drive, Passion, Career, Energy, Life Force, Creativity, Sexuality, Spirituality

Earth
Sovereignty, Law, Body, Physical World, Finance, Money, Prosperity, House, Health

Air

Truth, Life, Communication, Information, Knowledge, Breath, Perception, Memory

Sending the remains of our spell out into nature influences the spell. Scattering it to the winds can bring us information or send a message. Burying things helps them to either wither and rot away, returned to the land, or grow longterm roots for deep results. Releasing things to the water helps us heal and connect. Stagnant water helps us remove and reduce, like a swamp. Fresh water brings blessings, and ocean water is best for deep healing and cleansing. Burning things releases their energy, and the ashes can always be disposed of through one of the three other elements.

Our actions in ritual are a way to also correspond with our intention. If we want to stop something, neutralize it, we can freeze the object of our spell. If we want to make something flow, we melt it. If we want to bring something together, we literally bring the parts of the spell together. If we want to separate things, we literally break them apart. Ingredients in the natural shape of things we want to influence or heal are another form of correspondence. Working with lungwort can help heal the lungs. Solomon's seal root looks like a spine and is good for the back. Herbal healers, such as the famous alchemist and doctor Paracelsus, called this the Doctrine of Signatures, but Witches and tribal healers knew it for centuries before him. We can even see the planet's traditional colors, their majickal light, in the color of flowers, saps and oils, and in the minerals within stones and metals.

While spells are important, finding harmony with nature is even more important. Nature and the Universal Mind are the greatest teachers. One reflects the other. We all need to be conscious of nature in our daily lives and seek to attune to it. Pay attention to the rising and setting of the Sun, the coming and going of the tides, and the alignment of the stars. Feel the rise and fall of the cycles. Knowing where Venus and the Big Dipper are in the sky is a majickal act, just as much as any spell. Just being cognizant of their presence in the heavens, knowing what is up there above your head, changes you for the better.

From the great cycles of the above, bring it down below. Be regional about your majick. If you want to attune to your own location, use objects you gather locally. The flower petals, sand, and stones of your own town will be best. They will affect you, and you will affect them. Here in Salem, Massachusetts, mugwort is everywhere. You can also quite easily find St. John's wort, Queen Anne's lace, yarrow, and thistle. They grow right in the cracks of the streets, in the public green spaces, and near the roads. Learn your regional plants first. What are they used for?

What kinds of trees grow in your area? If you can't identify them through a book, call your local city planner and ask what is growing right on the streets and public parks. Call your local Audubon Society. There are many resources for us. If trees were felled during a lightning storm, can you get some bark? If you can't get to the fallen trees, do you know where they dispose of them? Lightning-struck wood, especially oak, is very powerful. Learn the patterns of your community along with your nature.

Then learn what is beneath your feet. What is below you in your own area? Volcanic rock will have a different light energy than a sandstone formation. Granite feels different than clay and will influence the people and communities that live upon it. When you know that, you can better understand some of the influences on the very different communities that can develop in your country.

Nature provides some of the greatest allies in majick in the form of majickal plants, stones and animals. Below is a guide to some wonderful ingredients, both traditional and modern, that I always have stocked in my own apothecary. I can find them at the store, available for all, and keep them in my own home for my majick and the making of my majickal products.

HERBAL MAJICK

An herb is technically any plant with a majickal or medicinal use to it. Many of the most powerful herbs are considered weeds by most gardeners, but it is often in the wild things that the power of nature is strongest.

When a Witch talks about majickal herbs, we include:

Green Plants – fresh dry plants consisting of roots, stalks, leaves, flowers or seeds. Some recipes might call for just part of the plant, such as the root, while others don't specify. Often the majickal and medicinal action of the root is different than the flower.

Woods – The bark of trees is used both majickally and medicinally. Some woods form a base for incense, and others have specific majickal properties.

Resins – Resins are the gummy excretions of trees and bushes that often dry to a harder mass. Droplets often form into hardened "tears." Resins are rich in essential oils, and often smell strong and pleasant when burned upon charcoal, liquefying before burning off.

Oils – Oils refer to both essential oils and base oils. Essential oils are powerful volatile chemicals extracted from large amounts of plant matter. They are extremely concentrated and aromatic, and usually have to be diluted with a base oil. They are used in aromatherapy practices. Base oils are usually liquid extractions of vegetable fats from the seeds or fruits of plants. Olive oil, apricot kernel, and grape seed oil are common base oils in majick and aromatherapy. Jojoba oil is ideal as it is technically not an oil, but a wax, and will not degrade as quickly as these other oils. Some majickal practitioners will use mineral-based oils or petroleum-based oils or jellies in majick, but this is not recommended.

Fixatives – Fixatives are substances that help mixtures retain scent and prevent the mixture from spoiling. Witches will use salt to prevent herbal potions made with a water base from fermenting and decaying, though several other substances can help preserve the potion or oil and its scent. Fixatives include orris root, frankincense, copal, balsam, sandalwood and clary sage. When making an ointment, petroleum jelly, vegetable fat and beeswax are considered fixatives as well. Vitamin E, while not a true fixative in terms of scent, can help preserve blends of essential oils and ointments. Add a few drops to any oil-based potion or ointment.

A Witch can gather and dry her own herbs for majick, either from a cultivated garden or in the wild. If gathering in the wild, a practice called wildcrafting, never pick more than one third of the herb available. Traditionally herbs are cut with a special knife, often copper as some folklore says that herbs are better for majick if no iron or steel touches them. Sometimes a crescent sickle or white-handled knife is used to cut herbs for majick. Yet I know other herbal Witches who harvest with a sharp pair of scissors.

Herbs must be dried, if they are not used in majick right away. If they are not dried properly, they will grow moldy. Herbs can be gathered by the stems, tied with string or elastic, and hung upside down to dry. If delicate flowers and seeds can fall, the bunch of herbs can be hung inside a paper bag, cut with slits for air around the herbs, so any seeds and flowers that fall will dry at the bottom of the bag. Flowers can be pressed in books or dried upon a screen. Dried herbs should be stored in air-tight glass containers, away from direct sun whenever possible. As long as the herb retains its color and scent, it is still good in majick and medicine. Always label the glass jars as many dried herbs look alike.

HERBS, PLANTS & TREES

Agrimony
Fire • Sun, Mars

Agrimony is a powerful herb use to break hexes and clear the air of unwanted energies. Use with other protection herbs to banish harmful energies. Use it to help you overcome enemies. it helps kindle your will to fight back in unjust situations. Carry in a black majick bag.

Allspice
Fire • Sun, Moon, Jupiter

Allspice aligns with high energies that can be called into your spell to do just about anything you want. Use it to unleash powerful mystical forces. It is particularly good for spells involving money, luck and healing.

Angelica Root
Fire, Water, Air • Sun, Moon, Venus, Uranus

The herb associated with the archangels, said to be a gift from the divine during the plague. It is used in spells of protection and healing. Hang this root in a majick bag with a quartz crystal in a child's room to bring angels to watch and protect the child. It helps bring peaceful, protected sleep and dreams to both children and adults, and can also be burned to attract the influence of the angels in your majick.

Amaranth
Earth • Saturn

Amaranth seeds are very mystically potent. They are a symbol of divine life and resurrection, and call upon higher forces beyond our simple day-to-day majick. Use them for immortality, invisibility, healing, and to call forth the dead.

Anise Seed
Water • Moon, Venus

Anise seed, different from Star Anise, is used for deep sleep and prevention of nightmares. Put into a small bag and place beneath your pillow. It is also an herb of love and romance, bringing peace and harmony to your relationships.

Balsam Fir (Balm of Gilead)
Water, Air • Moon, Jupiter

Carry balsam fir in a black majick bag for strength, insight and power. When used in a bath, it can help revive feelings of love when you believe love is lost. While balsam fir is known as Balm of Gilead, it differs from the plant that provides the popular aromatic buds also known as Balm of Gilead, which is *Populus balsamifera*. Balsam fir can be used as a majickal substitute for these buds , which have become expensive and hard to find.

Bay Leaf
Earth, Fire, Air • Earth, Sun, Jupiter

Bay leaf, or bay laurel, is an herb of legal success. To win in court, write the word "win" in black ink on a whole bay leaf and place it in your left shoe when you go to court. If your intentions are correct and harming none, you shall be victorious. Bay is also the herb of oracles, and can be burned in incense to increase psychic power and the ability to see and understand clearly.

Bat's Head Root
Earth, Fire • Saturn, Pluto

Bat's head root is actually a seedpod that gets its name from its resemblance to a bat's head. It is also known as goat's head root or devil's head root in Mexico. You can use it to make wishes come true and protect yourself from harm, including harmful sorcery and hexes. It evokes the power of the spirit of Bat, and the horned god of Witches.

Beth Root
Air, Water, Earth • Jupiter, Saturn, Venus

Beth root can be carried in a black majick bag with other herbs of protection for general protection or mixed with herbs of Jupiter for success. Native traditions associate it as both an aphrodisiac and an aid for childbirth, so it can be used in majick for either of those intentions as well.

Bilberry Leaves
Fire, Water • Sun, Moon, Saturn

Bilberry leaves help you harvest all that is good from the effort of your work and hobbies. It can also help you see where you need to be and what you do with your time and energy. It can also help attract earth spirits known as gnomes to help you with your majick. Use it in spells for money, pleasure, happiness and safety.

Birch Leaves
Air, Water, Earth, Fire • Mercury, Moon, Earth, Pluto

Birch is a very majickal Celtic tree of healing and blessing. Use it to keep your skin from getting any blemishes or disease and to help heal the cells in your body. Birch leaves are used to stop the "evil eye" or harmful majick, particularly gossip, and work best for this purpose when carried in a red bag.

Blackberry
Water • Venus, Jupiter

Blackberry is a sacred plant, associated with the Goddess, and the fruits are sacred to the goddess Brid. Blackberries, whether fresh or in the form of wine and cordials, can be used in her healing and inspiration rituals. Blackberry leaves are used to transform bad luck into good luck. If you feel someone is the source of your bad luck, you can sprinkle the leaves on their doorstep. Blackberry helps us overcome fear and can be used in general healing spells, healing any feminine health issues, or for money and protection spells.

Black Cohosh
Fire, Earth • Pluto, Saturn, Earth

Black cohosh has a powerful majick to attract and repel. It can be used in spells to attract to you all the things you want and need, and in particular, it is useful to find a home that is safe and happy. When burned or carried in a black bag, it can help neutralize your enemies.

Black Peppercorn
Fire, Earth • Venus, Mars, Saturn

Black peppercorns, by their very nature, evoke fire and passion. You can feel them upon your tongue when you taste them. Their majick can be used for sexual revitalization and intensity, especially when carried in a red bag. They can also be used as a spell for protection, in which case they work best carried in a black bag. We advise that the majick of peppercorns, or any other herb or stone, is not a responsible form of protection against STDs, HIV and pregnancy, so use common sense and traditional forms of medical protection. Do not burn black pepper on charcoal, as it is toxic in this form. It is used in chemical warfare gases and pepper spray for its strong, painful irritant qualities.

Black Walnut
Fire, Earth • Venus, Earth, Sun

Black walnut, due to the hard shell, is very protective. It can be used in spells to evoke the protection of the Knights of the Round Table, specifically to place Sir Gawain's shield of protection before you. It can block out "poison," be it psychic, majickal or emotional, and for this aim, works well when mixed with pieces of amber and mandrake and carried in a black bag.

Blessed Thistle
Fire, Water • Sun, Moon

Blessed thistle, being the sacred herb of Scotland, is one of those rare majickal herbs that can be used to add power and blessings to all majickal purposes. In particular it is used in child blessings to bring a triple blessing of love, beauty, and wisdom, and can be used in spells for adults with the same blessings and intentions.

Bloodroot
Fire, Water • Venus, Mars

Bloodroot is a powerful plant, one of the first to bloom after the winter snow thaws and spring begins. Majickally it is used to stir the heart, to bring love and beauty. When carried in a red or pink bag and mixed with rose quartz, strawberry leaves, and rose oil, it lets those who gaze upon you see your outer and inner beauty. You will warm their hearts as well as your own. You will radiate the feeling of love to those who need love. You can carry it with you as a charm or hang it by your bed or dressing table.

Blue Cohosh
Water, Fire • Moon, Sun

Blue cohosh is used to ease pain, both physical and psychological. It is also used for general protection from harm and works well at protecting both people and places. Carry blue cohosh in a black bag for personal protection or hang it on the premises to protect a location such as your home, office, or car.

Blue Malva
Earth, Water • Saturn, Jupiter

Blue malva flowers bring unexpected good luck, money, and other forms of fortune into your life and can continue the flow of blessings. It mixes well with other herbs for money and success, and can be carried in a charm bag with citrine and clear quartz for this purpose.

Blue Vervain
Earth, Water, Air • Saturn, Moon, Venus

Vervain is considered the Enchanter's herb, used for many forms of majick. The most common form of vervain in America is blue vervain, known for its many blue star-shaped flowers. Vervain's blessing is that it can soothe the nerves and help us stop living only in our mind, getting us back in touch with our bodies. It helps promote peaceful sleep and can be used in a dream pillow to banish nightmares and soothe dreams, especially when mixed with St. John's wort. It's an all-purpose herb that can aid the majick of love, money, healing, and protection.

Boldo
Air, Fire, Water, Earth • Mercury, Mars, Moon, Sun, Saturn

Boldo leaves are a faery herb. American Witches say they are sacred to the Welsh Faery God Bran, despite boldo being a native herb of Chile, and when placed in a bowl in your living space or carried in a green or purple bag, will attract the faery spirits to you. In spellcraft, Boldo can be used to enhance the majick of all spells with faery power, increase your majickal will and effectiveness, and grant the gift of vision and faery sight. Boldo mixes well with simple clear quartz, which amplifies its power.

Borage
Earth, Fire, Air • Earth, Jupiter

Borage can be used to grant courage in all difficult situations. It boosts confidence in all things and can ease the pain of a long-lost love. Its natural powers are cleansing and clearing, stopping unwanted energies. It can also be used for protection and to stimulate psychic powers while not lowering your psychic defenses. It works well when carried in a white, gray, or silver bag.

Bougainvillea
Water, Air • Moon, Mercury, Venus, Jupiter

Bougainvillea flowers are sacred to the Goddess Eostra, goddess of the dawn and the Earth. The power of Mother Earth and all of nature will be with you and your majick if you add a little bougainvillea to your spell. It adds prosperity and blessings to all things and can especially bring comfort in your home to you and your loved ones.

Broom Flowers
Air, Fire • Mercury, Mars

Broom flowers are used to sweep away bad thoughts from your mind and clear your home of unwanted energies. It can be made into a tea and sprinkled in the home to dispel these forces, or the flowers can be sprinkled on your path as you walk. Carry it with mandrake root and witch hazel in a white bag for a powerful clearing charm.

Buckthorn Bark
Air, Earth • Mercury, Saturn

The bark of the buckthorn tree is very powerful. It has a very masculine energy, yet is used to keep masculine energy in balance within. It is an herb of protection, and particularly powerful to help women in abusive situations. The most powerful gift of buckthorn is the ability to help one change their "destiny," or the current course they are on, and create a new future.

Burdock Root
Fire, Earth, Air, Water • Sun, Venus, Mars, Saturn, Uranus

Burdock's deep root gives us tenacity for long-term majick, including healing and protection. It wards off harmful energy and can be carried in a red bag for luck and blessings.

Calamus
Fire, Air • Sun, Mercury

Calamus root is an herb that can strengthen and bind any spell, so you can add it to any working to make your majick stronger. Its general uses for waxing Moon majick are to invoke healing, luck, and prosperity. On the waning Moon, it protects us by banishing harm and can banish ill health and mental suffering.

Calendula
Fire • Sun

Burning calendula flowers are sacred to the Witch Goddess. In majick, they stimulate psychic energy, clairvoyance, and dreams, all of her domains. Due to their golden color, they are used in prosperity majick. They can also be used in a charm or incense to bring back a straying lover. Avoid during pregnancy and lactation.

Caraway Seed
Fire, Water, Air • Sun, Moon, Mercury, Venus, Mars

Caraway seeds have a strong sexual power to them, as many of the herbs that produce a multitude of seeds usually do. Majickally they help keep you in the mind of a lover, or can increase your partner's lust for you, regardless of distance. Traditionally they are also used for healing, maintaining good health, and preventing theft. They can be carried loose in the pocket, wallet, or purse, scattered where you want them to have effect or carried in a red bag with rose quartz or garnet.

Cat's Claw
Fire, Water • Sun, Moon

Cat's claw bark, from the Amazon, is used to protect all that is valuable to you – your family, friends, business, and home. In ancient Scotland, the cat was considered a powerful majickal animal, and cat's claw can help evoke their majick. The Scottish saying, used as a shield, is "Beware of the cat that scratches." It's an herb of protection and health in general and is used in vision quest ceremonies to commune with the spirits and ancestors.

Catnip
Water • Venus

Both herbally and majickally, Catnip can help you relax, rest, and dream. It promotes general healing and good humor. Catnip is a favorite treat of our feline companions. Using catnip along with kindness and love, you can psychically bond with your cat so that he or she will become your majickal familiar.

Cedar
Fire • Jupiter, Sun

Cedar can be used in potions and charms and works well when burned, which releases its majickal power, bringing health, wealth, and protection. In particular it can be combined with cloves or cinnamon sticks and carried in a blue bag to get a loan, increase your business, or find a new and better job.

Chamomile
Water • Sun

Chamomile is a very healing herb, letting you rest and regenerate when you need to recover from illness or simply maintain good health. Chamomile can be used to aid dream majick and meditation. It is used in solar majick to bring a gentle, nurturing success, including more money, and works well in a charm with citrine in a gold bag.

Cherry
Water, Fire • Moon, Venus, Mars

The red color of the sweet cherry associates it with love and romance. Carry it in a red bag with rose quartz to bring wild love to you. It can also increase your skills with a divination tool, such as tarot or runes.

Chickweed
Water • Moon

Chickweed, also known as starweed, can cool down any situation and bring tranquility where there is anger. It is also used in spells designed to attract a love or maintain a current relationship.

Chili Peppers
Fire • Sun, Venus, Mars, Neptune

Chili peppers are a fiery catalyst for all majick, but in particular, they can bring the fires of lust to your life. Chili increases the libido and can bring intense sexual gratification when coupled with your majick. It works well in a red or black bag, with a garnet and a little bit of Midnight Sex Potion (see **Chapter Five**). Place the charm under your mattress.

Cinnamon
Fire • Jupiter

The spirit of cinnamon warms and invites. Being ruled by the good luck planet Jupiter, Cinnamon's energy can influence people in high places and create situations where everyone is good-natured and gregarious while doing business. It can be used in gambling spells. Carrying a bit with you when you play bingo or visit a casino is helpful. Cinnamon can keep you lucky.

Cloves
Sun, Jupiter, Vulcan

Cloves have a rich history as a valuable spice brought through the trade routes to Europe in Medieval times, but despite being a common and popular herb today, it is very majickal. Like cinnamon, cloves bring good fortune, luck, and success, as well as help improve business careers and generate fame. They also drive away hostile forces, especially when burned.

Coltsfoot
Fire, Air • Sun, Moon, Pluto

Coltsfoot is an herb of clear understanding and can help us find peace and tranquility, even when there is chaos around us. It can also be used for spells of love and acceptance. When burned, it can stimulate clairvoyant powers.

Comfrey
Earth • Venus, Mars, Saturn

Comfrey root carries a deep wisdom. It can help you remember past lives. It can also help ground into the present life. Some use it to stimulate thoughts of marriage and fidelity, a real commitment, in their partner. It can also be used to heal a broken heart or banish "the blues." When placed in a suitcase, it prevents your luggage from being lost. It works well with hematite and can be carried in a white bag.

Coriander
Fire • Mars

Coriander is the spice of love and lust, and generates a fire within those who use it. It can be used in powders, potions, and incense. It can turn lust to commitment and thoughts of marriage, and also bring a playful peace and goodwill between those who do not get along. For a powerful lust spell, place a dish of coriander seeds out under the Full Moon. To drive your lover mad with desire, toss a handful of the seeds into a wooded area and speak your lover's name aloud to the Moon.

Cumin
Water, Air • Moon, Mercury, Mars

Cumin keeps your face and name in your lover's mind and even dreams. It promotes fidelity in the relationship, preventing one from straying. Try using it in a majick box with love herbs and two jasper stones. It can also be used as a protection spell when mixed with frankincense and burned or scattered.

Damiana
Water, Fire • Venus, Mars

Damiana is a powerful aphrodisiac. It induces lust, love, and passion. It is often made into a sweet herbal liquor to be shared between lovers and can be used for the same reasons in majick. When burned, damiana can also help induce visions and aids in communing with the spirits and gods.

Dill
Air • Sun, Moon, Mercury

Dill, both dill weed and seed, can be used in majick. Dill is associated with speeding up majick and making spells manifest faster. You can add a pinch to spells, incense, and potions, or carry it in a black bag. In some lore, it is said to "rob Witches of the Will" meaning it can protect against harmful majick. It can help you recover from sadness when a lover leaves you, and the multitude of seeds from the dill is associated with virility and sexual fertility.

Dulse (Sea Weed)
Water • Neptune

Dulse is a form of seaweed that can be used for any form of water majick. It can help you connect with the energies of the oceans and the majick of the sea creatures and water elementals, even if you are far from the sea. Dulse can be used to enhance and increase your natural psychic abilities.

Echinacea
Fire, Air • Sun, Moon, Mercury, Earth

Echinacea, or coneflower, is known popularly as an herbal immune support. Likewise, its majick helps support and strengthen our majickal spells. It works best in a black majick bag for this purpose, to draw in power. Echinacea root is also used to stop snake venom, and majickally, it can be used to stop poisonous talk and actions from harming you and your loved ones.

Elder
Earth • Saturn, Earth, Sun, Moon

The elder tree holds powerful majick, rich in lore and medicine. It is associated with the spirit of Faeries, and a lone elder tree is said to be dedicated to the Faery Queen, the Hylde-Moer, the Elder Mother Tree. She can bring healing and protection against evil. The flowers are specifically used in a facial wash to bring beauty. Elder can be placed on the grave of the dead to help guide and protect them in the afterlife. Elder wood should never be burned, or you will "offend" the spirit of the elder.

Eucalyptus
Fire, Earth, Water • Saturn, Pluto, Sun, Moon

Eucalyptus is a very aromatic herb used in healing. It wards off illness and disinfects, making it good for healing majick against colds and flu. It works well with lavender and can be placed in a yellow bag with a clear quartz crystal for healing. Eucalyptus can also be used to aid investigations, to make sure the truth is revealed.

Eyebright
Air, Fire • Mercury, Sun

Eyebright is known for the little "dot" upon the flower, reminiscent of the eye, and it is used sympathetically for all things associated with both the physical eyes and the psychic eye. It can grant clear vision of your spiritual path and help you see the future. It gives insight into the unknown and helps grow psychic abilities, particularly to answer personal questions. Eyebright can also make you appear more attractive, even irresistible, to another.

Fennel
Water, Air • Moon, Mercury, Neptune

Fennel seeds can calm nervous energy, heal digestive ailments, and make one happy and content. Fennel can also multiply things, increasing the abundance of whatever it is directed towards, due to the multiplicity of its seeds.

Feverfew
Fire, Water • Sun, Moon, Venus

Feverfew can help with clear thinking. It helps prevent anxiety, including worry about whether or not someone loves you, and can keep you from focusing every moment upon a new love. Herbally, feverfew is known to cure headaches, and in spells, it can help heal all issues of the head and grant peaceful clear mind. It also helps those who are accident prone to be more grounded and prevents future accidents. Feverfew works well with amethyst and can be carried in a white bag.

Five-Finger Grass
Air • Mercury, Sun, Moon

Five-finger grass, also known as cinquefoil, carries the majick of holding, grabbing, and manifestation. Its leaves are associated with the hand, looking like it has five, or sometimes seven, fingers to each leaf, hence the name. It can be used as a protective herb, blocking harm. It is a "counter majick" herb, undoing curses. An old folk saying tells us that "anything five fingers can do, five-finger grass can undo," meaning anything anyone does against you, cinquefoil can help you undo. It can help you manifest the four elements, plus Spirit. It's a grounding herb, used to "bring Witches back" when added to flying ointments to induce visions. It can also bring a wealthy lover, or connect you to a Taurus person. It works well in a green majick bag.

Hemlock
Earth • Saturn, Mars, Jupiter, Pluto

Hemlock can refer to both the tree and the poisonous herb used to end Socrates' life. Most traditional lore refers to the very dangerous plant, while much modern lore is referring to the evergreen tree. The needles, cones, and bark of the tree can be used for knowledge of the astral world and to increase esoteric wisdom and understanding. It can also protect you from your enemies, stopping both physical and majickal harm. The poisonous plant is deadly, and should be avoided. Casual use of it can cause severe injury and death.

Hibiscus
Water • Venus, Jupiter, Sun

The beautiful hibiscus flower is used in love spells, especially when distance is a factor. They can be used to keep you in your lover's mind regardless of the distance between you. Hibiscus can also be used to launch a lover's spell over a larger distance.

Horehound
Air • Mercury, Moon

Horehound is an herb of overall good health and healing, to bolster the life force and immune system. Traditionally the herb is used in cough drops and syrups, so its majick carries a similar intention. It can also be used for protection, including spells against malicious majick, and it acts as an aid in any form of exorcism or banishment of unwanted spirits. For this purpose, it is effective when burned. It can increase mental powers and memory.

Horny Goat Weed
Fire • Mars, Pluto

Horny goat weed is an herbal aphrodisiac, and its majick helps drive a lover wild. You can carry it with you in a red bag or place the leaves under the mattress or bed. It will increase sexual passion and desire.

Hyssop
Air • Jupiter, Mercury, Sunday

Hyssop can influence people in positions of authority and power, and with its majick, you can have favors granted and gain good fortune. It is also a cleansing and purification herb, well known for healing issues of guilt and shame.

Irish Moss (Sea Weed)
Water • Jupiter, Neptune

Irish moss can be used to connect with the majick of the mermaids. It is also used for luck, money, and protection. Gamblers favor the use of Irish moss and carry it in a green bag.

Jalapeño
Fire • Mars

The hot jalapeño pepper, like many other hot spices, can be used for lust, passion, sex, and power. It can be a majickal catalyst, adding power to any working. When using it as a charm, jalapeño operates best when carried in a red bag. As with black pepper, do not burn on charcoal.

Jasmine
Water • Moon, Jupiter

Jasmine, a night-blooming flower, is filled with majick and mystery. The alluring scent speaks to its power to gain favor, either in romance or outward success. It attracts good fortune, prosperity, and luck, yet it is also effective in love powders, oils and potions. It is a dream herb, and used to enhance psychic awareness in dreams or to even bring dreams to guide your love or success. Jasmine can help guide us in understanding our past lives, and may also be used in majick to honor the Moon Goddess.

Juniper Berries
Fire • Venus, Mars, Sun, Jupiter

Juniper can be used for variety of majick. Primarily the berries are used for intentions as widely ranged as protection, hex breaking, anti-theft, psychic power, love and health. The juniper wood or leaves can be burned for a protective and purifying incense. Specifically the berries are used in beauty majick, to increase physical beauty and to help lose physical weight.

Kelp (Sea Weed)
Water • Neptune

Like other seaweeds, kelp is used for all forms of water and ocean majick. It connects you to the spirit of the seas even when far from them. Specifically kelp majick is great for protection, and in particular, protection while traveling over or in water.

Lady's Mantle
Water, Earth • Venus

Lady's mantle is a powerful herb of nature, said to unlock the mysteries of Mother Earth. It grants physical strength and health to women, and can be used to open the heart and attract love. Dew is caught in the "cup" of the lady's mantle flower, and according to legend, if one bathes in this dew on Beltane morning, one can remain young and beautiful. It is the premier herb of alchemists, as revealed by its Latin name of *Alchemilis vulgaris*. Alchemists seek to unlock the secrets of nature, and lady's mantle helps them do it.

Lavender
Air • Mercury, Jupiter, Uranus, Sun

Lavender is a multipurpose herb with many gifts. It can be used to bring peace and tranquility, and in particular, calm the nerves for sleep and active dream majick. It can enhance and stimulate psychic powers. In healing majick, it is great for sobriety spells and to cleanse and heal the blood. Burned, it provides a cleansing scent to banish harmful energy, but it also motivates you to fulfill your purpose in the world and seek deep wisdom.

Lemon Balm (Melissa)
Water, Air, Fire • Moon, Jupiter, Vulcan, Sun

Lemon Balm is one of the most helpful herbs available. It's Latin name, *Melissa officinalis*, indicates a connection both to the bee and the Greek priestess who aided the Pythia, the High Priestess and oracle at Delphi. According to alchemists, it has a large quantity of gentle life force, and can restore health. Majickally it adds color and brightness to the aura. It can be used in spells of love, healing, psychic power, success, and quick money. Any spell can be aided with a pinch of lemon balm.

Lemongrass
Water, Air, Fire • Venus, Uranus, Sun

Lemongrass is a great blessing. It can cleanse both our selves and our space to open the way for happiness and success. It brings riches and attracts friends or business partners with resources. It helps us find unseen treasures, literally or metaphorically within ourselves, and leads to our own recognition and riches. Lemongrass can also aid in health and beauty majick.

Lemon
Fire, Water • Sun, Moon

The peel of the citrus fruit lemon is used to discover who is a true friend and who is a false friend. It can be used as an ingredient in purification formulas. It also grants health and long life, and can be used in love majick. Just as the scent of lemon can uplift, the majick of lemon can raise your intention.

Lemon Verbena
Air, Fire • Mercury, Vulcan, Sun

Lemon verbena can be used in love majick to gain insight into a lover's fidelity, as well as help promote chastity when sex should be avoided. As a dream herb, it can help you relax and fall asleep. Lemon verbena is also an herb of success, used in money and wealth majick.

Licorice
Air, Earth • Mercury, Venus, Sun, Earth

Licorice is used in Mercurial majick, to help you speak eloquently and with a compelling voice. It can aid in creativity, especially when the task involves writing or words. Licorice root can be used in spells of love and lust, and to ensure fidelity. It is also a strong herb to be used in dream pillows, as it works well for dreams of eloquent speech, creative writing, and fidelity. Licorice is also used in spells to break addictions, especially smoking and other oral addictions.

Lovage
Water • Venus, Neptune, Sun

As the name would imply, lovage is used in all forms of love spells, to create, attract, and open to love. It can also be used to protect love and to grant beauty. Lovage works well with rose quartz in charm bags of pink, green, or rose red.

Lucky Hand Root
Fire • Venus, Jupiter, Sun

Named for its resemblance to a human hand, Lucky Hand Root is a powerful talisman to pull whatever you want to you and increase the dexterity of the hands. It has been used by musicians and craftsmen for that purpose, but most often, it is used in money majick and gambling charms.

Mandrake
Earth, Water • Saturn, Venus, Mercury, Moon

Mandrake is a powerful herb, though the name refers to several unrelated plants, including "true mandrake" or mandragora, English mandrake or white bryony, and American mandrake, or *Podophyllum peltatum*. The root of true mandragora is often shaped like a human figure, giving rise to the name. While all are different herbs, they often are used for the same majickal purposes, including protection, love, and as a majickal catalyst to add to the power of any spell.

Marjoram
Air • Mercury, Sun

Marjoram helps you clear your mind and see things as they truly are. It can bring love and happiness at work or in the home. Marjoram blesses handfastings and marriages. It can also help restore happiness when experiencing grief. It lifts sorrow and clears away the clouds that prevent you from being clear and peaceful.

Marshmallow
Water, Earth • Moon, Venus, Saturn, Pluto

Marshmallow root is an herb of softening and soothing. It brings gentle healing and comfort. When burned, it attracts spiritual assistance and blessings, pulling "good energy" to you. It can be used in love and sex majick as a force of attraction. It can also be used to soften and remove blocks to prosperity and riches.

Meadowsweet
Water, Earth • Moon, Saturn, Earth

Meadowsweet is used to inspire love and happiness. It relieves stress and tension, and fresh meadowsweet's scent is considered to induce merriment and joy. This herb can be strewn about the home for peace and goodwill, or placed in the four corners to prevent thieves from entering. Considered sacred by the Druids.

Mint
Air, Earth • Mercury, Moon, Earth

Mint, specifically peppermint and related species, is an herb of communication. It helps clear the air and clear the mind, so true communication can happen. Mint helps ease pain and aids healing of all kinds, including psychic healing. It's a great herb in spells to heal cold symptoms.

Milk Thistle
Fire, Water • Jupiter, Earth, Sun, Moon

Milk thistle seed is one of the few powerful Jupiter herbs that is not a rich spice. It's associated with Jupiter through its action upon the liver, the part of the body influenced by Jupiter. Milk thistle can be used to heal anger and rage, as well as for general health and well being, clearing out any unwanted energies. It increases strength and vitality while it lessens depression. Majickally it's used to keep "food on the table and money in your pocket," enough prosperity to live and feed yourself and family. Seeds can be carried in your wallet, in your shoe, or sprinkled around the home.

Mistletoe
Fire • Sun

Mistletoe is the preeminent herb of the Druids, known as the Heal-All because it could be used in all majick, and was considered a manifestation of the sacred gods upon the tree. Legend says it appeared where lighting struck. Mistletoe gathered from oak was considered more sacred, and special rituals were used to harvest it, not letting it touch the ground, else it would lose its power. Today we use mistletoe for health, wealth, money, and the wisdom of the ancient ancestors.

Motherwort
Water, Earth • Moon, Venus, Earth

Motherwort is the herb of the mother, and like many herbs that are used in reproductive health for women, it is used to majickally empower women and manifest the blessings of the Goddess. It strengthens a woman's body, including during pregnancy and birthing. A charm in a pink bag with rose quartz can soothe menstrual pains. For both women and men, it fosters self-nurturing and self-confidence, like a mother boosting a child to succeed in the world.

Mugwort
Water • Moon

Mugwort is an herb of psychic development. Used in potions and incense, it stimulates the third eye and opens up intuition and visions. Too much can bring a light euphoria that makes psychic work difficult to focus. It is also an herb of protection, banishing harmful forces. It is used by women for protection during pregnancy, though it should never be taken internally by a pregnant woman. It is best used for pregnancy protection as a charm, placed in a white or silver bag with a pentacle, and carried or burnt in the home.

Mustard Seeds
Fire • Mars, Jupiter, Sun

Like other plants with plentiful seeds, mustard is associated with prosperity and abundance. Classically it is used in majick for wealth, good fortune, luck, and winning in general. It mixes well with other herbs of a similar nature when carried in a blue or green charm bag. Others sprinkle a few seeds in the wallet, purse, pocket, or shoe. Mustard seeds also have the power to remove your enemies from your path, clearing the way for your own success.

Nettle
Fire • Mars, Venus, Earth

Nettle has the power to connect and the power to separate. Known as stinging nettle, due to little hairs that can sting like a bee, it deals with serious connections. When mixed into any love spell, it can turn love into a serious relationship headed toward marriage. But it also can help us heal when we've felt the sting of love lost.

Nutmeg
Fire, Earth • Venus, Mars, Earth

Nutmeg is a powerful spice. Its majick helps expand your aura and your majickal reach so you can touch the sky and stars out in the cosmos. On a more terrestrial level, it promotes general well-being and happiness, fidelity, and good fortune.

Orange
Fire • Sun, Venus, Jupiter

Orange is like a miniature Sun, for success and well-being. It can be used in love majick to turn a simple relationship into marriage. It aids the success of all business ventures. Orange increases health and the immune system. It can also aid in divination skills. Carry the orange peel in a majick bag to evoke these qualities.

Orchid
Air • Mercury, Venus

Orchid flowers are used in love and beauty spells. The root is considered to be an aphrodisiac and used in charms for men to increase their virility and women their beauty. Orchid can also enhance psychic powers, and works well when a little is burned as incense with other psychic herbs such as mugwort and myrrh.

Pumpkin Seeds
Fire, Water • Venus, Mars, Sun, Moon

Pumpkin seeds can be used for protection. Carry three seeds in your pocket or a majick bag for this purpose. You can do majick for prosperity by placing three seeds on your property. As the pumpkins grow, so too will your prosperity multiply. The seeds, due to their high zinc content, are associated as both a healing food and an aphrodisiac, and therefore can be used in healing and love spells. They are often used in dream majick, placed in a dream pillow to help you make your dreams come true.

Scullcap
Air • Mercury, Moon

Scullcap is the herb of the mind. It helps with memory recall and study skills to better take tests and learn new knowledge. It increases all our perceptions and mental faculties. It can bring clear thinking and relaxation to aid sleep and end insomnia. It mixes well with gotu kola and clear quartz, in a bowl or bag. Put it out when you are studying or on your nightstand when you go to bed. Scullcap is said to also bring money, but does so by increasing our skills and plans to make money, making us more clever, not by altering fortune.

Solomon's Seal
Earth, Fire • Saturn, Vulcan, Sun

Used as an incense, it can purify your aura and protect wherever it is burned. It is an herb of expansion and contraction, adding energy to make the majick work in harmony with divine wisdom and divine will. It can be used to get greater control, as King Solomon was a magician who could summon and control spirits, and as he was also a rich king, it can help us with money and success.

Spearmint
Water, Fire • Venus, Mars

Spearmint is one of the cooling mints, yet it has a very active power to it. Use it to instigate change in your life. It's very effective at bringing change in your love life or change at your job. Carry it in a pink bag with a rose quartz to catalyze a new love or carry it with a citrine in a blue, green, or yellow bag for a new job.

Star Anise
Water, Air • Moon, Venus

Star anise is the "wheel of joy" as it helps generate happiness and joy for you and your family. It can help soften a lover's heart and heal relationships that damaged through pain and misunderstanding. Place one whole "wheel" in a pink bag with a citrine stone and some glitter to evoke the joy.

St. John's Wort
Fire • Sun

St. John's wort is a very majickal plant with a rich history. It brings more light into any situation and is used both medically and majickally to ease depression, or mental darkness and other forms of mental illness. It can be used best majickally in combination with sunflower petals, gotu kola, and clear quartz in a blue or white bag. It also helps heal issues surrounding trauma, banishes nightmares, and is an overall protective herb, calling upon the protection of the faeries.

Sunflower
Fire • Sun

Sunflower is a plant imbued with all the blessings of the Sun. Use its petals and seeds to keep your heart light, attract joy, and bring prosperity and good fortune. Used in a dream pillow, it will put light upon the truth you are seeking and reveal the answers in your dreams. Sunflower can help heal a broken heart, raising your self-esteem and inner fire. Sunflower can be used to work with any solar deities. I use them to work with Lugh, in gaining his skills and protection.

Sweet Woodruff
Fire, Water • Mars, Venus, Pluto

Sweet woodruff is used to protect against evil, especially to protect your home from evil and your relationship from the malicious intentions of others. It can also be used to help increase self-love and self-esteem, and works best when in combination with serpentine and malachite. Carry it in a green bag to bring out these properties. May wine is made by steeping the fresh twigs of woodruff in German wine. Drinking some confers similar properties of protection and self-love.

Tansy
Water • Venus, Mercury, Vulcan, Sun

Tansy has a toxic nature; it is associated with the dead and funerary rites, but strangely also in majick that makes you immortal and in spells of health and well-being. Tansy is also a protective herb, as it's used herbally as a vermifuge to remove unwanted parasites, and majickally can remove those forces and people who are pesky and bothersome.

Tarragon
Fire • Earth, Sun, Mars

Tarragon is used to help a woman be more independent, strong, and happy. It is used to keep you warm in the wintertime and keep your choices tasteful. As revealed in its Latin name, *Artemesia dracunculus*, it indicates an association with dragons, and the genus name *Artemesia* relates to Artemis, linking it to other majickal herbs such as mugwort and wormwood.

Thyme
Fire, Air • Vulcan, Mercury, Sun

Chivalry is a key concept associated with thyme's power. Associated with the knight's sword, a pinch can be added to your athame or sword case. Thyme can manifest any wish quickly, as it speeds up majickal results. When carried with beeswax, it is used best for love and protection, and can be carried in a black bag.

Tonka Beans
Fire • Jupiter

Tonka beans are used in majick for love, luck, prosperity, and power. Carry them alone or with other herbs in a purple, blue, or black majick bag.

Uva Ursi
Earth •Saturn

Uva ursi is used for psychic power and personal strength. Sprinkle it in the room when burning candles for clear vision during psychic consultations. It can be used in spells and potions to communicate with the spirits of the elves. It is mixed with tobacco in Native American smoking mixtures to help communicate with the divine.

Valerian Root
Water • Venus, Mercury

Herbally, valerian is a powerful sedative, so majickally it is used to help us sleep and get deep rejuvenating rest. Mixed with other psychic herbs, it can help us speak to our deceased loved ones in our dreams. It is also used in spells of love, protection, and purification. The smell of valerian has been compared to dirty socks, and while it is not the most pleasant odor, it is a very powerful herb.

Vanilla
Fire, Water • Venus, Mars, Pluto

Vanilla bean is traditionally used in spells of love and lust. Its inviting and intoxicating scent is surprisingly sensual and can induce lusty thoughts in another. It also helps increase mental powers.

Vetivert
Air, Water • Uranus, Mercury, Moon

Vetivert is used to aid in psychic "flight" or astral travel. It can be placed in a majick bag and tied to your broom. It uplifts and brings relaxation and tranquility. It is also used for protection, specifically from thieves, curses, and other intentional harm.

Wild Yam Root
Fire, Water • Jupiter

Wild Yam, also known as Chinese Yam, is considered an aphrodisiac in Chinese medicine. In majick, it is used in love majick and is well known for healing the hunger suffered when we lose a love. Wild yam can be used to heal issues around infertility and aid conception. Overall its majick is like a tonic, increasing life force and vitality. It can fortify you to handle stress and strain at work and home. Yam can be used to bring goodness and blessings into your home. Works best when placed in a pink or gold bag.

Willow
Water • Moon

Willow bark aids us in all forms of healing majick, reduces pain, brings relief, and grants protection. Willow is associated with the realm of the faeries and can be used in all forms of faery majick. It also increases psychic ability. Willow wands make excellent tools for handfasting rituals.

Witch Hazel
Air, Water, Fire • Mercury, Moon, Sun

A popular herb made into an astringent wash, witch hazel is also used for many majickal reasons. When carried in a black bag, it protects you from harmful energies and psychic attack. In a blue bag, it can be used to mend a broken heart. In the home or workplace, it can create harmony when scattered about, aid in astral travel or psychic "flight," and when used under the pillow, grant prophetic dreams.

Wood Betony
Fire, Earth • Sun, Earth

Wood betony's majick protects both your body and soul. It helps you attend to and manifest your physical needs. When you put it under your pillow, it shields you from harmful dreams and nightmares. During Midsummer, you can burn it in a bonfire to purify yourself.

Yarrow
Water • Venus

Yarrow is used in spells of courage and power, as well as for love and psychic ability. It can attract beneficial friends and allies to you and connect you with the faery realm. Yarrow is associated with boundary and protection, and can strengthen your psychic shields and help you disconnect from harmful people and things.

Yellow Dock
Air • Jupiter

Yellow dock root works well in majick for healing, prosperity, and fertility. The plant itself creates a multitude of seeds at the end of its life cycle, which shows that it is good at manifesting an abundance of your specific intention.

Yerba Santa
Air • Venus

Use yerba santa in majick for beauty and healing, as well as in spells to increase your psychic powers and protect you. Yerba santa is quite effective in dream majick, letting you communicate with spirits and allies in your dreams.

RESINS & GUMS

Amber
Fire • Sun

While most Witch shops classify amber as a stone or mineral and carry it in their stone and mineral section, either by the piece or fastened into jewelry, softer grades are powdered and used herbally in incense and majick. Like solid amber pieces, it evokes the power of the Sun and healing, balance, and purification. As a talisman, it can prevent poisoning both physically and psychically.

Benzoin
Fire, Water, Earth • Sun, Moon, Earth

Benzoin resin was burned by Cleopatra to see visions of the future, as it does increase our psychic and divination skills. You may also use it in potions to fix or stabilize the scent and spell.

Camphor
Water • Moon

Camphor's scent is powerful and healing, used to ward off illness as an herb of purification. It can increase awareness and aid in our divination skills, and in classical lore, it was a scent associated with the faeries.

Copal
Earth, Water, Fire • Earth, Neptune

The South American resin copal is used in its native territory to invite the beneficial spirits and gods to ceremony. If making a poppet, a piece of copal works well as the "heart" of the doll, anchoring the majick and bringing the doll to life. When burned, it brings ease to our lives, creating fulfillment and happiness. Copal blends well with frankincense and myrrh.

Dragon's Blood
Fire • Mars

Blood red is the color of majick all around the world, symbolizing the life force found within us all. Using anything this color taps into that life force. Dragon's blood, a red resin used to varnish violins, is a powerful herb of love and protection. It can attract a lover to you or banish unwanted forces and even harmful spirits as a powerful incense of exorcism. While it can be used dry in powders or dissolved in potions and carried in charm bags, it often works best when burned in incense. Dragon's blood is a powerful catalyst that can super-charge any spell you perform.

Frankincense
Fire • Sun, Moon, Jupiter

One of the most powerful and popular resins used as a temple incense, frankincense creates a peaceful sanctum and promotes meditation and introspection. It can be used to neutralize, bind together, or protect, uplifting and healing as it protects us from harm.

Guar Powder
Water • Moon

Guar powder is used to capture the passion of the howling wolf, the wild Moon majick of the forest. It is also used to fix the intention of spells.

Gum Mastic
Fire, Earth, Air • Sun, Saturn, Uranus

Gum Mastic can also carry or bind a spell, and it can prevent someone, or a situation, from doing harm.

Myrrh
Water • Moon, Saturn

Myrrh is a very protective and preserving herb, used to neutralize harm, to purify, and to summon rainbows after a storm. Myrrh was used in ancient Egypt in the mummification process.

Storax
Water, Air, Earth • Moon, Mercury

Storax resin—not to be confused with styrax resin, or benzoin—is the resin of the sweet gum tree, though the resins of several evergreen trees are sometimes referred to as storax. Much like frankincense and myrrh, it can neutralize harm and cleanse. It can help purify the senses and tranquilize the mind, as well as induce a deep healing trance when burned.

Tragacanth Powder
Fire, Water, Air, Earth • Sun, Moon, Mercury, Earth

Tragacanth powder is the binding agent found in many shaped incenses because it acts like a glue and has a neutral scent. It is calming and clearing in a very gentle way. It is also used to honor the Faery King and connect to his power. To align with the Faery King, carry tragacanth in a green bag.

MAJICKAL OILS: ESSENTIAL, INFUSED & FRAGRANCE

Oils form a huge aspect of our majickal apothecary, though their use can be confusing, as we can't go out and pick oils in our garden or gather them in the woods. We usually purchase them from Witchcraft supply shops, health food stores, and perfumers. The different types used in this book are not always clearly distinguished, as you should work with what is available for you. Majick doesn't have to be expensive to be effective. The most important ingredient is your intention.

The scent of oils is a powerful trigger. We often key into certain memories through associated scents. The smell of fresh bread or apple pie can bring us right back to a particularly powerful memory when those smells were present. Likewise in majick, the power of scent triggers our majick, helping us access trance-like states and recall far off majickal lands. Many Witches regularly use scented oils not only in ritual, but also in daily life to evoke energy, power, and blessings.

Oils can be divided into essential oils, fragrance oils, and infused oils. Each is made differently, but all can be used in majick. Essential oils are technically not oils at all, but the volatile chemicals of plants that give them their unique scent, and often their medicinal qualities. They are extracted from large amounts of the plant and can be quite expensive. Affordable ones (that are also easily available) include lavender, peppermint, lemon, and sweet orange. Essential oils are used in herbal medicine and aromatherapy and come in various "grades" for medicinal use. Unless the label says 100% essential oil, it is either a diluted oil or a fragrance oil.

Fragrance oils are not purely natural oils extracted from one plant, but often contain mixes of oils, natural and synthetic, to simulate the scent of a particular plant or to simulate the chemical structure of a particularly oil. Some of the most evocative majickal oils are either very expensive for the average majickal practitioner, such as rose and jasmine, or are made from a plant that has a strong scent, but extraction of the scent is quite difficult and costly, perhaps even impossible. The process of extraction can destroy the scent or change it radically. Other scents that were very popular in the occult movements are made from animals—oils such as musk, civet, and ambergris—and while still listed in formulas, practitioners today use synthetics for these evocative scents, or herbal substitutes. While most essential oils are extracted from steam distillation, some use CO_2 or other solvents. Popular scents like strawberry, lilac, gardenia, carnation, and apple are usually only available as fragrance oils. Mixes of pure essential oils that mimic the scent of another plant are known as bouquets, though one must keep in mind the original corresponding energies of plants in the bouquet. Due to their popular scents affecting the mind and memory, many of the formulas of this book use fragrance oils to stimulate the psyche and unlock the doors of enchantment. Those who trained in majick and occultism in an earlier era, prior to the holistic and natural movements, have grown attached to scents that are only available synthetically, but use those scents as majickal memory triggers.

Infused oils are true oils, made by placing amounts of herbal matter in an oil; they have little scent. The oil-herb mixture is either left out in the sun to infuse or heated gently on the stove or a double boiler to let the colors, scents and properties of the plant get into the oil. The oil will not smell strong, but will have the majick, and often the medicine, in the oil. Witches will often crush dragon's blood or other resins and infuse them in a base oil. Just gently stir in the powdered resin and apply a low level of heat in a saucepan. Let it cool, strain out the plant matter, and bottle it.

These true oils, infused or alone with their natural properties, can be used as a base to mix the more expensive essential oils and fragrance oils. Such base oils include almond oil, grape seed oil, hazelnut oil, sunflower oil, and apricot kernel oil. Many will use olive oil, but it is most likely to go rancid and makes a poor base for expensive essential oils. Use it only when you are going to use up all the oil quickly. A few drops of Vitamin E oil will slow down the decomposition process. While it makes a poor infused oil, as it is really an expensive liquid wax, jojoba "oil" is an excellent base for blends of expensive essential oils, as it will not spoil easily.

As with all herbs, consult a reputable medical resource or practitioner before using any oils, particularly if there are any medical concerns or contraindications. Many oils are very dangerous to pregnant women. When wearing oils, always use diluted oils and try a small test patch of diluted oil on your skin, to make sure there is no allergic reaction. Never consume these oils internally. The purpose of this book is to illustrate their majickal properties, not medicinal uses or dangers.

Here is a list of majickal scents for your majick.

Allspice – success in love and money matters, determination

Ambergris – to bind all majick

Ambrette Seed – substitute for musk, animal power, primal energy

Angelica – connecting to helpful spirits, protection

Anise – happiness, peace, good fortune

Apple – protection, love, empowerment

Apple Blossom – psychic vision of the Otherworld, faery majick

Balsam – power to overcome, insight, awareness

Basil – love, sex, prosperity

Bay – legal success, divination, psychic powers

Bayberry – to calm wild weather, to bring blessings of the winter

Benzoin – for psychic visions, stabilize a situation

Bergamot – for money and success

Black Pepper – lust, protection
Camphor – healing, divination, faery majick
Cardamon – lust, love, protection and wards
Carnation – protection, clearing, ancestors
Catnip – to bring success in love, attractiveness, and seduction
Cedar – for protection and long life, create and maintain sacred space
Chamomile – to heal, relax and bring to center
Cherry – love spells, kissing, romance, fun
Citronella – to cleanse and purify, to energize
Clary Sage – dreaming and good cheer
Clove – healing, strength and memories
Clover – the majick of the plant spirits, psychic travel to Ireland
Coriander – lust, passion and kindling the spirit
Cypress – comforting, centering, working with the spirits
Dragon's Blood – adds power to any majick
Elder – energy of the Dark Goddess, faery majick
Eucalyptus – to clear, cleanse and open the way
Fennel – for fertility, public speaking, protection and majickal power
Fir – eternal life, freshness, good fortune
Frangipani – sexual and sensual majick, altered states of awareness, trance
Frankincense – good luck, career success, purification, protection
Geranium – happiness, centering, grounding, protection
Ginger – for love, money and health, energy
Grapefruit – for healing and uplifting
Heather – the majick of Scotland, faery majick
Heliotrope – adds the power of the Sun, success, health, wealth, happiness
Honeysuckle – the majick of Wales
Hyssop – heals guilt, protection, cleansing
Jasmine – lunar majick, success, psychic powers, speaking with spirits

Juniper – for purity, protection and success

Labdanum – success in business and money, protection, solar fire

Lavender – peace, tranquility, good communication, faery contact

Lemon – purification, love

Lemongrass – cleansing, good fortune, fresh starts

Lilac – power, balance, truth, harmony, childhood

Lime – cleansing, purify, removal of obstacles

Lily of the Valley – faery power, healing the heart

Lotus Blossom – opening psychic centers, vision, spiritual awareness

Marjoram – clarity, love, happiness and home

Mimosa – enchantment, glamour, shapeshifting, self image

Mugwort – psychic powers, dreams, intuition

Musk – lust, romance, Stag God of the wild wood

Myrrh – purification, protection, ancestors, Dark Goddess

Neroloi – stimulating, protecting, cleansing

Nutmeg – physical and psychic energy, prosperity

Oak-moss – manifestation, grounding, money, home

Orange – health, success, happiness

Orris – fixative, binding harm

Palmarosa – love, harmony, blessings

Patchouli – love, protection, manifestation

Pennyroyal – initiation, protection (*caution* essential oil is an abortificient)

Peppermint – clear communication

Pine – for Merlin and the Morrighan, leadership, power

Rose – majick of England, love, healing, dreams

Rosemary – increases memory, purifies

Sage – clears and cleanses, encourages wisdom

Sandalwood – to increase psychic powers, lunar energy, meditation, stillness

Spearmint – for love majick

Star Anise – joy, blessings

Strawberry – love, to open to love's power

Tea Tree – purification, protection

Tonka – fixative, money, success, power

Valerian – dreams and rejuvenation

Vanilla – love, lust, power

Vetiver – astral travel, protection, nature spirits

Violet – love, past lives, getting over shyness

Wintergreen – success in love and money, gambling, strength

Wormwood – attracts the spirits, protection, kindles fire energy

Ylang Ylang – enhances all majick and psychic work, peace, love, happiness

Oils are measured by volume. One measurement you'll see often in old Witch and occult books is a dram. An archaic measurement of both weight and volume in ancient Greece, and used as an apothecary measurement, though a somewhat imprecise measurement. Today, by volume, a dram is considered to be 1/8 of an ounce. It used to be considered a full teaspoon, but teaspoon have gotten larger over the decades. In majickal work, a dram was often considered twenty drops of liquid, but we know that different droppers will measure out different drops by volume. But for the sake of these formulas, you can use the twenty drops equals one dram rule of measurement.

If you are using fragrance oils in incense, you should always test them first on charcoal. Many fragrance oils are not designed to be burned, and when they do burn, they smell like smoldering plastic. Oils that are designed to be heated in potpourri simmering dishes are usually okay for incense blends, but whenever possible, try to use all-natural oils for your incense.

Essential oils and other fragrances should not be confused with flower essences, which are very dilute solutions of flowers preserved in water and alcohol. Flower essences are used as remedies for mental and emotional imbalances in a similar way to homeopathy and are available in health food stores. A popular line is the Bach Flower Remedies, as Dr. Bach is considered the modern inventor of our flower essence healing traditions. Aromatherapy and Flower Essence Therapy are often mistaken for each other, but are very different healing techniques.

STONES, MINERALS, AND METALS

Majickal crystals are really any minerals infused with an intention. Before the days of crystals and stones from around the world being so available to us, we would use stones we found in our yards, on the beach, or in the woods. All stones have power. But the tradition of exotic stone use is found in ancient majick. Gemstones and minerals would be traded from faraway lands in the ancient world and made into majickal talismans and amulets.

I think we are drawn to certain stones by their color, and their beauty. If we are using them for majick, and if it works, we always seem to go back to that same stone. We don't experiment enough. Experimentation is part of how we learn. While you can favor particular stones, please make sure you experiment. First, do research to find out the attributes of the stone and learn how to incorporate it in a spell. There are specific stones for each type of majick. Carry the stone on your body for a short time and see how your own vibrations, your own energy, changes. Use this information in your own stone majick.

Below is a list of stones I use in my own majick, mixing "new" or newly discovered stones with minerals possessing a rich ancient lore.

Amber
Fire • Sun

Amber is a fossilized resin of tree sap, associated with Witchcraft and healing in many ancient cultures. Use amber to prevent poisoning of the body, mind, and spirit. Amber brings energy and healing, drawing out anything that harms and replacing it with beneficial energy. Amber prevents poisoning on both literal and metaphoric levels. It is a resin of the Goddess and God, to signify priestesses and priests in Witchcraft. It has a high level of vibration and can balance male and female energy.

Ametrine
Fire/Water • Sun, Jupiter

Carry ametrine for balance and intellectual stimulation. It clears your aura of unwanted energies. Citrine is ruled by the Sun and brings success and healing. Amethyst is for psychological balance and also Jupiter, for success. So Ametrine draws in the powers of both, along with everything they have to offer. It is a stone of partnership, as the two stones are partnered within it. It can be used for success and career advancement in all its forms. It is a very powerful stone.

Amethyst
Water • Jupiter, Neptune

Wearing amethyst brings courage and strength. It is a powerful healing stone that gives peace and clarity of mind. Amethyst literally means "not drunk" and can be used in majick for sobriety and addictions. Amethyst is a stone of psychological balance and also a stone of Jupiter, used for success.

Andalusite
Air • Earth

Carry andalusite as a charm to enhance memory and balance and to aid you in attaining a clear mind for meditation. Also known as faery cross, it can help us commune with the faery folk. Andalusite is a good stone to use before you cast a spell, to make sure you are thinking straight, so you are thinking correctly prior to casting the spell. Use it for clarity to be cognizant of your spell intention.

Aquamarine
Water •Neptune

Aquamarine is a stone of spiritual and emotional healing. It can bring awareness and clarity to any situation. Aquamarine is a mermaid stone. It is the stone of the siren song. It is a stone of the voice, and can help make your voice pleasing. Wear it near your throat so you will have a beautiful voice. Its energy is of motion, fluidity, and creativity. Use an aquamarine in order to create an appropriate majickal atmosphere. It will bring your mind to those creative stages in planning your spells and rituals.

Aragonite
Earth • Earth

Carrying aragonite gives self-confidence to anyone. It relieves stress and fatigue. It can also be used to disperse the stress of a household, office, or where the Earth has been disturbed. Many who are very needy in love, and who have been for years, create a high level of stress within. Aragonite can help relieve this inner stress, so you can allow in a new vibration of love and change your life.

Aventurine
Air • Venus

Aventurine is an excellent stone for money majick, including gambling and luck. Aventurine is a prosperity stone. Sometimes you don't have to have money in your pocket or gold on your wrist to be prosperous. Aventurine can help you understand what you already have, including appreciating your job, home, and resources. It helps you have a good vibe so people will respond best to you. It is a stone of compatibility.

Azurite
Water • Jupiter, Neptune

Azurite heightens psychic awareness and opens the third eye. Carry it and follow your intuition. It aids in envisioning what is correct for you. It helps you develop foresight and vision of your intentions and with manifesting your majick.

Bloodstone
Fire • Mars

Use bloodstone in legal matters to gain success and invincibility in your work. Bloodstone can also help you detect that which is being hidden or obscured from you. Carry bloodstone for protection and to prevent you from being deceived. Any illness of the blood can be aided with healing majick using bloodstone.

Botswana Agate
Air, Earth • Mercury

Carry Botswana agate for emotional comfort and stress relief. This type of agate helps promote friendship. Keep it by your doorway or carry it in your pocket to both attract friends and to know who is really your friend. You, or your guests, do not even have to be touching the stone.

Leave the stone in the room, and it will still work its majick. It is also a stone of protection, and used when traveling.

Blue Goldstone
Earth, Fire, Air • Jupiter, Uranus

Though a human-created "stone," blue goldstone can bring wisdom, energy, and inspiration to its user. Even though it's manmade, it still reflects and refracts light and has a lot of majickal lore. It reflects the energy of healing, success, and abundance, as well as wisdom and inspiration

Boulder Opal
Water • Moon, Venus

All types of opal can help scatter energy. It can be used in protection majick to disperse harmful forces. It also helps remove blocks from the energy system and the chakra centers, but it does not add to your overall energy. Use it first to clear before doing healing work. Opal can also clear away blocks to perceiving your spirit guides. Carry boulder opal in a majick bag to aid you in communicating with your spirit guides.

Calcite
Variable • Variable

Calcite is a wide range of colored stones, each with its own properties based upon the colors and their correspondences to the elements and planets. In general, calcite of any kind is used in healing, to remove blocks associated with the chakra of the calcite's color, as well as for general spirituality and wealth. Calcite's energy reaches outward, sending your intention outward to manifest what you want. It is a very powerful aid in spells and healing. Optical calcite, which looks like a natural magnifying glass, can double your spells. When you put it over any writing or pictures, it creates two images. Put it over your written spells and symbols to double your majickal power.

Carnelian
Fire • Mercury

A powerful gem for healing and energy, carnelian promotes courage and the healthy flow of sexual energy. Carnelian is said to be the blood of the goddess Isis, and it was used by the Egyptians for healing, calling upon her power and blessings.

Cat's Eye
Earth • Moon, Venus

Cat's eye grants the user beauty, wealth, and protection, in particular protection against infidelity or losing your wealth. In Vedic Astrology, cat's eye is a talisman for Ketu, or the South Node of the Moon, the heavenly body of our karmic past, so it helps us avoid past mistakes. Cat's eye gathers the energy from all the phases of the Moon, so it has a lot of lunar power to it. It pulls the tides of the lunar energy. A real cat's eye, the eye of the animal, almost looks like the phases of the Moon when cats shift their eyes from side to side. Cat's eye is a projection stone, helping you tune into your desires and project for them. The different colors of cat's eye influence its energy and use.

Chrysocolla
Water • Venus

Chrysocolla brings peace, wisdom, and love into all things. It clears the throat chakra so we can speak with more clarity and harmony, helpful in difficult situations. Chrysocolla is good for children to use, because it helps them feel calm and comfortable. It's particularly good for teenagers concerned about the troubles of the world and life. Chrysocolla can help them feel that everything will be okay. In many ways, this is a very motherly stone, helping us feel calm and speak up when we need to speak.

Citrine
Fire • Sun

Citrine is a powerful form of yellow quartz created due to an impurity of iron. It promotes health, wealth, money, and good restful sleep. Citrine is considered to be a "shower of prosperity."

Emerald
Earth • Venus

A stone with a rich history of majick, emerald helps us find answers to our problems psychically. It is associated with the eyes, and can be used both to heal the eyes and to heal in general with its green color stimulating the immune system. The wisdom of the deep Earth is said to be found within emerald. Witches of the Cabot Tradition meditate upon the emerald tablet, scrying into a vision of an emerald within our hand to find answers, so it is not only a stone of Hermetic wisdom, but of prophecy.

Fire Agate
Fire • Mercury, Mars

Fire agate looks as if it is shining with a fire within. It opens up your creativity. It increases stamina and encourages a zest for life and its pleasure. It ignites your intentions. It sets the spark going. Add it to a spell to speed things up, to make them go quickly, or to ignite your own feelings and motivate you. Fire agate is a "get up and go" stone. If someone is lethargic, depressed, or simply sad and unmotivated, fire agate is a good stone to carry.

Fuchsite
Air • Venus

Fuchsite can be used to send our love a long distance. It promotes blessings and good fortune, and it can be used to enhance any herbal healing formula. Fuchsite can also be used to commune with the faeries and nature spirits.

Garnet
Fire • Mars

Garnet is an energetic stone used for passion, sexual energy, and creativity. It is a stone of the Goddess. Red is the color of majick in most cultures, and while I think that all colors are majickal, it's the color of life force. Garnet can be considered the blood of the Goddess, and with that power, it can bring forth manifestation, creation, upon the Earth. It is a stone of sovereignty, a queen stone or king stone, much more so than ruby. We generally don't use rubies or diamonds because their energy is tainted in the way they are mined and traded. I only wear them when I have been gifted one from someone I know. Garnet can be grounding and protective when you want to retain your energy.

Green Goldstone
Earth, Fire • Venus

Another version of this human-crafted "stone," Green Goldstone is used for majick involving money, healing, and grounding.

Hematite
Earth, Fire • Mars

Hematite is a stone of healing and vitality. As it is composed of iron oxide, many use it as a grounding stone due to its heavy nature. It helps balance you when you are scattered. It metaphysically "nails things down" in your life.

Howlite
Earth, Water • Earth, Venus, Neptune, Sun

Howlite is an adaptable stone used for many purposes, including spiritual healing, awareness, clarity, and vision. It is often dyed and mistaken for turquoise. Howlite's name always reminds me of owls, and I feel it grants clarity beyond simple vision. It allows you to see in the darkness of your life, beyond what you would normally see.

Jasper
Earth, Air, Fire, Water • Earth, Jupiter

Jasper is a stone of beauty and self-esteem. It can be used for protection, pain relief. and even in weather majick to help it rain. Jasper is also a stone of success, bringing money, prosperity, and increased esteem in the eyes of others.

Jet (Witch's Amber)
Earth, Spirit • Earth, Saturn, Pluto

Jet is a fossilized wood similar to coal, often known as Witch's amber and often paired with the orange amber. It is a "stone" of protection, power, luck, and communion with the ancestors. Witch's amber is often paired with true amber in the necklace of a priestess or priest. Jet is the power of life itself, and it draws upon universal energies and deep knowledge. It is protective because it also grants you greater knowledge, and the more you know, the more protected you can be.

Kyanite
Air • Mercury

Kyanite promotes tranquility and peace when carried on your person. It can also aid in communication, clearing the throat chakra and stimulating psychic awareness. Kyanite can help you sleep when you are suffering from restlessness or insomnia. It easily puts you into a comfortable dream state.

Labradorite
Air • Uranus, Pluto

Labradorite encourages patience, clarity, and courage in difficult situation. It is also an excellent aid to meditation, dreams, and psychic development. Despite its otherworldly attributes, labradorite opens you up to nature, to the natural connections we have with all things. It can connect us to the stones, trees, and wild animals, as well as the planets, stars, and swirling galaxies.

Lapis
Water • Venus, Jupiter

Lapis, or lapis lazuli, is a stone of meditation, and regular use of it can aid psychic development and the skills of divination. Lapis can be used to connect with the gods of ancient Egypt. It is also used to encourage loyalty in others. Use lapis lazuli as a power stone.

Lodestone
Earth • Venus

Loadstone is a natural magnet used to magnetize, to command, and to draw to you all that your spell demands. This stone will enhance all of your spells. It can be part of a larger charm designed to draw your desires to you. It can be used like a key to unlock things in your life and open the way to their manifestation. Lodestone can also be used to ground if you are unfocused and scattered.

Malachite
Water, Earth • Venus

Malachite is a stone for both love and business, helping attract and manifest the things you desire. It is a pure Venusian stone of love, what is known as agape or divine love, and wearing it can put you in touch with that divine love, but it is also useful in spells for romance and relationship. It is also considered protective from physical harm. The powdered form of malachite is toxic, so be careful using it. Don't soak it in water.

Mookaite
Earth • Earth

Mookaite, also known as mookalite, helps Mother Nature grow most lush and abundant plants. Mookaite also helps with slow, gradual healing when carried as a charm. It protects you from overwhelming feelings and lets you be in the present moment.

Moonstone
Water • Moon

Moonstone is the Moon upon Earth. It draws down the Moon and uses its energy. It can help attune the user to the Moon. Moonstone enhances all Moon-related activities, including peaceful sleep, dream work, divination, and enhancing psychic power. If you are a Moon Child, influenced by the Moon or born under the sign of Cancer, it will greatly enhance your strength and energy. All Witches and psychics should wear it to enhance our connection to the Moon's phases. It is also a great stone for those lacking in compassion, empathy, or emotion, as it helps them feel deeply.

Moss Agate
Earth • Earth, Mercury

Moss agate is used to heal, increase energy, aid in any skin ailments where your emotions are expressing themselves through your skin, attract money, and make friends. It helps you be compatible, or attract more compatible people to you. It increases your own sense of beauty, letting your confidence grow so that you might get to know others.

Obsidian
Fire • Mars, Pluto

Obsidian is associated with the Dark Goddess and is used for scrying and spirit contact. It can also be used to grant wishes and for protection. Make sure to clear and balance obsidian, more than any other stone, as its energy can be chaotic and disruptive if not properly cleansed and charged. I use an obsidian ball charged and fixed to bring order and organization to my life.

Onyx
Fire, Earth • Mars, Saturn

Onyx majick is for physical strength, extreme courage, and exorcism majick. Onyx can be used to scatter energy and neutralize majick used against you. Best used by those who are Capricorn Sun signs or have Capricorn and/or Saturn well-placed within their chart.

Peridot
Earth • Venus, Sun

Peridot is a stone of healing, restful sleep, and money. It eases stress and pressure in the emotions. It can also help manifest fame and fortune.

Petrified Wood
Air • Saturn

Petrified Wood, since it had another "life," is an excellent aid in doing past life regression work. It is also a stone of healing and longevity. It aids in being present, in grounding and centering and being stable. It also helps connect to nature.

Prehnite
Water • Venus

Prehnite is a stone of healing and unconditional love. It helps open your heart and connect you to the planet. It can also help connect to the root causes and issues of problems and illnesses so that you can solve them more clearly.

Quartz Crystal
Earth, Air, Fire, Water • Sun, Moon

Quartz crystal can be used for all majickal purposes, amplifying any intention. It is one of my favorite stones because it does everything and can enhance anything. Quartz contains an electrical resonance—the larger the crystal, the stronger the resonance in it. Like a radio, which has a quartz crystal in it, quartz will carry your words and intentions far across the universe to manifest.

Rainbow Moonstone
Water • Moon

Rainbow moonstone strengthens your intuition and psychic powers. It helps connect you to the Goddess of the Moon and brings balance and harmony to all things. By weaving a connection between the Earth and the Moon, you can open to your intuition. Rainbow moonstone brings in all of the light of the rainbow, all the colors of psychic power, and can be used in many different forms of majick.

Rhodocrosite
Earth • Mars, Venus

Rhodocrosite is used for love, self-esteem, and happiness, helping the user feel connected to others and themselves. The stone can generate feelings of loyalty in the user, and in those around anyone who carries it. The love of rhodocrosite can almost be considered a form of patriotic love, inspiring love of groups as well as individuals. It is the love of family, tribe, community, and country. This stone can also be used in active dreaming.

Rhodonite
Earth • Venus

Rhodonite, similar to Rhodocrosite, is a stone of peace, balance, and happiness. The small specks of black help draw in more light, making rhodonite more powerful.

Rose Quartz
Earth, Water • Venus

Rose Quartz is one of the most powerful yet gentle stones for love, compassion, and spirituality. It helps open the heart to the essential spirit and self-worth within.

Rutilated Smoky Quartz
Fire, Earth • Earth, Saturn

Rutilated smoky quartz is a stone that enhanced mental telepathy, psychic ability, and healing work. It is also used in some forms of weather majick. I must admit that smoky quartz is not my favorite stone to work with, though the rutile brings out special qualities.

Sapphire
Earth • Jupiter

Sapphire helps you open your awareness and ground yourself. It can also be used to enhance study and to bring good fortune. People will recognize your talents and abilities when you use sapphire. You'll be better able to influence situations to your advantage with its energy.

Sea Salt
Earth, Water • Moon, Saturn

While usually seen as part of the herbal inventory, technically sea salt is a mineral. It is used for protection and clearing, and to help stabilize water-based potions. If sea salt is not available, kosher salt is an excellent substitute.

Selenite
Water • Moon

Selenite is a water soluble crystal, so do not cleanse with water or it will melt. It promotes peace, meditation, and clear judgment. Selenite can also open and balance the crown chakra. Some use selenite wands to clear other crystals and tools, by placing objects on the selenite for a few minutes. Selenite has a pure and clear energy. Like quartz, selenite is a versatile and powerful stone, able to be programmed for any intention, as it will direct and magnify that intention.

Seraphinite
Earth, Air • Venus

Seraphinite, named after the angelic Seraphim, is used for healing, clearing, and enhancing cooperation between people. It can also be used to connect with higher dimensional beings as well as nature spirits and elementals. Seraphinite, due its green color, can be used for the regeneration of cells within your body, and for emotional healing and inner awareness of patterns that harm you so they can be neutralized and transformed.

Serpentine
Fire • Earth, Mars

Serpentine is used to double any blessings given from the Goddess and God. In particular it's good for blessings with money and good fortune. It is also a charm against poisoning and bites from insects and snakes. It can be used for grounding and attuning to nature. Due to the serpentine characteristics, it is associated with kundalini, the serpent power at the base of the spine.

Smoky Quartz
Fire, Earth • Sun, Moon, Saturn

Smoky quartz is a stone of meditation and clarity. It helps open and amplify your intentions, while still remaining grounded and calm within your body. Smoky quartz can be carried as a protective stone.

Snowflake Obsidian
Fire, Water • Mars, Saturn, Pluto

Snowflake obsidian is used to bring peace and balance to mind and body. It is a protective and grounding stone. It is also a stone that can balance polarities. While obsidian can bring either order or chaos to a situation, the white flecks of the "snowflake" help balance the energies of obsidian.

Sodalite
Fire, Air • Jupiter

Sodalite helps transform anxiety into success, particularly success in business. Sodalite can also help facilitate clear communication between people who are having disagreements. Sodalite has many similar qualities to lapis, and can be used as a lapis substitute when necessary.

Sugilite
Air, Water • Jupiter, Neptune

Sugilite enhances any work with the third eye. Place it upon your brow to activate your third eye. If using it with the intention to open the psychic powers, it can feel like a hole is being opened all the way through the head. It can also be used to calm down psychic abilities that are overactive, or when worry and despair claim your imagination and inner vision. It helps clear away emotional patterns that limit you, as well as balance any disorders associated with the head or brain. Use it to help with headaches, dyslexia, cognition, and motor dysfunction.

Tektite
Fire, Earth, Air • Uranus, Pluto

Tektite, created from the fall of a meteorite mixing with natural minerals upon the Earth, can be used for courage, protection, and to facilitate astral travel.

Tiger's Eye
Fire • Mars

Tiger's eye is a stone of power and energy. It increases health and life force. Carry it to bolster your will to succeed and overcome difficult odds.

Tiger Iron
Fire • Mars

Tiger iron is used to increase energy, common sense, and grounding. It's similar to tiger's eye, but much more grounding.

Tourmaline
Various • Various

Tourmaline is a mineral that comes in a wide range of colors, including black, blue, green, pink, red, and a "watermelon" of green outside and pink inside. The different colors determine the best type of majick it can be used in, as each color is associated with a planetary force. Tourmaline can be used for healing of mind, body, and spirit, and the color influences the specific type of majick. Tourmaline really moves majick and removes blocks to healing and manifestation.

Tourmaline Quartz
Earth, Air, Fire, Water • Sun, Pluto

Tourmaline Quartz is clear quartz that has black tourmaline within it. A powerful all-purpose stone, it is best used for money majick, business, success, courage, and protection.

Tree Agate
Earth • Mercury

Tree agate is an excellent stone for gentle grounding, protection, and healing. Like moss agate, it helps connect you to nature and can encourage friendships.

Turquoise
Earth • Jupiter

Turquoise is a sacred stone wherever it is found in the world, particularly to many Native American tribes. It is a stone of friendship, protection, and courage. Its blessings are many, and its gentle vibrations can be used for healing and empowerment. In my own experiences, turquoise is a stone of time travel, specifically moving backward in time. Though I don't know any traditional lore about such uses, it takes me back in time, usually as a past life regression. I'm not sure if it works well that way for others, but that is how it works for me.

Unakite
Water • Neptune

Unakite is a stone of emotional balance and clear spirituality. It can be used to promote a healthy pregnancy, and it is also associated with better communion with your familiars and animals in general.

Zebra Jasper
Earth • Mercury

Zebra jasper is a stone used for stamina, endurance, and balance. The balance is brought about by the alternating colors, the stripes of the zebra. Otherwise it has similar qualities to other jaspers.

Zebra Serpentine
Fire • Pluto

Zebra serpentine has all the associations of serpentine, along with a particular specialty in creating balance, bravery, and courage. It is particularly good for balancing mood swings and hormonal imbalances.

Zoisite
Earth, Fire • Venus, Mars

Zoisite is used to draw love and happiness. Sometimes it is found with small amounts of ruby and is particularly good in healing the heart after a bad break-up. It can increase vital energy, particularly if found with ruby, which appears as small red spots upon the green and black, and is an overall healer of the body.

METALS

Like minerals, metals can also be used for majickal intentions. While sometimes available in a raw form, metals are most likely to be worked with in the form of jewelry or other tools. We can empower anything metallic as part of a majickal spell and wear it without anyone knowing our majick is at work.

Gold
Fire • Sun

Gold is the king of metals, what alchemists were seeking in their spiritual transformations. It is the symbol of enlightenment and of the sovereign, the king or queen. It is used for success, health, happiness, wealth, power, and spiritual evolution. Gold is the metal of the God.

Silver
Water • Moon

Silver is the metal of the Moon. Wearing it enhances psychic abilities, as silver conducts psychic energy and helps store the blessings of the Moon. It can also be used in majick for fertility, creativity, and emotional healing. It is the metal of the Goddess. It helps us follow our soul's path in this life.

Quicksilver
Air • Mercury

Quicksilver, or liquid mercury, captures our fascination because it is the only metal that is a liquid at room temperature. I'm of a certain generation where children played with the mercury of thermometers before our society realized how dangerous it is, being highly toxic and easily absorbed into our skin, which creates all sorts of sensory, neurological, and nervous problems, all of which the planet Mercury rules over. I don't recommend using mercury in your majick unless it's in a tightly sealed bottle and left unopened.

Copper
Earth, Air • Venus

Copper is the metal of love. It tarnishes green, the color of Venus. Used in the form of copper jewelry worn near the joints to treat aches and pains, it is also a metal that attracts love and luxury to us. Today, copper is most easily found in mineral shops, but it can also be found in U.S. pennies prior to 1982, but such pennies must be cleansed and neutralized of all previous energies before using them for majick.

Iron
Earth, Fire • Mars

Iron can come in the form of iron powder, often called lodestone food, as these iron shavings are used to "feed" lodestones for majick that is used to draw wealth and other desires to the natural magnet. Iron can also come in the form of antique iron nails. Iron is sometimes called the blood of the Earth, as it oxides as red rust. Traditionally iron is used in majick for protection and defense. It's a component of the Witch's Bottle spell for protection. It is said that faeries usually shun iron, but it is also used to disrupt unwanted spirits and energies. Steel, an alloy of iron, has similar majickal properties, but many find that pure iron itself is best for majick. As steel, particularly carbon steel, is also transformed, or improved upon, iron, it could also be found under the rulership of Pluto, a "higher octave" of the energy of Mars.

Tin
Water, Fire, Air • Jupiter

Tin is a silvery, shiny metal that is both malleable and ductile, and is considered more 'brittle" than some of the other metals. It has a crystalline structure, and when bent, emits a sound as the structure is disrupted; that sound is known as a "tin cry." Ruled by Jupiter, tin evokes the power of prosperity, abundance, and good fortune. It is useful in any type of legal matters. In the past, tin was easily available through actual tin cans, but today most tin cans are made from steel. Traditional tin foil is not easily available, as it has been replaced with aluminum foil. Tin can still be obtained through chemical supply shops.

Lead
Earth • Saturn

Lead is a soft, heavy, malleable metal that was used throughout the ancient world both in majick and in construction. Unfortunately lead is toxic, and is considered a neurotoxin that builds up in the tissue and bones, leading to disorders of the brain and nervous system. Today, it is used in buildings and alloys, but most of us experience it as a radiation shield, particularly when getting X-rays. Lead's nature is protective and serves as a barrier, as all things toxic have the properties of setting boundaries between what is safe and what is harmful. Lead is also a metal of silence, to help you listen to your inner voice.

Aluminum
Air, Water • Mercury, Uranus, Neptune

Aluminum is sometimes used as a substitute for quicksilver. Like quicksilver, it is reflective, and therefore associated with majick mirrors, scrying, and reflection. Some use it with, or in place of, a majick mirror for psychic scrying, communication, and protection. Due to its lightness, it can help you feel uplifted and free when you would otherwise feel bound and too grounded in your problems. Various magicians have associated aluminum with either Neptune or Uranus. Aluminum is now considered toxic and should not be used in food preparation.

Brass
Air, Fire • Sun, Venus, Uranus

Brass is an alloy of copper and zinc. It is an excellent conductor of all forms of majickal energy. Brass candlestick holders are the best due to this conductive nature. Due to the golden color, it is associated with the Sun, and can be a substitute for true gold, though its copper gives it a natural affinity to Venus and its zinc to Uranus as well.

Bronze
Fire, Air • Venus, Jupiter

Bronze is an alloy of copper and tin, though some alloys that are a mix of copper with some other metal, such as aluminum, are sometimes called bronze. Brass and bronze are often mistaken for each other. While they have similar appearances, they are different energetically. Bronze mixes the energies of two of the most beneficial planets, Venus and Jupiter, bringing beauty, success, and self-confidence in majick.

Electrum
Fire, Water • Sun, Moon

Electrum is an alloy made mostly of gold and silver. It can occur naturally with other metals, particularly copper, though it is also created artificially and used in majickal talismans and tools. It balances the properties of the Sun and Moon, male and female, active and receptive.

Pewter
Air, Earth • Jupiter, Saturn

Pewter is a tin alloy, traditionally made by mixing tin and lead, though today most pewter is "lead free" and is an alloy of mainly tin mixed with copper, antimony, bismuth, or even silver. As traditionally a mix of the Jupiter energies of tin and the Saturn energies of lead, pewter has the power of regeneration and protection. Pewter can also help us accept our worldly responsibilities and have success with them.

Platinum
Water, Earth • Moon, Saturn

Platinum is not used often in majick, but is said to have similar qualities to both lead and silver, without the toxicity of lead. It is considered a "wise" metal that can help you see both into the past and into the future.

Zinc
Air • Mercury, Uranus

Zinc is a metal that bolsters the immune system and helps regulate the signals within the body, particularly the electrical and majickal impulses. Worn as jewelry, or taken as a supplement, zinc can help reduce excess nervous energy.

Other metals are associated with the outer planets in astrology, but due to their dangerous radioactivity are impossible to obtain and dangerous to use. Uranus is associated with uranium. Neptune corresponds with neptunium, and Pluto with plutonium. We simply include this occult information to help Witches better understand the volatile and "radioactive" power these outer planets can have.

ANIMALS

In older majickal books, such ingredients were said to come from the "Bestiary." While it might sound strange to us, animal parts have long been used in both majick and medicine, and many forms of traditional Chinese and Indian medicine still do mix animal parts with herbs and minerals to make powerful remedies.

Modern Witches, however, are very sensitive to the energy of animals and to the rights of animals as our allies in majick and kin upon the Earth. We generally only take that which has been shed from a live, healthy animal. Fur or skin obtained this way will have a living, healthy energy to be used in our majick. We never harm any animal to obtain ingredients for our spells, and we would never create a commercial market for animal parts, endangering the animals.

When I reclaimed my path as a Witch in my adulthood, I made friends with a curator at the local Franklin Park Zoo. I explained to him that I was using these things as a part of my religion, not making a product out of it to create a market and endanger the animals. He gave me many exotic ingredients not available to most Witches today, such as lion claws, leopard fur, and bear fur. Here are some animal ingredients for spells that are more readily available.

Abalone Shell
Water • Neptune

Use abalone shell for spiritual healing on all levels. It can release tears of joy and open up blocked emotions. The goddesses and gods of the sea work through the vibration of abalone.

Bee Pollen and Bee's Wax
All Elements • Sun, Venus

All the products of bees—including pollen, wax, and honey—are considered blessed and majickal ingredients for our work. Bees are like sacred alchemists. They transform nature in quite amazing ways, making majick and medicine, just like Witches. The honey bee, or *melissa*, is also the name of the ancient Greek priestesses who attended the priestess of Delphi in her oracular prophecies. The pollen can be mixed with rose petals and a love oil for a very powerful spell for romance. Carry it in a red bag. The wax can be mixed with thyme and carried in a black bag for protection.

Cat Hair
Water • Moon, Venus

Cats help us connect to the power of the psychic world, as cats can see into the Otherworld quite clearly. They know to follow their intuition and respond to the unseen. If the cat is your own majickal familiar, using the fur helps empower all your majick and deepen your relationship.

Dog Hair
Earth • Earth

Dogs help us stay grounded in the world, being present for simple joys. They are teachers of loyalty and also great protectors. Dog hair can be used as a substitute for wolf hair when necessary, particularly when it's from a more wolf-like dog. Other dog species bring out different qualities.

Eggshell
All Elements • Earth

White powdered eggshell, known as *cascarilla* in the African traditions, is a powerful component in majick. Eggs hold the energy of life and birth, helping us bring new things into manifestation. They are said to be catalysts for our majick for this reason. Traditionally, a shell is also a protection for the egg, and powdered eggshell can be used in protective markings. (Cascarilla is also the name of a Caribbean plant and should not be confused with powdered eggshell.)

Feathers
Air • Mercury

Feathers are used in a wide range of majick, depending on the color and type. Generally they are associated with the element of Air, for clear communication, and the planet of Mercury, for swiftness of thought, word, and deed. Dyed feathers, or naturally colored bright feathers, can be associated with their corresponding elemental or planetary colors in spells. Feathers are used in message and travel majick. Specific feathers can be associated with deities. Crows are associated with the Morgan. Though technically possessing crow feathers, and the feathers of any raptors is illegal in the United States now, we often used black colored feathers in place of crow feathers. Feather spells can be "launched" by blowing the feathers into the wind, just as lighting a candle sends the spell in fire majick. The direction in which you blow the feathers can influence the spell. Feathers could be blown towards New York City or Hollywood, relative to your position, for fame and fortune. Working on the top of a hill on a windy day is an excellent way to work with feathers in majick. Using feathers to demonstrate your control over the wind, summing the winds at will, is an aspect of traditional Witchcraft as taught to me by my teacher Felicity. Use the following list of specific bird feathers in crafting your majickal intentions, or as a form of divination, a way to receive a message from the animal world.

Bluebird– happiness, luck, blessings
Bluejay – resourcefulness, adaptability, communication, speaking up
Cardinal – vitality, self-love, self-esteem, pride
Crow – intelligence, majick, warrior spirit, prophecy, sacred law, spirit travel
Chickadee – truthfulness
Crane – longevity, creativity, intelligence
Dove – peace, motherhood, prophecy, exploration
Duck – comfort, protection, adaptability
Eagle – inspiration, courage, healing, creativity, spirit messages, true path, clear sight

Finch – energy, vitality, action, potential

Goose – travel, quests, awakening, ancestors

Hawk – psychic vision, protection, strength, warrior, hunter

Hummingbird – joy, fertility, healing

Kingfisher – prosperity, love

Magpie – majick, intelligence, psychic strength

Owl – wisdom, prophecy, healing, fertility, mystery, darkness

Raven – majick, creation, resolve, cleverness

Robin – fertility, rejuvenation

Sparrow – victory, dignity, self-worth, success

Starling – family unity, hope, protection, messages, communication, clarity

Swan – beauty, truth, self-knowledge, ancestors, faeries

Swift – speed, agility, perception

Vulture – death, rebirth, purification, ancestors, underworld

Woodpecker – insight, rhythm, healing, love

Wren – boldness, resourcefulness, rulership, ingenuity

Fleece
Earth • Earth

Fleece is the wool of a sheep or long-haired goat before it is turned into yarn. Either can be used in majick for creating peace, comfort, dream majick, guidance, and purity. The majick of sheep energy can help people accept help from others, guidance when they are lost.

Horse Hair
Fire, Earth • Mars, Earth

Horse majick brings power, freedom, and the ability to travel. Horses are a sign of civilization, as they were one of the first animals domesticated. They are the shamanic steeds to visit the Otherworld and are associated with the goddesses Epona, Rhiannon, and Macha. Horse hair adds power to any spell.

Rabbit Fur
Air • Mercury, Moon

Rabbit fur will speed up any spell, making it "quick like a bunny." When you want to make something happen immediately, add a little rabbit fur.

Snake Skin
Earth • Saturn

The snake is a totem of the Goddess, symbolizing psychic ability, change, and transformation. Snake skin is used in majick when you must regenerate, shedding your skin and becoming something new. You can use it in spells of healing and protection. Mix the skin with melted beeswax and warm olive oil. When it cools, you have a salve to heal the skin and increase majickal power.

Stag Antlers
Earth • Earth, Sun

The stag is the totem of the Lord of the Forest, the horned god Cernunnos. In alchemy, the stag is a symbol of the Sun. Stag confers the powers of strength, alertness, independence, nobility, manifestation, and regeneration. The stag sheds its antlers in the spring and regrows them. Powdered antlers were used in medieval medicine, and antler "velvet" is still used in Chinese traditional medicine and some modern alternative medicine. Antler found from a shedding stag can be used to add power and health to any spell. It is particularly potent for spells involving personal sovereignty.

Wolf Hair
Earth, Fire • Mars

Wolf fur is very powerful for protection. Witches mix it with herbs ands stones of protection in our protection potions or carry it in a black majick bag. It, like other animal hair, should be taken from a live and shedding animal. It would be good for the postman to carry wolf fur, particularly for protection from strange dogs and other unknown dangers.

Other ingredients from animals—items such as crab shells, wasp's nests, red ants, gator claws, rabbit's feet and various animal bones and teeth—can be found in majick shops, but they are not used in the Cabot Tradition of majick.

GRAVEYARD DIRT

Witches often gather dirt, also known as graveyard dust, from the graves of people they admire or people who had skills they aspire to have and use in their majick. We primarily use it in our protection potions, using a pinch from the grave of someone admired for bravery. While other majickal traditions have more invasive methods of gathering the dirt, I suggest that you take dirt from the top of the grave, without disturbing the grave. Replace any sod you remove to gather the dirt, and do not use a shovel. If you simply want to commune with the ancestors, you can gather dirt from the highest monument in the graveyard or at the gate. It is traditional to make an offering to the spirits of the grave itself, and at the gate, usually a few coins or a libation of water or alcohol.

COLOR, SYMBOLS & OTHER MAJICKAL TOOLS

While we often think of nature strictly as the animal, vegetable, and mineral realms, all things comes from nature, and even if they are crafted by human hands, they have an inherent majick in them due to their shape, symbol, and color. Several tools do not fall into the more traditional ingredient lists above, but are nonetheless important to the Witch.

Anything of a particular color will carry the vibration, the majick, of the color it has. Stones of a particular color, whether natural or synthetic, reflect a particular vibration for majick. You can use any type of color in your life, from the color of your clothing to the color of your nails and hair. You can do majick with the color of your car. Color influences everything in majick. The various tools below are influenced by color.

Color	Element	Planet	Signs	Majick
Red	Fire	Mars	Aries	passion, creation, partnership, marriage
Black	All	Pluto	Scorpio	secrets, discovery, balance
Orange	Air, Fire	Mercury	Gemini	directions, writing, schooling
Gold	Fire	Sun	Leo	dominance, searching, healing, success, treasure
Yellow	Fire, Air	Sun	Leo	coins, treasure
Green	Earth, Air	Venus	Taurus, Libra	balance, love, beauty, comfort
Sea Green	Water	Neptune	Pisces	psychic ability, art, beauty, healing
Royal Blue	Air, Water	Jupiter	Sagittarius	influencing people in high places, humor, adventure
Light Green	Water	Neptune	Pisces	love of family, shapeshifting, art, creation
Wine	Earth	Saturn	Capricorn	hard work, dedication, teaching
Indigo	Air, Earth	Jupiter	Sagittarius	deep thought, night sky,

Burgundy	Earth	Saturn	Capricorn	keeping silent, attaining greatness, youth
Purple	Air	Jupiter	Sagittarius	parties, sports, sculpting
Orchid	Water	Moon	Cancer, Pisces	emotions, acting, psychology
Pink	Earth, Air, Water	Venus	Taurus, Libra	self-adornment, self-love, choosing a mate
Rose	Earth, Air, Water	Venus	Taurus, Libra	Goddess majick, law, protection
Brown	Earth	Venus, Earth	Virgo	teaching, critic, decision making, grounding
Black	Earth, Fire, Water, Air	Saturn	Capricorn	absorbing knowledge, study, healing
Gray	Earth, Air	Mercury	Gemini, Virgo	inventing, psychological insight, clearing
White	Earth, Fire, Water, Air	Uranus	Aquarius	lightning, quickness, revolution, teaching lessons
Iridescent	Water	Neptune	Pisces	intuition, psychic power
Opalescent	Water	Moon	Cancer	protection, hidden things, faerie contact

Likewise, certain symbols have built up power and meaning over time. Some are from esoteric systems, such as the Norse runes or Celtic Ogham script, while others are much more simple. They can be symbols such as the Sun, Moon, star, skull and crossbones, or dollar signs. All symbols can be tools in your majick.

Planet Glyph	Name	Colors	Majick
☉	Sun	Gold, Yellow, Orange, Red	Physical Strength, Success, health, winning, creativity, obtaining goals, wealth, illumination

Symbol	Planet	Colors	Attributes
☾	Moon	Silver, Light Blue, Lavender, Orchid, Opalescent Colors	Psychic Ability, Psychological Balance, beauty, feminine force, dreams, astral travel, protection, intuition
☿	Mercury	Orange, Gray, Silver	Wisdom, all knowledge, motion, communication, travel, transportation, speed, healing, motivation, creativity
♀	Venus	Green, Pink, Rose, Brown	Love, growth, health, fertility, new projects, beauty, sensuality, money, jewelry, cosmetics, pleasure, friendship, prosperity
♂	Mars	Red	Action, force, protection, partnership, marriage, passion, sexual love, courage, clothing, determination, furniture
♃	Jupiter	Royal Blue, Purple, Indigo, Turquoise	Good fortune, wealth, success, law, influence people in high places, business, officials, honors, expansion, material logic
♄	Saturn	Black, Wine, Indigo	Testing, binding, to inhibit, manifestation, crystalization, science, concentration, maturity, discipline, invention, pragmatic, neutralization, longevity
♅	Uranus	Dazzling White	Eccentric ideas, invention, publicity, reform, electricity, bizarre happenings, unexpected changes, revolution, divine mind
♆	Neptune	Iridescent Colors, Sea Green, Dark Blue	Visions, dreams, ideals, fantasies, asrtistic abilities, psychic awareness, healing, images, water, illusions, chemical change, unconditional love
♇	Pluto	Black, Red	Bring order to chaos, group ideas, sudden manifestation of spells and projections, power, unification or disruption, wishes

◇	Earth	Brown, Rust, Beige, Green	Action, force, passion, partnership, building, gardening, marriage, balance, decisions, grounding, nesting, stability
▷	Vulcan	Rainbow of Primary Colors	Total force in all majick
◈	Sparta	Brown	Grounding, balance, harmony, pragmatic

For those unfamiliar with the planets Vulcan and Sparta, they are two "esoteric" planets of occult tradition used in the Cabot Tradition. Vulcan is said to be an inter-Mercurial planet, within the orbit of Mercury. Vulcan is known as the "Jeweler of the Gods" and the master of the forge, putting total power into your majick. Sparta is considered a "twin" to Earth, on the opposite side of Earth's orbit, mirroring many of the qualities of our own planet. As traditions of astrology develop and diverge, some have given many of the associations of Vulcan to the planetoid Chiron, and the associations of Sparta to the hypothesized planet believed to be beyond Pluto, sometimes referred to as Persephone or Proserpina.

Zodiac Glyph	Name	Colors	Planet	Majick
♈	Aries	Red	Mars	Warrior, protection, athletics, competition
♉	Taurus	Green, Pink, Red-Orange	Venus	Grounding, prosperity, sensuality, health
♊	Gemini	Orange	Mercury	Communication, writing, speaking, humor, social activities
♋	Cancer	Yellow-Orange, Silver	Moon	Mothering, nourishment, care taking, creation, life

♌	Leo	Yellow, Gold	Sun	Creativity, art, music, theater, fame, showmanship
♍	Virgo	Yellow-Green, Brown, Gray	Mercury	Healing, daily job, healing anxiety, processing, discernment
♎	Libra	Green, Pastels	Venus	Balance, meditation, justice, romance, art, decisions
♏	Scorpio	Blue-Green, Red, Black	Pluto, Mars	Power, secrets, psychic ability, mystery, occultism, sexuality
♐	Sagittarius	Blue, Purple	Jupiter	Education, travel, philosophy, athletics, adventure, freedom
♑	Capricorn	Indigo, Black	Saturn	Responsibility, career, leadership, discipline, tradition
♒	Aquarius	White, Purple	Uranus, Saturn	Social consciousness, individuality, technology, utopian ideals, equality
♓	Pisces	Violet	Neptune	Creativity, self expression, dance and art, trance, resolving inner saboteur

The colors and symbols of a variety of tools and ingredients can aid us in our spellcraft. Candles are functional for light and for setting an atmosphere of enchantment, but the color of the candles adds to the majick, as each color is associated with certain elements, planets, and zodiac signs. If you want to draw the influence of a particular planet, use the charts below to determine what color candle for your altar. In addition to the traditional candles on the altar—black for the Goddess, placed on the left of the altar to absorb light for our majick, and white for the God, placed on the right of the altar to send out light for our majick—a third candle, matched by color to your intention for the overall working, maybe be used in between, even if the spell you are performing is not primarily a candle spell.

The clothing you wear during majick, and even during your day, influences your energy. I suggest matching the colors of your clothing to the primary planetary influences and aspects of the day, an excellent way to take advantage of their power. Ritual clothing is often called vestments, and many Witches choose to wear special clothes in ritual, such as robes and cloaks. They are primarily black. We wear black because it absorbs light. The more light you absorb, the more energy you have. Black draws in all colors, all light. Wearing black is important when doing spells because you want to absorb all the light energy that you can. It will fill your aura with that power and make a more successful spell.

The jewelry a Witch wears is also part of her majick. The various metals have properties, and the stones and shapes set into jewelry bring a particular influence. Many Witches wear the pentacle, the five-pointed star in a circle, as a symbol of majick, Witchcraft, and protection, but it is also a symbol of alpha and of information. Much of its majick and protection come from having greater access to psychic information, and through your intuition, being in the right place at the right time.

In the old days, writing was only done with a quill pen. Today we have magic markers, felt pens, and many other writing options, though some Witches, including myself, still prefer quill pen and ink. The pen is the wand. Written spells can use special ink. While a simple, good quality black pen is useful for most spell petitions, special colored ink can be used to align with the planets. Herbs, oils, and stones, charged in ritual, can be added to the ink, making it a potion. Planetary inks can be made best on the day of the week associated with the planet (see the following table).

I always use potions and stones in my inks to enhance the power. An artist's ink pen or brush can be used to write spells with this ink. Many modern Witches, rather than making ink, instead clear and charge a set of colored pens or markers for their majick. When I write a spell to bring something to me, I use a black feather pen. The color black contains all colors; therefore it absorbs all light, energy, and majick. I actually have two black feather pens. One is only for protection spells. When I write a protection spell, I put a drop of Black Feather Potion into the ink and adorn the ink bottle with a small pentacle. The other black pen is for my personal needs, and I use appropriate ink for the type of spell I am writing.

Day of the Week	Planet
Sunday	Sun
Monday	Moon
Tuesday	Mars
Wednesday	Mercury
Thursday	Jupiter
Friday	Venus
Saturday	Saturn

Likewise parchment, a special paper, is most often used in written majick. Traditional parchment was made from animal skin, but today parchment refers to a fancy printing paper, not the parchment paper used for cooking. Parchment printing paper comes in a variety of styles and colors and can be matched by color to your intention.

Various containers are used for majickal ingredients to create a charm or talisman. Small colored bags can be purchased or sewn to carry stones, roots, and herbs. Such bundles can be called a mojo bag. Mojo refers to majickal power; the term mojo bag was first used in the American tradition of majick known as Hoodoo, but many Witches in America have adopted it. Those who don't have an aptitude for sewing can take small squares of cloth with the ingredients in the center, bundle up the ends, and tie it together to form a small bag.

Bottles are another important device for majick. Small sealable bottles and jars are used to contain various ingredients and charms, making a vessel for a particular spell intention. Some bottles are hung in the home or business. Others are buried or placed in your freezer. If you are going to display the bottle as a part of the majick, then obtaining beautiful decorative bottles will be essential.

In order to create a spell bottle, you must decide your intention. Find a bottle, preferably new. I prefer a cork-topped bottle. Take a small piece of parchment paper and write your spell. Roll the spell up and tie with a proper color ribbon. Find a crystal or stone that you can charge to place into the bottle. If you can find a charm or herb that will help ignite the power to have the spell bottle work, once you have placed the ingredients in the bottle, seal the cork with glue. If you wish, you can embellish the cork and the top of the bottle with a crystal bead and other charms. Cast a circle and send the spell. You can keep the bottle or give it to a friend.

Our majickal potions in the Cabot Tradition tend to come into two basic types. The first is made from a water infusion of dried or fresh herbs, and the second is made in an oil base. Water-based potions are like herbal teas, but are typically preserved with sea salt. They do not always have a strong or pleasing scent to them. Oil-based potions are more of the traditional Witchcraft perfumes, with essential oils or fragrance oils infused—along with various plants, stones, or animal hair—into the oil. One of the more majickal measurements of classic potion formulas is the dram, meaning twenty drops, though many bottles that are 1/8th of a fluid ounce are marked dram bottles. Dry "potions" are known as philters; they are majickal powders that can be scattered, kept in a bowl, put in a charm bag, or burned as incense.

All liquid potions can use a little bit of heat, and can be made on a stove. Gas or wood stoves are best, as electrical stoves can interfere with the energy. I prefer enamel pans and pots to make potions, but enamel can be difficult to find nowadays. Heatproof glass and ceramic are also good. Iron and steel pots can be used for protection potions only. They will diffuse other kinds of majick. Aluminum pots should not be used in potion making at all. My former student and co-author Christopher likes to use a large ceramic potpourri pot, heated by a tea light, which can be kept in the center of the altar rather than in the kitchen. Properly prepared potions can last a traditional four days, as their energy infuses your own energy with intention, lasting well beyond how long their scent is noticeable. The containers used to store potions should be majickally decorated in harmony with the potion's intention.

Chapter Four: Protection Majick

Living life as a Witch means living with majick every day and night. Practicing your spells and projections comes naturally. Am I routinely surprised at the outcomes? Oh yes, it's a great delight when a spell to ward off a financial crisis or to increase finances to meet the need comes to fruition the very next day.

Once while walking a fast pace near Salem Harbor, I noticed the wind beginning to pick up, becoming so strong it wrapped my robes around my legs, slowing me down so much I could hardly walk. Slowing me down so I wouldn't get hurt by the car that lost control and sped across the sidewalk in my path. My protection spells are not because I am paranoid, no. They are for the unexpected danger.

Today, I decided to take that same stroll near Salem Harbor. The sky is blue, and the ocean water mirrors the same color. It is autumn, my favorite time of year. The air is cool, so I have put on a cape over my robe. Every step stirs up the orange-brown leaves in my path.

While drawing in all the beauty around me, my thoughts drifted to a vision of all the people who would read my book and benefit from the majick and spells it holds. You can live the same majickal life I live here in Salem, Massachusetts, simply by practicing the spells I have created, the spells Penny has created, and the spells handed down to us from Witches from the past. Penny and I are sharing majick from our Book of Shadows.

To feel protected is a very real need. We need to feel safe and secure to be able to pursue our relationships, creativity, and dreams. Protection majick ensures that no one can really harm you, except perhaps yourself. When you perform protection majick, it affords you the luxury of feeling free to be who you are, including being overt about your own majickal practices as much as possible. Protection majick puts you in the right place and the right time, doing the right thing to avoid harm. Protection majick shields you from the ill intentions of others. Psychic shielding helps you energetically prepare for the unexpected, even when it is consciously impossible to prepare. When we have our shielding up, a potentially harmful experience is not going to be as harmful as it could have been.

People seek out a Witch's help when they feel unsafe. Sometimes they seek spells to protect them from people who would do harm. Other times, they seek protection from unknown spiritual ills and entities. When you understand the fundamentals of protection majick, you can be protected from all these things and hopefully get an awareness of yourself, to protect you from the biggest danger there is— yourself and your unconscious actions.

HARM

Witches don't believe in a source of evil. We don't believe there is any Devil orchestrating harm in our lives as part of a great manipulative plan. We define what we seek protection from as "harm." Harm is something that causes injury or damage, so we seek to avoid this damage.

We really don't know what is harmful. We think we know, but we don't know harm absolutely. Harm can be relative. What is harmful for one person might not be harmful to another. Something can be harmful over a long period of time, but relatively harmless in a short dose. Media like television can make us afraid of all sorts of harm—home invasion, crime, war, economic ruin. Certain foods are harmful. Even good foods raised in improper environments can be harmful, and we'd never know it just by looking at it. We fear these things and think of them as harmful.

Sometimes harm is less tangible. Going to the wrong place at the wrong time is harmful, in terms of energy. It doesn't always mean something truly harmful will happen to us objectively, but sometimes there are places where we just shouldn't be. The energy is debilitating for us. Other times, it's not the place, but the human-created environment. Thought patterns, our own and others', can affect us. Emotions like jealousy, rage, fear, and shame can harm us. Even the energy of a business deal or bank loan, when someone decides they don't want to work with us, can create an energetic harm as well. Many factors can be harming us, all without our conscious knowledge.

We describe harm as what is incorrect for you, for your highest good. Energies described as positive are not always good for you, just as energies described as negative are not always bad for you. They are simply opposite ends of the same spectrum. The true wisdom is in finding balance and harmony. Sometimes things that feel uncomfortable for us, things we think are harmful, are actually the impetus to make good changes in our life. Sometimes things that feel good to us are actually stagnant and harmful, and change is necessary, so we describe our "good" and "correctness" in terms of our highest good. Sometimes what we need might not be what we want.

Protection majick helps protect us from harm, even if we don't know what we need protection from. The intention of protection is clear, and the majick will do its own work, operating physically, mentally, and spiritually on our behalf.

HARMING NONE

One of the primary ethical teachings of Witchcraft is "harm none." It's a fairly modern addition to the Witch's lore in its current form, but it speaks to the deeper wisdom of the Witch. I wasn't taught the "harm none" rule by my teachers in the Witches of Kent, but I was taught that if you properly protected yourself, you didn't have to do harm to another. I only heard the phrase "harm none" when I started practicing openly as a Witch, meeting other Witches and reading about other traditions, particularly from the teachings of Gerald Gardner. Even though it was not a part of the original teachings I received, I like the phrase "harming none" because it fits so well with what my teachers of Kent taught me. You can waste a lot of time worrying about others, but if you protect yourself properly, you don't have to worry about it.

Witches believe in the Three-fold Law. Everything you do comes back to you three-fold, or so they say. Sometimes I think it comes back to you twenty-fold, or even a thousand-fold. But it returns to you energetically. It's not a moral law, like a dogmatic commandment, but more akin to a scientific principle, like gravity. Other cultures call this return by many other names. Sometimes it is called karma, or other times wyrd, but it is the consequences of your actions. Cabot Witches believe it is ruled by the Hermetic Principle of Cause and Effect: "Every effect has its cause. Every cause has its effect." We might judge something "good" or "bad" based on how pleasant or unpleasant its effects are, but it is simply returning to its source.

NEUTRALIZATION

A key teaching to true protection majick is understanding the need to neutralize harm. You do not have to harm someone else to protect yourself. If you do, you are simply doing the same thing, perpetuating harm. There is an old saying, "If you wish to murder someone, you should dig your own grave because you will also die from the wish." Harming another will ultimately harm yourself. Everyone and everything is connected. While in other religions, this teaching is emphasized by a spiritual sense of threat and reward, in Witchcraft, our threat and reward is our own. There is no God or Goddess who threatens us. No one is hanging the threat of hell over us. You will create your own version of hell on Earth when you cause harm, but it is not the making of any deity.

Witches choose not to harm based upon our understanding of the universe and our own psychic power. Power is neutral, and can be used to heal or harm. The misuse of power can harm ourselves, so we seek to avoid harm for the good of all involved. If all people could learn this basic principle, the world would truly change.

When some majickal practitioners work protection spells, they send the harm directed at them back to its source. If you know the techniques of neutralization, you do not have to do that. Neutralization, rather than reflection, allows you stop the harm at the edge of your protection shield. It will dissolve or dissipate harmlessly, rather than redirecting the harm. Think of harm as a bullet shot towards you. Reflection is simply sending the deadly bullet back. Not only will it harm the sender, but it could also harm anyone unfortunate enough to step in front of it while it's on the return journey. Neutralization is like snatching the bullet out of the air and putting it on the ground. You take all the majickal momentum out of it. Neutralization is based upon the science of the Craft and an understanding of light energy. Because many do not approach their majick as both a science and art, sometimes these principles are overlooked.

A basic first step in neutralization is learning to take responsibility for your own thoughts, words, and actions. When you know how to effectively neutralize the unwanted energies you generate, you can more effectively neutralize other forces, both consciously as they approach you, and unconsciously through establishing appropriate shields.

When you say think of something and realize you do not want to empower that thought with your majick as it would be harmful to you or others, hold your Instant Alpha Trigger and think to yourself, "I neutralize that." When you speak something harmful, again hold your trigger and say, "I neutralize that." When you envision something harmful in your mind's eye, envision putting a white light "X" through it while holding your trigger, or literally lift your fingers and draw an "X" before you in white light, neutralizing the vision. These thoughts, words, and visions are a normal part of our unhealthy programming in our culture. People think, speak, and imagine all sorts of harmful, self-defeating behavior, but constant neutralization will transform how you think, speak, and imagine. While at first you will feel like all you do is neutralization, you will eventually transform your own process, replacing harmful programming with new, helpful patterns.

When you come across other people's words and deeds that are harmful, you can silently hold your trigger and neutralize it. And you can program your own protection spells and shields with the power to neutralize harm automatically. Neutralized energies are then free to be put to constructive use. They are no longer trapped in a pattern of harm, and can manifest blessings.

PROTECTION SHIELD

A protection shield is the most basic form of protection majick. To cast a protection shield, you are using your own psychic light energy, the aura of your body. From your own molecular structure, there is light that oscillates out from and into your body. Just as if you were swimming through a pool at night with shards of Moonlight coming through the water, universal light shards come through the pool of your body. Your thoughts control your energy, your light. Your thoughts control what you put out to the world, and what you choose to take in, or not take in. Your intentions program the flow of light from the body, like a computer driving a vehicle. When you project the shield around you, you are sending oscillating light beyond your body, neutralizing unwanted energies and banishing anything that is harmful. It acts like a filter, preventing harm from reaching you. It will allow only the energies that are good for you, that you want for your highest good, to enter. The protection shield will increase your intuition, perception, and wisdom, allowing you to know where you should be at any given time and less afraid of what you don't know or understand.

To cast a protection shield, get into an alpha state, or hold your Instant Alpha Trigger. Envision the energy around your body, your aura, becoming like an enormous crystal egg or crystal sphere. Imagine the crystal shield forming around you now. The crystal light expands above your head and beyond the reach of your fingers, surrounding you completely. Visualize yourself inside the crystal egg, sparkling bright. Hold your hands out in front of you to test the shield's distance. Explore the shield all around you. Program the shield for peace and safety with these words three times in your mind:

"This shield will protect me from all negative and positive energies and forces that may come to do me harm. So mote it be, it is done."

When done, return from alpha level. While this shield is theoretically permanent, it can be helpful to re-affirm it and energize it periodically, strengthening its power.

PROTECTION FROM GHOSTS AND SPIRITS

Many people seek out Witches because they fear ghosts, spirits, and all manner of night things. Don't be afraid of ghosts. More often than not, they will help you, not hurt you. I really don't believe you need protection from ghosts. I've never known a ghost who could truly harm anyone in this plane. They can scare you when manifesting. They frighten us because we do not expect them, and people have been misled to think that ghosts are harmful.

Most religions today tell us to fear ghosts. Most ghosts are unwilling to move on to the next plane of existence. Some stay because they feel they have a purpose. When we are passed, we have full control. We can stay here or move on to a higher level. Most people want to stay near their loved ones.

Spirits can visit us, and not be haunting us. Spirits of loved ones often show up in the readings I do for people. Once a spirit crosses over to the Otherworld, things change. Their perspective shifts. They understand the consequences of their actions across lifetimes, their karma. Often the spirit will realize they were not a nice person, or that they created a terrible life.

As I was sitting in my office waiting with anticipation for the two people who had booked a half hour psychic reading with me, I wondered, as I always did, wonder who are these people? What do they wish to know? The candlelight on my desk gave sparkle to the chandelier above me. Shortly an older woman and her forty-eight-year-old son came in and then introduced themselves. The mother looked like she had stopped shopping during the fifties and was still wearing the fashions of that time. Her son was tall and lean and appeared to never leave his mother's side. As I started to look psychically into their lives, a figure of a man appeared to me, standing behind the mother. He spoke to me in my psychic mind and said, "I am her husband and the 'boy' is my son. I just passed away two weeks ago. I was not a good husband and a worse father. Please tell my son I am so sorry I only took him to see one baseball game, when I could have taken him to all of them. I love my wife and son."

When I relayed the message to them, they both cried, and the son said, "My father was a fan of baseball and never missed a game." His mother thanked me for the surprise message. She said she was never quite sure if he loved her, but now she understood. She had only come for a general reading and never expected to hear from him.

The spirit of the father then explained a bit about his karma and his son's karma to experience that type of relationship. Once you experience a certain thing and understand its lesson, you don't have to experience it again. The son then understood the lesson, and it eased his pain. It elevated both their spirits. As we constantly grow towards the universal mind, total intelligence, we have to experience all things in order to attain that high level of intelligence and spirit. This was one step toward that goal. Visiting spirits can help us understand these lessons.

Many ghosts are not truly ghosts at all. When a ghost sighting repeats, such as the same scene, over and over again, with no variation or interaction, the haunting is a hologram, not the spirit of a deceased person. Typically we have the image of the ghostly person going down the stairs repeatedly, or a man with a knife working in the kitchen. There is no variation. It is simply a holographic "picture" of them etched upon the ethers, and every so often it gets "played" like a skipping record.

Disturbed living people are often the root of a "haunting." When someone is out of balance and has psychic ability, they can send out energy that will manifest their own fears and problems. If they are indoctrinated to fear demons and devils, the phenomenon will manifest as demons and devils. They project out what they are experience. Most poltergeist experiences are caused by someone who is alive. They can manifest some powerful "proof" of the haunting, including tapping, rapping, scratching, or moving objects, though there is no ghost present. The source of the distress is always near the manifestations, but they don't have to be living where the poltergeist is reported. Those with good shields for themselves and their home usually don't report such things.

HOME PROTECTION

Protection majick can be used to protect your home, your mode of travel, your possessions, and your land, even your family and animals. Your majick can either extend your own shield around them or ignite their own majickal shields for protection. I never use my own shield to help defend others, but I take the natural energies of person, animal, place, or object and catalyze them, along with any of my spell components, to shield them from harm.

THE WRIT OF PROTECTION

The Writ of Protection, or the Writ of Enemies, is an old folk tradition used by Witches to warn people who may come to your home or business with wrong intentions. It is a psychic message to let them know on some level that you are protected by majick and that they are fully responsible for their actions. You aren't responsible for their actions. While our intention is to manifest our protection shields to neutralize and bind harm, or keep it entirely away, you never know how our protection can manifest in conjunction with someone's karma. Many people can approach us with wrong intentions, even if they do not realize it. Creating a majickal warning, a writ, is considered the ethical thing to do by Witches to give everyone the chance to act with better intentions.

Some traditions used a tied knot, or series of tied knots, in terms of Witch's cord, to say "beware." Many would hang charms or holed stones from it. That would be enough to let anyone who approached understand that home was protected by Witchcraft. The cord said "beware" and such a warning can sound ominous. Perhaps it should. Today, people don't recognize the cord as a warning, and in our modern society, our warnings are more often on the subtle, psychic level than an obvious sign.

My own Writ of Protection is written in Theban, the alphabet of the Witches. It says:

WARNING TO THOSE WHO COME TO DO HARM
I AM NOT RESPONSIBLE FOR WHAT COMES AFTER YOU

ꑊꑌꓔꑌꍀꀎꍀꀎ ꓜꑌ ꓜꓩꑊꓤꓜꑊ ꓜꓩꓩꑊꑊ ꓔꑊꑊꑊꑊ ꓜꑌ ꑊꑊ ꓩꓩꑊꑊꑊ
ꀎ ꓔꑌ ꍀꑌꑊ ꑊꑌꓤꑊꑊꓤꀎꑊꑊ ꓩꑊꑊ ꓜꓩꓩꑊ ꑊꑊꑊꑊꑊ
ꓩꓩꑊꑊꑊ ꓤꑌꑊ

This is carved upon a red clay tablet, visible when you enter my home. The protection is reinforced as the red coloring is caused by iron powder, the metal of Mars that oxidizes to a red color. It was added to the clay before it was hardened in a kiln.

Your own writ can be in Theban, another majickal alphabet such as Ogham or Runes. It doesn't have to be explicit as it is broadcasting on a psychic level. Your writ can use whatever wording you feel is appropriate, including simple verses such as:

BEWARE – 

TURN BACK – 

HARM NONE – 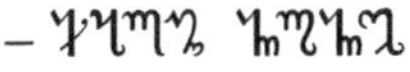

THIS WAY OUT – 

Once you've posted a warning, you've fulfilled your moral duty to warn all who enter about the forces at work. I believe Witches are obligated to post something on some level.

Protection Potion

One of my favorite versions of protection potion—first shared in my book, *Power of the Witch*—is used by many practitioners of the Cabot Tradition of Witchcraft (and has spread even beyond that tradition).

2-4 Cups of spring water
2 Tablespoons of sea salt
2 Tablespoons of myrrh
2 Tablespoons of frankincense
1 Tablespoon of iron powder (iron shavings)
1 Teaspoon of vervain

Pinch of wolf hair from a live, shedding wolf
Pinch of graveyard dirt from someone you revere for courage or bravery

Charge all the ingredients and place them in a pan or pot used for protection potion. Simmer them slowly. and using your Instant Alpha Trigger, make a clockwise motion over the mix, saying,

"I charge this potion to protect me (and anyone I designate) from all positive or negative forces that may come to do me harm. So shall it be!"

Let the potion cool, bottle it, and label it. Use it on your wrists, forehead, and behind your neck to invoke the powers of protection. It can also be used on objects, vehicles, and the windows and doors of your home or office.

Protection Oil
1 dram of patchouli oil
1 dram of frankincense oil
1 dram of myrrh oil
1 teaspoon of mandrake root
3 teaspoons of sea salt
Pinch of wolf hair (from a living, shedding wolf or a pinch of fur from your familiar)

A variation of the water-based protection potion, this rich Earth scent contains the power of the majickal mandrake. While most mandrake root sold in the United States is may apple, a wonderful plant, it is even better to obtain traditional mandrake, or mandragora root. English mandrake, or white bryony, which was carved to resemble mandrake root and sold to the unsuspecting, is not a good substitute, as its majick is more about deception than protection or power.

Protection Incense

2 cups of nettle leaf

2 tablespoons of frankincense

2 tablespoons of myrrh

½ teaspoon of benzoin powder

1 ¼ teaspoon of storax resin

Powder all ingredients with a mortar and pestle. Keep in a tightly sealed jar. Sprinkle on charcoal and walk through your home with the burning incense, moving into closets and other small spaces to clear out any harm.

Sator Square

An old bit of borrowed majick is the use of the Sator Majickal Square. It's a mysterious palindrome in Latin that dates back at least to Pompeii. Scholars have associated it with the Greeks, Hebrews, and even the Celts. It has been used by various traditions for healing and protection. I use it for protection. It works extremely well. Simply put the square on a piece of paper and frame it. Place it over a door or window. The square can be visible in the frame, or behind a photo or print. The Sator square seems to constantly work. Whoever created this bit of majick originally was extremely good at it, and we get the benefit of their creation.

SATOR

AREPO

TENET

OPERA

ROTAS

Iron Nails and Horse Shoes

Iron is an extremely effective tool in all protection majick. Like a lighting rod, it attracts harm and grounds it, preventing it from reaching you. Iron nails, railroad spikes, and horseshoes are a great way to bring its energy into your home.

Place two nails at the base and one nail at the top of all your windows, forming a triangle of protection. Railroad spikes are also good at the windowsill. You can lay a single spike down on the windowsill. While some majickal supply stores carry railroad spikes, you can often find them alongside of a local railroad track, as they are just discarded when they are replaced by the railroad company.

Place a horseshoe, upward pointing like a cauldron, over your door for protection. It will redirect energy that is harmful before it enters your home. The traditions of the village blacksmith were intimately connected to the village Witch, and many of the tools of the blacksmith and horseman were used in majick.

White Light Pentacles

You can add additional protection to any protection shield by entering into alpha and conjuring white light pentacles on all four sides, above and below. They can be drawn around your home, office, car, and animals. Whenever I ride in someone else's car, I draw white light pentacles all around it to protect us while driving. Some of my friends are not good drivers. My friend Margie will stop in the middle of a very busy highway to turn and talk with me. It is very frightening. I feel better when I have the white light pentacles around the car.

White Light Shield

Just as a protection shield can be created around you using the energy of your aura, a similar protection shield can be created around other people, your vehicle, and other places. You can start by drawing white light pentacles on all the windows and doors, repeating them often until you feel they are strongly in place. Likewise, you can charge the energy of your home, office, or vehicle. Go into alpha and envision your shield. You can imagine it as a crystalline geometry, whatever will fit around the entire home. People use spheres, pyramids, or other shapes. Say to the shield:

"Protect me from all negative and positive forces that might cause harm. So mote it be!"

Dragons of Protection

The dragons of protection are allies to help you protect your home, calling upon the primal power of the dragons. Call upon the protection dragons, and they will encircle your house. They appear to be slumbering and will only awaken and activate if someone comes to do mortal harm to you or someone in the household. Then the dragons would use their power to stop your enemy and send them away.

While in an alpha state in your home, usually done after the White Light Pentacle Shield, envision two dragons, tail to tail, around your home. Say to them, "Protect me from anyone or anything that will do mortal harm to me, my loved ones, or my household." Envision the dragons in white light. Mine look as if they are made from living, moving crystal. These dragons gleam and sparkle as they slumber. You can go back and strengthen your connection to the dragons periodically by repeating this work.

One of the most powerful experiences with the dragons of protection came when I was being pursued by a stalker. He found my home and came to it when we were not home. Something happened. The stalker actually went to the police to complain about my house, warning them something dangerous was there. He reported going outside of the house and seeing things. He got so frightened that he never came back and then left me alone.

Dragon Queen Protection Spell

1 tablespoon of dragon's blood resin
1 tablespoon of nettle
Several pieces of mandrake
Oak leaves
Hemlock cones
1 jet stone
Red fabric square or red majick bag
Protection potion

To keep oneself and home safe from evil and harm, use this spell. On a waning Moon, in the night air, place the stone and herbs on the square of red fabric or in the red bag. Put a drop of protection potion on your wrists, forehead, and the back of your neck. Say these words out loud while envisioning a beautiful red dragon flying above you with her flames surrounding you:

By the waning Moon and the power of the herbs
Protection shall surround me and my home.
The fire of the Dragon Queen will protect me.

Put a drop of potion on the mix and place it in the bag. Carry this bag with you always for the Dragon Queen's protection. You can triple the spell and make three bags, putting one in your car, one in your home, and one in your work place.

Feathers of Justice

A powerful act of majick is to call an act of injustice to the attention of the gods. Witches in the Cabot Tradition do not believe in vengeance or retribution. We seek to protect ourselves while harming none. Vengeance is not our decision. We should not try to decide what will happen to people who do harm. Revenge has a way of turning sour, ultimately harming you as much as it harms another. We don't believe in harming anyone, as our creed is to harm none. Yet our deities are often gods of justice.

In the Celtic traditions, the goddess known as the Morrighan, and one of her specific aspects, Macha, are known for justice. The Morrighan and Macha can make up their own mind regarding what should happen to someone who has done harm. If you wish to call their attention to a situation, to petition them for help and justice, use a black feather. This should ideally only be used for someone who has perpetuated violence or material harm on some level. It's not used for petty squabbles and personal fights.

Ideally you can call upon them in a majick circle. Light a black candle and call upon them in the circle. Have a black feather. It can be a dyed feather from a craft store or a found crow feather, but make sure it is black. Make the sound of a cawing crow to call them to you. Only use the caw of the crow for important matters, like justice. This lets them know you are not just visiting, but have something very serious on your mind. The caw indicates you feel you are "at war" and need help. You need the matter taken out of your hands and placed into the hands of the gods. Talk to them about your situation. You should have a relationship with the goddesses and gods prior to this, so they know you are sincere and will recognize them in good times as well as bad. I use a small shelf as an altar for Macha. I place a crow feather and a majick wand on it. After I step in front of the altar, I talk to her just to tell her that I honor her. Remember, the gods and goddesses are your allies and ancestors, but they are not at your beck and call. They have their own work in the Otherworld.

Charge your black feather in the circle, and when done, mail that feather to the person who needs to be pointed out to the goddesses. If others are involved, have them also mail black feathers to this person. Even if you are not comfortable speaking to the goddesses in a circle, then simply mail the feather. This act focuses the energy of the Morrighan and

Macha upon the perpetrator and lets them decide what is the best course of action. You then let it go. Don't envision any harm or outcome. Just let it go. It is out of your hands now. Simply point the way.

One rapist was sent black feathers from people all around the world. He moved several times, but the feathers still found their way to him. Soon his actions caught up to him, and he was never able to harm anyone else again.

Black Feather Salt
6 cups of sea salt
1 or more crow feathers cut into very small pieces

Mixed together, these form a majickal symbol commonly used as a call for justice. Place this salt in a bowl wherever you wish to keep harm away, or carry it with Black Feather Oil in a black majick bag and burn black feather incense.

Black Feather Oil
1 ounce of sunflower oil
2 drams of heliotrope oil
1 crow feather cut into small pieces

Infused with shavings of crow feather, this potion brings to justice those who have wronged you or others. Use cautiously.

Protection Spell
1 hematite stone
Black Feather Oil
Black mojo bag
Protection Herb Mixture – patchouli, nettle, sea salt, wolf hair
Optional Additions – henbane, datura, mandrake, hemlock
Black candle
White candle

Light both the black and white candles. Mix the herbs and oils together and place them in the majick bag. Place your hands onto the majick bag and say aloud:

By the power of the Morrigan
I neutralize and bind the unjust actions and deeds
of those who come to do harm and evil.
So it is done!

Faery Protection Candle
1 black candle
Green leaves and flower petals

Light the black candle for protection, drawing protection to you. Sprinkle the leaves and petals around the base of the candle and recite the following spell:

May helpful Elves
And Faeries bright
Bless this candle
with majick light.
Bring me protection!

When the candle is done, save the leaves and petals for further majick. You can also put them in a black bag and hang them in your house or scatter them in your yard.

Excalibur Protection Spell
White candle
Crow feather
Sword or blade

Light the white candle to reflect the harm away. Place a crow feather at the base of the candle. Hold a sword (or other blade) over your head as you speak this spell:

Excalibur
Bring me Power
in this very hour,
Feather black
Flame so bright
help me be safe
This night!

Cabot Witches use an Excalibur replica sword, but any sword will do. While we favor this design, no one really knows what Excalibur looked like.

Unicorn Protection

The Unicorn is the protector of women, and its power can be called upon for that purpose. Take four antique keys, charge them with the blessings of the unicorn, and place them over your outside doors to keep harm away from your home. Put up a picture of a unicorn in your home. It will bring in the energy of the Unicorn.

Pentacle Tattoo

You can tattoo a pentacle on your body for protection. I have one tattooed on my arm where no one can see it. I always wear long sleeves. It is also a statement: "I am a Witch. I am marked as one."

Protection of the Broom

Witches place their besom, or broom, bristles up behind the door to keep away unwanted visitors. Any broom will do; however, a besom charged in a circle for protection and anointed with protection oil or potion is best.

The Knockers Protection Spell

The Knockers are faeries and sprites that warn you when something harmful is coming. I learned this spell from my teacher Felicity. The Knockers used to help miners in Wales avoid danger. My sister from a past life, Faith Cox, lives in Cornwall. She has told me that the Cornish miners would always listen for the Knockers. They knew these spirits would protect them in case there was danger in their mines. This Knocker Spell is still performed in Cornwall to this day.

While we can sometimes see the future, we often don't see our own clearly, and other entities—such as these faeries, being between the worlds—can see things in the future more clearly and help us. When you ask them to warn you about danger, they will bang on the wall, door, or headboard to tell you that you are in danger. When you check, no one will be there. If you are asleep and in danger, they will bang to wake you. The Knockers once woke me up to let us know the door was unlocked. Usually when you listen to their warning, the danger will pass you by if you are careful.

To call the Knockers, find three small pebbles. Sit inside your front door. Say out loud:

Knockers come help me.
Save me from any danger.
Knock for me.

Throw each pebble at the door of your home, making a tapping sound. Makes sure to do this for the front and back doors, plus any other entrances you have.

Destroy Evil Incense
1 cup of black cohosh

1 cup of nettle leaves

2 tablespoons of copal

1 tablespoon of myrrh

Burn to completely remove any evil influences from your life or home.

Don't Come Back Incense
1 crow feather, cut small

1 cup of nettle leaves

1 teaspoon of dragon's blood

Burn to completely remove someone from your life. Can be used as a part of a more complex banishment spell.

Faery Protection Majick Herbal Mix
1 teaspoon of elderberries

1 teaspoon of rowan berries

1 teaspoon of oak leaves

1 teaspoon of dried fern leaves

Green majick bag

Grind all ingredients into a powder using a mortar and pestle. Carry in a green majick bag.

Acorn Majick Spell
During the Burning Times, Witches carried acorns with them to become invisible. They also gave acorns to other Witches as a secret sign. It was a way to share their hidden majick. When you want to remain "invisible," place the three acorns in the majick bag and carry with you.

Invisible Incense
3 acorns

11 oak leaves, powdered

Bark from a lightning-struck tree, powdered

1 lodestone

Black majick bag

Mix the acorns and leaves together and burn—or carry in a black majick bag with a lodestone—when you don't want to be seen.

Jinx Removing Incense
1 cup of rose petals, dried and crushed

1 cup of yellow flowers

1 tablespoon of benzoin powder

1 tablespoon of cinquefoil

Burn on charcoal to remove any jinxes or bad luck.

The following protection spells, for protection of the home and self-protection, come from my daughter Penny's majickal work.

For Protection of the Home
Compass

4 iron horseshoes or 4 railroad spikes

For this you must use a compass to determine magnetic north. Set this spell up in a place where it will not be disturbed. Once you've found magnetic north, place the old iron horseshoes or rail spikes around the edges o the house, either inside, or buried outside the home, in the cardinal directions , starting in the North and moving clockwise around. Again starting in the north and moving clockwise, sprinkle salt over the iron. When you reach the north point again, say:

I protect this house and the people in it from any negative or positive energies or forces that may come to do us harm. So mote it be.

Self-Protection
Wolf hair

Sea salt

Item from a Crone, such as a strand of hair or a mother image

Black cloth, possibly from an old robe or cape

Black string

Carry wolf hair, sea salt, and something given to you from a Crone, a woman over sixty-five years of age. In our culture, the elders are not only the wise, but also the protectors. If you do not have access to wolf hair, you can substitute with dog hair or cat hair from a live and shedding animal. Animals are the great protectors on this planet. They do this of their own free will with purity in their hearts, which is the most powerful form of protection. Wrap these items in the black cloth and wrap a string clockwise around it as you tie it, forming a charm bag for your protection spell. Carry the charm in your left pocket.

Triangle Spell to Learn Your Enemies
On a piece of yellow poster board, cut out an isosceles triangle with the measurements 33" by 13". With a black marker, draw an equilateral triangle within it. When it is done, place it on the floor facing north. Sprinkle yellow flower petals over it. Leave it out so you will find out who your enemies are and also who is speaking against you. Place the yellow petals in a bowl or add them to an herb mixture to stop gossip or grant protection. Pick up the triangle and put it away until you need again.

Rid of Enemies
1 lemon

Iron nail

9 pins

Dish

White candle

Protection potion or protection oil

Sit in a majick circle. Place the lemon in a dish. Light a white candle anointed with protection potion or protection oil. Put the nail into the lemon, and then stick all nine pins into the lemon and say:

All enemies of mine shall find attention to other things and turn to do good forever. So mote it be!

Release the circle. Snuff the candle. Bury the lemon in the ground and it is done.

Antique Key Protection Spell

Find four different antique keys. Light a white candle and take each key, one at a time, and hold it in your hands. Focus your majickal power into each key. Say out loud:

This key shall keep away any and all harm to me and my home. All harm is locked away. So shall it be!

Then hang the keys outside over your front door. If you wish, you can do the same at your back door. You may even add one more key and then wear it on a cord around your neck.

Chapter Five: Love & Romance

So many people want love, but do they really know what they want? In the American use of the English language, our words change meaning almost daily. The word "love" is used in so many ways, it can be unclear what anyone means by it. Love is applied to inanimate objects, to the Earth, to people in a wide range of relationships. It can apply to things we desire, anything we simply like, or even anything that is comfortable to us. What is love really?

In the ancient world, love is agape, a Greek word that is often translated as love. The Greeks, among other Pagan cultures, used many different words for different kinds of relationships and loves. Agape is the deep, thoughtful love, a spiritual love that was later absorbed into Christian theologies as unconditional love. To a Witch, we might think of this deep and spiritual love as Perfect Love.

Love majick is not all about the mystical connection between two romantic partners, be they straight, gay, lesbian, or any other identification and combination. Love has a wide range of associations, including our love of the goddesses and gods and their love for us, and our loving connection to the planet and the people in our lives.

When most people look to a Witch for love majick, they are looking for the romantic, chemical connection, the sexual attraction. When people have visited me in my shops over the years, seeking a love spell, this is what they have been looking to get. So this is how the spells of the chapter will be focused. There are many ways our majick can help ignite the love, and these items and rituals are what we have incorporated into our love spells. But when we seek love in these forms, it's important for a

Witch to know that love will seek us back. We should use our quest for romance to also heal us through love, starting with self-esteem and enhancing our connection to each other, the gods, and the planet.

SELF-ESTEEM

Self-esteem is the key to not only love majick, but all majick. Cabot Witches learn to use the majick mirror. While mirrors can be used in all sorts of majick, from psychic scrying to protection, the first use we learn is for self-esteem. It's a simple spell. Anyone can do it, but most people feel too silly to make it a part of their practice. Those brave and wise Witches who do are transformed.

Stare into a mirror, looking directly at your face, into your own eyes, and say, "I love you." You have to say it and hear it. It seems selfish. It is not. It is selfless. Part of majick is to "know thyself" as the ancient Greek temple of Delphi had carved over its entrance. To know yourself, you have to really see yourself for who you are and accept yourself. Then you can start to understand who you are and what you are here to do. Telling yourself that you love yourself helps this process. You have to learn to enjoy who you are and what you've accomplished. You have to fall in love with your own character and personality. The things that you might not like about yourself, you have to accept, but for traits that are harmful to you and can be changed, you must also willing to change. Transform yourself through your majick, but also through taking responsibility for your personal choices and actions and the consequences they bring. That's really the true meaning of karma. It might happen in this lifetime or the next, but take responsibility.

When you are able to love yourself, you've found the love that is most important. Then, while you might want love and romance from a partner, you won't need it. You may want it, however.

I recommend that you do it every day, perhaps even two or three times a day, until it begins to sink in to your consciousness. This catalyzes the process of self-love and self-acceptance. It takes time. Doing it for a day, a week, or even a few months won't counter everything else you've experienced in your life. You have to make self-love the foundation stone for further majick. Most of us do it in the bathroom. You can turn on the shower or radio. You may be embarrassed that someone will hear you, but do it.

Essentially this is a part of doing your own self-parenting. Many of us come from families where saying "I love you" is not an option. Some families are very gregarious, but many are not. Some people never hear "I love you" and learn not to say it to themselves or others. But we need to hear it, out loud and often. When we do it, we start to process the effect that the previous lack has had upon our psyche and our own personal balance and self-image. You can feel love by loving yourself, literally. Then it is more readily acceptable from others. When you can recognize love from yourself, you can more easily see it and feel it from those who truly do love us. Sometimes we don't even realize who loves us.

With a great understanding of love on a basic level, we can then begin to parse out the different types of love and how these variant meanings of love apply to our lives. You can love someone, but hate their behavior. Love can be separated from behavior, and many people don't realize that. The different types of love, from family and friendship to romance, can all apply to us. And through it we understand the bigger meaning of love, the spiritual love that is a connecting force between us all.

Sadly, when people are in great need of love, they do not want to hear any of this. No one wants to talk about self-esteem when they are in the throes of lust. I know that many people reading this (if they have even gotten this far before skipping right to the spells) are in great need without even realizing what they need, and are therefore going to find this boring. That is why it is important to do this self-esteem work before doing love majick. Those who go right to it without proper preparation don't care, as they believe they know what they want and what is best for them, so they will be disappointed when the love spell seems to be not working. However, if they take a moment to reflect, to see a greater pattern they have been following, they will see that love from another without love from yourself is not the path to happiness. Take this time and use this majick, like the mirror exercise, to start the path of transformation and self-esteem.

ROMANCE

Romance is a necessary and very helpful part of love, and even more importantly, self-love. Romance is not simply a relationship, but it is the feeling of majick and mystery that we associate with relationships. It is a key to going deeper when getting to know someone, but also keeping the passion alive with new adventure and pageantry. We have to be able to romance ourselves, our whole majickal lives, to know how to incorporate true romance into our relationships. Remember, your first relationship is with yourself. Romance helps us understand the enchantment of love and love majick.

Romance is decorating your room in your home with everything you love. For women, it might be lace and chandeliers and gorgeous art upon the wall. For men, it might be a comfortable, warm place, with twelve pillows on the bed and a big wide-screen television. Anything you feel excited and happy about creates the atmosphere of true romance.

By putting thought and emotion, energy and intention, into your own surroundings and life, you begin to have a truly romantic life. Beauty triggers romance. Beauty is not always facial beauty. Beauty is found in your surroundings as well. Think of how the beauty of nature triggers a deep response in so many of us. That is romance and enchantment just as much as a candlelit dinner.

When you surround yourself in beauty in your daily life, it makes you more beautiful. When you are in an environment that supports your feelings of love, you are able to love yourself and others more easily. That's not to say that you shouldn't be able to love yourself without these things, or love others in a more spartan environment, but taking the time to make yourself and your surroundings pleasing to you is an act of self-love and can help you build this foundation of esteem.

If you live in a place that is barren, you are not going to get the same feelings you get from certain colors, flowers, scents, textures, images, and music. These are all majickal tools. Part of majick is picturing how you want your life to be. Surrounding yourself with things that make you feel like the image you are envisioning helps anchor that majick in your life. You don't have to be rich to do this. Take pictures of things you like. Find them in magazines or online. Print them out, arrange them, and frame them in your home. Put them up on the wall. The images will inspire you. Have more mirrors in your space, so you can see yourself in your space rather than feeling disconnected from it. You don't have to look in all the mirrors all the time, but the awareness of yourself surrounded by beauty will really sink into your mind. It's the peripheral awareness that lets you know you are there, constantly reminding you to live a romantic life and embody your beautiful self. This will help bring you love on all levels faster than ignoring these things.

Sharing your space with another is a part of the romance with relationship. When a potential partner sees your living space, they start to understand you better when the space really expresses your own hopes, dreams, and feelings. When they spend time in this space with you, you are sharing not only your time and attention, but the very energy, the romantic vibration, of your life.

Food, whether eaten alone or with others, is a part of romance. Food that is ruled by Venus and Mars, the two planets of attraction and energy, stimulate an aura of love majick around you. The aura's energy is what connects you to both the vibration of love and to others whom you love. You can make your own love meal for yourself or to share. You can also regularly eat something that you consider loving, and when you consume it, remember that it is an act of loving yourself when you do. An apple is ideal, as it's shaped like a heart and heals the heart. It makes the heart feel good. It is also an ideal majickal food for Witches as the seeds form a pentagram, the five-pointed star associated with Witchcraft, and its red and white colors are associated with the realm of faeries and the Isle of Avalon.

One of the most important flowers for romance is the rose. Roses are always very important in majick. They are a flower intimately associated with the Goddess as the Great Mother and source of all things. Roses can be used fresh or dry, though they should be natural, with no artificial chemicals on them. Roses will bring the vibration of love. They can be used in potpourri or herbal mixes to infuse love majick into your surroundings. Just having them around will automatically affect your aura and energy.

Use all the things around you to heal your heart and accept self-love, and then you'll be ready for a true and lasting relationship.

ETHICS AND PROBLEMS IN LOVE MAJICK

Majick doesn't insure a perfect outcome. Don't think just because your intention involves love that it will always be happily-ever-after for you both. Casting a love spell, especially if you cast it for one particular person, can get you into trouble. Your majick can interfere with the other person's karma. If this person has not already shown any interest in you, I would strongly advise you not to use that person's name in your spell. Attempts to interfere with someone's free will and their own karma always backfire in the end, and while you might initially get what you think you want, it rarely works out that way.

The best love spell we can cast is to have love in our lives, and when asking for a relationship, to ask for a "correct" relationship, or in other words, a "compatible" one. You are asking for a good, caring person that is right for you. Otherwise, you can get hung up on the love interests that are "incorrect" for you, even though you think it will make you happy. Many of the ladies, and a few of the guys, like the "bad boy" types because they are exciting. Many men like the femme fatale type. You might get a look from someone and end up daydreaming about that one look, probably exaggerated or misinterpreted in your mind. It may have simply been a twitch in their eye. The daydream can turn into a months-long fantasy, yet your love interest has never made a move, never contacted you for something more. Casting a spell to fulfill one of those fantasies is not a good idea. You have not really had any type of relationship with this person, let alone a romance. You don't know the nature of this potential interest. That fixation with a lack of knowledge can get you into a lot of trouble. So in your love spells, ask for the person "who is correct and good" for you.

If you insist on focusing on one person, then until you have some sort of real relationship with your interest, one not based in delusion or fantasy, it is better to use your majick to project for a real relationship, to get to know the person better, rather than using your majick for a permanent relationship or even marriage. It will give you time to get to know the person, and will provide the wisdom to learn if this relationship would be right and good for you.

When you project for marriage with someone, a complete connection that is legally recognized, you are going to get everything that comes with that person, and there can be many things hidden. Many will assume that all has been said, while your partner will believe if there is no direct question about it, then nothing was hidden. When you marry, you get not just love and companionship, but you might get debts, concerns with in-laws, problematic social groups, health issues, karma – everything. When you are in a place desiring a partnership, but not in desperate need because you have your own self-esteem, you'll be able to evaluate this better and ask the appropriate questions before taking that leap.

I believe you should always cast a spell for what you want, but be open enough to the wisdom of the universe to let the universe decide what is best for you. You are definitely going to receive your own karma, your own lessons about love. Your karma can result in a very good lesson on love. Karma does not mean it will be bad. Karma is not a punishment. Karma is the lesson that results from your actions. We have many lessons in school that we can enjoy quite a bit. Life is like that. Your karma can result in a wonderful relationship that lasts your lifetime.

Your majick can influence your karma. Your intentions and actions change your "fate." By taking the time to list the qualities you want in a person, you can clearly communicate this to the universe, and your karmic lessons can be delivered with more clarity. There is always give-and-take in the majickal life. Make a list of the qualities you want in a partner. But if you do an off–the-cuff spell for anything involving love, then you have to expect anything. At the very least, ask that your love spell be "correct and for the good of all" to make sure it is the best possible thing for you at the time.

My daughter Penny says that she did a lot of love spells when she was younger and every one of them worked, but didn't always work in the way she envisioned. She met interesting and famous people—and had relationships, some long and some short—but she learned from her love majick. When she projected for someone with a specific physical description, like *The Witches of Eastwick* – tall, dark, handsome, and looking for a long-term relationship—she manifested her love interest, but one of the men was married. She got what she asked for, but she didn't look at her words and intentions in the eyes of the All, the Divine Mind, from a bigger perspective. A lot of her spells, and all of our spells, can come with personal interjections that are mostly subconscious. We get what we ask for, plus a lot of other things that come with it. From these experiences, we live and we learn.

Sometimes people will seek out a Witch in hopes of breaking up an established couple because they desire one of the partners. As modern Witches, we truly believe it is forbidden to break up a couple because you are simply attracted to or fascinated by one of them. It's manipulative and alters the natural path. To do so will cause far more problems than it helps, and most Witches and I would never do such a thing for themselves or on behalf of others. Many seek to have an affair with a married man or woman, yet they are really not taking a good look at their needs. If someone is married and is willing to cheat with you, you'll know it. To use majick to try to force their will is completely unethical. Remember what they do to their current partner they will do to you.

The biggest enemy to successful love majick is unhealthy fantasy. While fantasy as entertainment and escape is one thing, some people get stuck in fantasy. Their mind describes what a relationship "should" be like, usually from unrealistic expectations from books, television, and movies. They build an image of how someone should respond, how the sex should be, and how perfect life should be like as a couple. Either you can never find it, or once you find someone as a partner, they can never live up to these superhuman expectations. This is not reality, but we become very good at expecting it to be our reality. While spiritually counseling others, I find women are more prone to this than men, but men also do it. Part of successful love majick is deciding we can spend our lives fantasizing about our perfect relationship that does not exist, or we can try to have real, authentic relationships where we can share love, learn, and grow.

Many times our fantasy can lead us into giving love away to those who don't realize it, and who don't necessarily want it. Instead of a partnership where love is shared, we can do great harm. One woman who came for a reading explained she hadn't heard from her man for six months, but was waiting for him to get in touch. I had to break it to her that they were no longer together. No one takes a break for six months without telling you and without any other communication. Yet she was pouring her love energy to him day after day. I had to explain to her how such behavior is harmful. We had to go back to the foundation of self-love. I asked her, "Why would you put yourself in a position of hurt and need like that?" While we need love, the first love we need is from within. With that, we can better judge what are appropriate and inappropriate relationships and actions. With that love, we can step out of delusion and harmful fantasy. When we have self-love, we can share that love, not throw it away on those who are oblivious to our feelings.

SUSTAINING LOVE

Many people have the "happily-ever-after syndrome" when it comes to love majick. They think that just because you find someone who is good and compatible, then your job is over, and eternal happiness is guaranteed. Yet in real life, there is always more work to be done. Majick can bring you together, but what you do after that is up to you. You must choose wisely. Your actions can grow your relationship . . . or end it, even when the spell was successful. Take responsibility for your actions and continue the romance.

Sustained love is aided by having some separation. Just because you have a partner doesn't mean your lives are completely joined and there is no separation. You have to keep your own hobbies, your own routines, and your own identity while also creating a tradition of routines, actions, and hobbies you can do together. A good relationship requires both. Some think no time apart is a measure of success, but a little separation is good. There is such a thing as smothering each other.

Develop habits to respect and honor each other. Hold hands with each other. Physical contact outside of sex is important, even though sex is important too. Have a date night, instead of just the routine of work, dinner, bed, and then work again. After work, make plans. Take a class, or go to a special restaurant or coffee shop. Weekends can be hard. By the time they come, everyone is often too tired from the work week to do anything, but if you take some time for fun during the week, you might find you have more energy during the weekend. Doing things both together and alone can inspire you. Stay active and inspired.

A nice weekend away, breaking routines and habits overnight in a hotel someplace, can be just what is needed to infuse more romance and mystery into the relationship. It doesn't need to be expensive. No flights to New York City, Los Angeles, London, or Bombay required. Just go to the nearest city to you and experience a little culture and night life. Or get room service. Stay in and pamper yourselves. Go to the pool. Getting out of the everyday can change the relationship. The lack of everyday stress helps you build up your friendship and connection along with the romance. It is both relaxing and fun.

Sustaining love includes not only with a partner, but with yourself. You have to continue to love yourself and take care of yourself. Once you find self-esteem, it doesn't not mean the work is over. It's a lifelong love affair you must have with yourself. If you sustain your own love, you'll be able to manifest what you desire more easily.

If you are feeling stuck looking for love, different environments create different perspectives. If you are in the same routine over and over again, that won't happen. In the Rosicrucian traditions, they have a lesson based upon the pond. A pond has no movement to the water. It's peaceful, but there is no change. It can grow stagnant. Throw a rock out into the water, and the waves move out to the edge but return to the center. Any movement changes the vibration, and the vibration will return to you at the center. Nothing happens unless you do it. You must initiate it. Throw that rock out there and make things change. You will not find your Prince or Princess Charming riding in on a white horse while you watch television in your living room. If you need help in your relationship, with yourself or with your partner, you have to do something to make the shift. You have to change how you do things to create the vibration you want, to draw in love to you.

Love Perfume

While commercial perfumes might simply be striking scents to get attention, it can be helpful to align your perfume with your intention. I suggest adding a few drops of your own majickal potion to your favorite perfume to attract the correct person. I suggest the following formula as a successful addition to commercial scents.

2 drams patchouli oil
2 drams styrax oil (benzoin oil)
2 drams lotus oil
2 drams heliotrope oil
2 drams olive oil
10 drops of vitamin E oil

Charge each ingredient for love. The vitamin E oil, available at most health food stores, helps prevent the olive oil from going rancid.

Another variation, using a water base rather than an oil base, is to mix the following:

2 cups of spring water
1 tablespoon of sea salt
1 cut apple
1 teaspoon of clove
1 teaspoon of lovage root
A few dried rose petals
Pinch of basil

Put a dab of the love potion on a doorknob, letter, or on the car door handle of someone you are attracted to. Adding a dab to your bellybutton, as well as your wrists, increases its power and effectiveness.

Love Philter

To attract love into your life, particularly a general love and self-esteem, make the following philter.

1 tablespoon of rose petals
1 tablespoon of patchouli leaves
1 tablespoon of hibiscus flowers
1 tablespoon of yarrow
1 tablespoon of passion leaves
1 tablespoon of strawberry leaves
1 tablespoon of damiana
1 tablespoon of motherwort
1 tablespoon of red poppy flowers
4 Adam and Eve roots
1 tablespoon of lovage root powder

Charge each ingredient for love as you blend them together. Add the following oils to the mixture of dry herbs:

20 drops of rose oil
10 drops of strawberry oil
8 drops of musk oil
5 drops of patchouli oil

Blend the oils and herbs together, and then fix both the scent and the majick with two tablespoons of orris root powder. Do not eat or drink orris root for it comes from the iris, which is toxic. When complete, charge the mix while in alpha by making clockwise circles with your hand or wand and saying the words:

I ask that a lover or companion be attracted to me, and that there be love between us. I ask that this be correct and for the good of all people. So mote it be.

Carry this philter in a red or pink bag with you. Do not consume this, or any of the philters in this book. While the scent is powerful, it is the energy of the mix altering your aura to attract the correct person, not the scent, that will attract a love to you, starting with self-love.

Love Incense
1 tablespoon of dragon's blood
3 tablespoons of crushed rose petals
1 tablespoon of yarrow
2 tablespoons of basil
1 tablespoon of patchouli

Carry this in a red bag. Burn this mixture every Friday and visualize the end result of the type of love you wish to conjure.

Love Candle Spell
Pink candle
Black candle

Carve the word "Love" down the side of the candles. Anoint both candles with Love Oil.

Majick candle
Spark the fire
Bring to me
My heart's desire.
Spell of love
Grant me this spell
The one I do love

Shall love me as well.
So Mote It Be!

Moonlight Love Spell

Three nights before the Full Moon, place a jar of spring water outside where the moonlight will enter the water. Two hours before the Full Moon, step outdoors and wash your hands and face with the Moon water. Touch your jewelry to the Moon water. Repeat this spell three times as you do:

By the light of the moon
And mystical power
Love will come
Hour by hour.

Any Moon water left over should be poured on your front steps or near your front door.

Faery Queen Love Spell

To call the Fey, place a miniature piece of furniture outside where you recite this spell. Recite this spell outside at a place that is pleasing to you, while calling upon the faerie folk to aid your majick.

By the light of the Moon
And mystical power
Love will come
hour by hour.
Faerie Queen, stay with me
Bring a love that is meant to be.

Repeat the spell three times!

Love Feather Spell
13 feathers dyed pink, red, and green
Extra feathers of the same colors

Place in your hand the colored feathers. Hold the feathers in your left hand and blow them into the sky and say:

Feather light, feather gay
Bring a love to me this day.
So Shall It Be!

For three more days, release more feathers to the sky to complete your spell.

Two Hearts Love Spell
Rose quartz
Heart cut out of red paper
Pink candle

This spell is from the Cabot Family Book of Shadows. Perform it on a Friday evening during the waxing moon. Put the rose quartz on top of the paper heart and light the candle. Say the following aloud:

This majick symbol shall bring me lasting love and marriage to my life. I ask that this be done for the good of all. So Mote It Be!

Burn the heart talisman in the flame of the candle and place the ashes in a majickal place. Let the candle burn out. Do not blow out the candle with your breath. It will ruin the spell. The correct love for you will come in the proper time.

Avalon Spell
Avalon symbol
Apple

The apple is a sacred symbol of the Witch. This symbol makes two into one. Use it to draw a love partner and potential marriage partner. Paste the symbol onto your apple and hang it in the bedroom.

Avalon Symbol

Come to Me Oil
12 drops of coconut oil
6 drops of patchouli oil
3 drops of jasmine oil
2 drops of cinnamon oil

Come to Me Oil is a multipurpose oil. While it is often used to draw a new love, it can really attract anything you desire, including a new job, prosperity, friends, or a specific object. You can use it in spells and charms for a wide range of intentions.

Love Herbal Mix
1 cup of basil
1 cup of rose buds and petals
½ cup of patchouli leaves
½ cup of lavender flowers
2 tablespoons of dragon's blood

Place this mix of herbs in a bowl in your home to bring you love.

Love, Sex and Passion Majick Herbal Mix
1 cup of rose petals and buds
½ cup of horny goat weed
½ cup of red pepper
12 drops of amber oil

Carry this herbal mix in a red bag to ignite more passion in your life. Carry it with you or put it under your bed.

Faery Passion Majick Herbal Mix
½ cup of fern (dried)
½ cup of maiden fern (dried)
¼ cup of acorns (crushed)
¼ cup of pine needles
12 drops of lavender oil
1 garnet

Carry the herbal mix in a majick bag with a garnet stone to have the faeries kindle passion in your life and with your lover.

Midnight Sex Oil
2 drams of coconut oil
1 dram of cinnamon oil
1 dram of mugwort oil

1 teaspoon of horny goat weed
1 teaspoon of damiana
1 teaspoon of hibiscus

Infuse the herbs in the mix of oils for a month, and then strain the plant matter out of the mix. Use this potion to help bring about sexual attraction, passion, and lust. Using it to anoint a red candle and then burning it for a sexual partner, or to have sex with the partner you have, is an effective and powerful spell. You can wear this potion, use it for massage oil, or just add a few drops to your regular perfume.

Midnight Sex Incense
1 cup of sugar
3 drops of purple food coloring
½ cup of damiana
¼ cup of rose petals
¼ cup of hibiscus flowers

Burn in spells and ritual for sexual attraction. Excellent in combination with the Midnight Sex Oil.

Midnight Sex Herbal Mix
½ cup of sugar
½ cup of horny goat weed
½ cup of damiana
½ cup of red pepper
1 cup of rose petals
1 garnet

Mix all the herbs together. Add the garnet stone. To empower it, prick your finger and place three drops of your blood in the mix. Place this mix of herbs in a bowl in your bedroom to bring you sex.

Midnight Sex Spell
Red candle
Midnight Sex Potion
Midnight Sex Herbal Mix
Red majick bag
Sexy outfit

On a night when the moon is waxing, stand in front of a full length mirror. Anoint the candle, your neck, wrists, and forehead with the Midnight Sex Potion. Light the candle. Take the bag of Midnight Sex Potpourri and hold it in your hands. Take the herbs out of the bag and place them around the candle. Stare into the flame and visualize your night of passionate love-making. Take three very deep breaths, and say aloud:

Herb and Fire, bring to me the passion
I desire, by the power of three times three,
fill my nights with ecstasy.
For the good of all, So Mote It Be.

Close the spell by letting the candle burn out or snuffing it out (never use your breath to blow out a candle). Empty the herbs into the bag and place under your mattress. To enhance this spell, perform when the waxing moon is in the sign of Scorpio. Wear your sexiest and most attractive outfit.

Return to Me Powder
1 black feather, cut
¼ cup of rosemary
¼ cup of nettle
1 lodestone
Lodestone food (iron filings)

With this spell, it is a case of "be careful what you want." Most being will use it to bring back a lost lover. However, you can use it to have lost things returned or replaced. Charge this mix on a Waxing Moon. You do not need to burn it as an incense, like other powders in this book, as the lodestone food will not burn, but you can carry it in a black bag.

Happy Ever-After Spell
Black candle
One of your own shoes you no longer need

Before a Full Moon, light the black candle. Place the shoe near the candle. Write this spell below on white paper. Hold the shoe in your hands and say the spell out loud. Snuff out the candle. Take the shoe to a crowded place, such as a park or a mall. Drop the shoe, then turn and run away.

I cast this spell to have Love come to me,
to have my Prince Charming find me
and Love me forever so I may be
Happy Ever After.
I ask this be for the good
Of all. So Mote It Be!

Love Spell
Spell paper
Red candle
2 red paper hearts
Rose quartz
2 tablespoons of rose petals
2 tablespoons of basil
Red majick bag

2 red ribbons
Love potion

Write out the spell previous to starting. One Friday afternoon or evening, take the red candle into your bedroom and anoint the candle with love potion. Put the hearts and stone in front of you. Put a drop of love potion on each item. Sprinkle rose petals and basil over them. Put a drop of love potion on your wrists, forehead, and the back of your neck, and then say the spell out loud:

Mix and stir and blend it so
my Lover's heart to grow and grow
With love for me and greater desire
The very thought of me
Will thrill like fire!
So mote it be!

Roll up the spell paper and tie it with the red ribbon. Place it in front of the candle with the other items and let the candle burn down. Place everything into the red bag and tie the bag to the red ribbon. Wear it around your neck for nine days and nine nights. Following the nine days, tie it to your bed.

Love Moon Spell
Spell paper
Green ink/green pen
Green ribbon

Performing this spell when the Moon is full, or when the Waxing Moon is in the sign of Taurus or Libra. Write this spell in green ink.

Magic Moonlight, hear this spell.
My words shall travel on the Moon's breeze

Sending my love calls with ease.
Capture my love with your shimmery light
Bring Him/Her to me on a moonlit night.
By the power of three
He/She shall love me
For the Good of All
So Mote it Be!

Take this spell outside to a wooded area. Speak the spell out loud. Then roll the spell up with green ribbon and throw it into the woods.

The following love spells—the Human Candle Love Spell, Chocolate Love Tea, and the Rose Petal Penny Quick Love Spell—come from my daughter Penny's Book of Shadows:

Human Candle Love Spell

1 white candle
1 black candle
2 red human-shaped candles
Mortal and pestle
Adam and Eve root
Strawberry leaves
Mandrake root
Rose petals
Dragon's bloodstone
Rose oil
Fine-tip marker
Cake pan – one inch deep
2 red ribbons

When the Moon is waxing, take your black and white candles and place the black one on the left of your altar and the white one on the right. Grind a small amount of each of the herbs together, except for the Adam and Eve root, in your mortar and pestle and add 1 drop of rose oil. Leave the Adam and Eve root separate. Adam and Eve root is usually sold as a pair, a "female" and "male" root.

Take your red human-shaped candles (they can be male and female, male and male, or female and female, depending on your gender and the gender of the person you want to attract). Bore a hole in each candle, where the heart would be. Make sure the hole is deep because you need to place both the herbal mixture and your Adam and Eve root into the heart. Start with the herbal mixture and leave room for the root. Before you place the root in the candle, write your name with a fine-tip marker on one root, and the name of the person you are interested in on the other. Place one root in one candle to represent you, and the other in the candle of the person you are interested in. Cover the holes with a bit of melted wax so the herbs do not fall out.

Place a piece of red ribbon across the bottom of the cake pan so there is a tab hanging over the edge, enough for you to grab and pull the wax out when you are done. Now write your name on the candle representing the other person, and their name on the candle representing you. Take one more ribbon and face the candles together, tying the two figures together, wrapping the ribbon clockwise. Scatter rose petals and any remaining herbs at the bottom of the pan. Place your human-shaped candles in the pan and light them. Let them burn until there is only a pool of wax. Let it cool and pull the ribbon and wax out. Bury it all on the full Moon. You will have more attention that you expected. Make sure this is what you want because this is a very powerful spell. It's a variation of another spell that is actually more powerful and permanent. Like my mom says, "Be careful what you wish for because you'll get it and everything that comes with it.

Chocolate Love Tea

1 tablespoon strawberry leaves

Water

1 piece of chocolate

A pin

Make strawberry leaf tea by boiling strawberry leaves with one cup of hot water. Take a small piece of chocolate, and with a pin, inscribe your name and the name of your love interest into the chocolate. Put the chocolate into the hot tea, letting it dissolve. Serve it to your person of interest, and you will get their attention.

Rose Petal Penny Quick Love Spell

1 copper penny

Rose petals

Copper is the metal of Venus, the planet of love. Take a copper penny and some rose petals. Hold them in your left hand. Place your right hand over your left hand and close your eyes. Say your love interest's name three times, then say your own name three times. Keep the penny and petals on your right side for three days. You can place them in your pocket or tie them up in a red cloth and pin it to your clothing.

Golden Star Love Spell

A powerful spell to protect your lover when you are physically apart is the Golden Star Love Spell, created by my daughters and me as a part of our own family tradition. You will need:

1 gold pentacle

1 piece of black velvet cloth to drape around a jar (or a black velvet drawstring pouch)

1 quart glass jar

3 feet of thick black cord

Enter into an alpha state, hold the pentacle, and charge it with the rhyme:

A golden ring around a star
Placed in black velvet and hung in a jar
Will keep you, my love,
When you are afar.

While visualizing your lover on the screen of your mind, suspend the pentacle from the silk cord so that it hangs freely inside the glass jar. Hold the cord in place by screwing on the lid. Wrap the whole jar in black velvet and hang the entire thing from the ceiling for as long as you want the spell to last. It is best to be done when you are apart for some time, not just leaving for work. When the need is over, remove the hanging, take it out of the black cloth, and open the jar. The ingredients can be reused as often as you cast the spell.

Spell to Have a Child

To start a family or to increase the family you have, use this spellcraft. Before casting your spell, take your partner to a place away from the home, preferably a place that is fun. You don't have to take a long vacation, only an overnight. Go to a hotel in your area that has room service and a pool. Stay overnight. Call room service for breakfast. Take a swim in the pool. Check out and go home, but make sure to have fun. Gather all the ingredients you need for the spell.

3 leaves
3 tree twigs
Sunflower seeds
1 black majick bag
2 rings
Black ribbon

Put all the spell contents on a table. Sit down, close your eyes, and envision a child in your life. Open your eyes and light your black candle. Say out loud while tying the rings together with the black ribbon:

Baby mine, we two entwine.
I shall care for you, you are mine.

Place the tree twigs, three leaves, sunflower seeds, and the rings that are tied together in the black bag. Place your flower arrangement in a place where you can see it daily. Tie the majick bag to your bed or place it under the mattress.

At the birth of a child, there should be a naming ritual. One must whisper the child's name in its ear so no one else can hear it. This will prevent the faeries from exchanging the baby for one of their own (the name may be changed at initiation).

Spell to Ease a Broken Heart

This is a powerful spell for when you feel you can't move on from a lover who has moved on from you. You will need:

Strawberry tea (one bag or one tablespoon of strawberry leaves in an
unbleached muslin bag)
Sea salt
Willow wood wand (or stick)
2 pink candles
1 mirror
Pink drawstring majick bag
1 quartz crystal
1 copper penny
1 china or crystal bowl that is special to you
1 teaspoon dried jasmine flowers
1 teaspoon orris root powder

1 teaspoon yarrow flowers
10 drops of apple blossom oil or peach oil
10 drops of strawberry oil

Start this spell on Friday, the day of Venus, in the early morning or early evening hours. Venus travels close to the Sun, and the planet is most visible near sunrise and sunset. Start by making yourself a cup of strawberry tea. You can sweeten it with honey if you like, but save it until after. Prepare a majickal bath with the sea salt and light one of the two pink candles as you bathe. Release any sorrow or pain to the water. When done, have your tea as you dry off, and use the strawberry oil as an after bath perfume. Make yourself feel luxurious and beautiful, and once you feel this way, start your ritual.

Using your willow wand, cast a majick circle around a prepared table with all your other tools and ingredients for the spell. Light the second pink candle for love and healing and then mix all your herbs and oils in the special bowl you have. Gaze into the mirror and say:

O Greater Mother Goddess
enclose me in your loving arms
and nurture and bring forth
the Goddess within me!

Take in the scent of the herbs and oils. Then turn back to the mirror and say:

I represent the Great Goddess
Mother of All things.
I shine in the light of the Golden Wings of Isis.
All that is good and all that is great and loving only belongs to me.

Put half the mixture in the pink bag, adding the charged penny and crystal. Leave the other half in the bowl where you can see it and smell it often. This spell is one you can repeat as often as you feel necessary.

To Mend a Broken Heart

If you are female, you will need:

1 rose thorn

1 silk rose

1 piece of parchment paper

1 white candle

If you are male, you will need:

1 rose thorn

1 fabric handkerchief

1 piece of parchment paper

1 white candle

Female

Go to a place out of doors and away from home. Place your candle in a candleholder and set it down. Light the candle. Before going out of doors, write this spell on your parchment paper. Use a black pen.

My Love is lost, but love remains. I shall always remember how romantic it was, and I shall always feel the pain of loss. I place this thorn into my left arm. It represents the pain and sorrow. When I place this thorn in my arm, it opens my heart to love once more.

Take the rose thorn and push it into your left arm, leaving a phantom there forever. Hold the silk rose and light the white candle and say out loud:

The pain of lost love shall go away
Candle light, ease my pain.

Close your eyes and understand that from this moment on, when you want to remember the love lost, all you have to do is push your fingers on your arm where you once placed the rose thorn. Every time you push the phantom thorn, you might feel sad or cry over the love lost. Each time you do this, hold the silk rose. The open petals represent your open heart, reminding you of love to come.

Male

Go to a place out of doors and away from home. Place the white candle in a candleholder and set it down. Before going out of doors, write this spell on the piece of paper. Use a black pen.

My Love is lost, but love remains. I shall always remember how romantic it was, and I shall always feel the pain of loss. I place this thorn into my left arm. It represents the pain and sorrow. When I place this thorn in my arm, it opens my heart to love once more.

Light the candle and say out loud:

The pain of lost love shall go away,
Candle light, ease my pain.

Close your eyes and understand that from this moment on, when you want to remember your love lost, all you have to do is push your fingers on your arm where you once placed the rose thorn. Every time you push the place where the thorn was, you may feel sad or cry over the lost love. Each time you do this, tie a knot in your handkerchief and then untie it. The untied knot represents your heart opening for love to come.

Black Moon Courage to Love Again Spell
Black Moon oil
1 dram of almond oil
1 dram of vanilla oil
1 dram of amber oil

While warming the oil on the stove in a small pan or cauldron, say the following:

From morning to noon, and noon to dusk,
the power of love surrounds me.
With the scent of flowers and herb and musk,
love's power ignites and grounds me.
Goddess of the midnight sky,
Goddess of Crone Love!

At the crossroads at midnight, leave a food offering (such as an apple) and touch your forehead, wrists, and the back of your neck with Black Moon Oil. Say out loud:

I go into the nightmares, Goddess of the Dark Moon; give me your courage to love again. I ask for your help. I leave this token of love.

Pour a few drops of Black Moon Oil onto the Earth at the crossroads.

Chapter Six: Prosperity

People turn to majick for money, success and prosperity all the time, not realizing that a truly wise Witch knows the secrets of prosperity, and that our mysteries are different from the ideas of popular culture. Witches have always been on the outside of the village, at the edge, helping people as priestesses and counselors. This ability to see things from a different perspective gives us an advantage when navigating the successes and challenges of money and teaches us how to truly prosper with the use of majick.

Modern culture tells us that to be truly successful and prosperous we need to have a large house with every possible amenity there is, a million or more dollars in the bank, and a fancy car in the driveway. Our image for a successful life is outrageously undoable and unhealthy. If everyone succeeded, our planet would be in worse shape than it already is, and we would have created a model of success that can neither be reached by all nor sustained over the long term of our culture.

Everyone follows this model because everyone has been hypnotized by the mass media. Our role models become those seemingly glamorous and famous figures on television, movies, and the music industry. People seek to become those figures, not realizing that stories and songs about human relationships, families, and the possibilities of seemingly ordinary life are really the places where we can identify, as the world of fame is illusionary. But no one wants to identify with the characters in the primetime sitcom with everyday problems and mishaps when there are rich and famous figures to emulate. Yet how many of those figures are happy? How many are satisfied? Our tabloids are filled with stories of their own personal tragedies and misfortunes, and it doesn't seem like all their money and fame brings them true happiness and success.

People are usually not satisfied with their own condition in life. They believe the images that massive levels of financial success will make them happy. They believe that if they don't seek it out, there must be something wrong with them. They allow their jobs, homes, cars, and bank accounts to become the problem rather than looking within for the problem. A desire to want to be successful and improve one's financial situation is great, but what is the motivation? Even though the values of modern consumer cultures have become global, those values don't exist everywhere. There have been people and places, and there still are, where people know how to prosper in harmony. They are not unhappy due to their lack of luxury; instead, they look at luxury as a perk. Happiness and success become more of a state of mind than a number in a bank account. You can be happy, healthy, and successful and live a life of meaning and satisfaction without millions of dollars. Happiness is found in doing what you love and loving life. Creating a life you love that can provide a means of support is the true mystery of prosperity majick.

To be prosperous is to be aware, daily, of how you are living and how you are feeling. Do you feel happy? Do you feel good? Are you comfortable and satisfied when you go to bed at night? If not, why not? With that awareness, you move towards slow growth. Think of the plants that are prospering under the light of the Sun and the rain of the sky. Do they suddenly grow six feet in one day? No, they slowly move towards the light, grow strong and bear fruit over a season. We reap the fruits of our harvest, literally and metaphorically. Many prosperous actions start as little seeds that take time to grow and require patience, care, and nourishment. The get-rich-quick schemes many people seek have no place in nature.

Prosperity grows through gratefully realizing what you already have. This is one of the greatest teachings. Are you thankful for all the things you have? We take many things for granted, particularly in modern American culture, yet there are many people—both around the world and right around us—that do not share in our good fortune. When you go to bed at night, are you thankful for the roof over your head and the bed you are sleeping in? You could be sleeping in the streets, with no bed, no home, and no food. Prosperity is relative, based upon what we have allowed ourselves to be programmed to believe prosperity is. A big part of any majickal training is learning to un-brainwash yourself, to see things as they really are and decide what beliefs and programs we want to retain or create, and which ones no longer serve our highest good.

With that understanding, I don't think there is anything wrong with having a luxurious four-thousand-square-foot house with granite countertops, stainless steel appliances, three garages, and even an elevator, if you have worked for it. If your life purpose leads you to that level of earning and life style, then by all means, you can enjoy it responsibility. But don't base your happiness upon having that, or you'll find if you no longer have it, your enjoyment of life will change. Luxuries can be blessings and benefits if we do not base our self-esteem and emotional stability upon them. Objects—or at least our ownership of them, along with all financial resources—are impermanent. Our material fortunes go up and go down, like the Wheel of Fortune. We have times in our lives where it is like the harvest of summer, and other times when it is the cold of winter. That is the reality of life upon Earth, and it's reflected in our finances, in this life, and across lifetimes. A majickal person knows how to weather these changes. The problem comes when we believe we are entitled to something. We are not entitled to anything, but we can be granted a great deal.

Our karma, the results of our actions from this life and past lives, often influence our prosperity. Karma is not reward and punishment, in terms of an almighty divinity doling out merits and demerits. It is more like the law of gravity. You throw something up in the air, and the consequence is that it falls down. It's not a punishment or a reward, but simply a consequence. Karma is essentially the same, but much more complicated, as the results are not always that immediate or noticeable as karma spans lifetimes. Majick can help us shape our karma, creating new majickal actions to change our life, but it does not negate our past karma. If your life leads you to a level of immense earning and luxury, then that is your karma. Sometimes people seemingly do not work for wealth; it appears handed to them. It's a result of past karma. If that is where you should be to experience your karma, it will happen. If it is unnecessary in your life, then you probably won't have those things. Often our desire to do majick, prosperity or otherwise, is a part of our karmic heritage, and working with the majick helps us work out our karma.

Ultimately, true prosperity is being comfortable in your own skin and your own surroundings, to use the resources that you have to thrive and succeed. The end result of your desire might not require money. Sometimes money is necessary, as we live in a currency-based society. But sometimes it is not necessary. Witches know to use our majick to project for the end result of our intention, and the way it manifests might not require money. We are open to success from many different sources.

CAREER

Career is immensely important to your prosperity because it is a part of your identity, self-esteem, and ultimately, your purpose or work in the world, though not everyone's true purpose is found in an area that generates financial compensation. Master Thompson of the Rosicrucian Lodge of Brookline Massachusetts, a very wise man, told me fame and fortune are only an offshoot of your life's goals. Those using career majick to prosper are looking to create a job where they can love what they do, be successful, and be paid for what they love. As Joseph Campbell says, "Follow your bliss," which is great advice on many different levels, but certainly applies to both the spiritual journey and developing a healthy, successful career.

To truly prosper, you need a sense of love or true purpose. Going into a vocation that you hate simply because it's profitable will not let you prosper. Sure, you might acquire a large bank account, but what does it really do for you? Ultimately it's disastrous. It never works out, even if you don't realize it until the end of your life. You have to care about what you are doing.

In the end, what you are doing matters less than your sense of purpose and connection to it. A baker is as valuable as an actor, environmentalist, solider, or banker, if you truly love the work. While the job becomes part of your identity, Witches know that identity in this world comes and goes with each lifetime. What are you here to do now, in this lifetime, in this moment? Passion and love are the keys to success. The prospering plant loves the Sun and reaches out to the light each day. Do you yearn for your own purpose and work? I do. I couldn't imagine doing anything else.

When you use majick to project for a career, don't pick something simply because it is stable what others think you should do. What do you feel called to do? I remember my mother telling me I had to learn to type because at the time, women who wanted to work were secretaries. They needed to know how to type and take shorthand. In that day, it was hard to imagine a woman being a lawyer or doctor. She thought typing was a skill I could always fall back on when I needed it. That was how I was taught, programmed, when I was fifteen years old. But I knew I didn't love to type. If I had taken the lessons and learned how, I probably would have fallen back on it as a career, and I didn't want that. I would rather work on a farm than sit behind a desk and work for someone else in an office. I knew in my heart that I wouldn't love that life. So I consciously decided not to learn how to type. I didn't take the lessons, much to my mother's disappointment. But I learned not to limit myself.

If you like to type, if you like the focused work of an office and working in a group environment like that, there is nothing wrong with it. Having the security and salary of an office job can be wonderful if you are called to do it. Anything can be fulfilling and majickal if you are called to do it. Many people are quite happy in this job because it is meant for them.

When I thought of a career that would satisfy me, I knew it had to creative. Many people are so afraid to think outside of what is provided for them by society, yet many of the most majickal and successful people do just that. Whether you are an artist or a CEO of a corporation, it is simply a vocation. So many people are afraid of owning their own business, of venturing out on their own to create the perfect job. I can understand the fear quite well, but being an entrepreneur is very doable. Why not try? Anyone can try it.

A friend of mine was working in an office and hated it. She realized that she loved to paint furniture by picking up discarded furniture found on the side of the road and at yard sales. She would sand the pieces, paint them, and sell them to decorators. This woman could take a beaten-up old chair she got for free and transform it through her creativity. She started making some money through her hobby, working nights and weekends to just make her office job more bearable. Soon she realized she could make a career out of this. She saved a bit and eventually left her office job and opened her own business, starting in her garage and eventually opening a little shop. She proved to me that there are so many different angles to creating your own blissful career. You can do what you want and enjoy it, but you have to dream, dare, and actually do it. Don't let fear of failure stop you.

Use your majick to not only have money and acquire the things you desire, but also to plan for your long-term happiness and satisfaction by following your blissful desires. Be thankful for what you have and use that gratitude as a foundation to prosper. Yearn for your purpose. Seek it out and fulfill it, every day.

Money Perfume Potion

A simple money potion can be used just like any other majickal perfume. It is particularly good to dab on your solar plexus as well as the traditional wrists, brow, and back of the neck. I also use small amounts on bank deposit slips, checks, and any other correspondences or exchanges of money, to bring even greater prosperity back to me. You can even put some on job resumes and applications when using paper. Those working electronically for a new job can wear the perfume before typing and hitting "send" on an email. To make this perfume, you will need:

> 2 cups of spring water
> 2 tablespoons of sea salt
> 20 drops of heliotrope oil
> 4 cinnamon sticks
> 1 teaspoon of heather flower (or a few drops of heather oil)
> 1 teaspoon of chamomile (or a chamomile teabag)
> 1 teaspoon of red clover (or a red clover teabag)
> 1 candle of gold, yellow or blue
> Gold or silver jewelry (not plated)
> 1 large denomination bill (such as a $100 bill)

If using loose herbs, you can first place them in an unbleached muslin bag to keep the herbal material filtered from the rest of the liquid. Tea bags can be excellent if you can find the appropriate herbs in a single bag; otherwise, mix the herbs together in one muslin bag and tie it off so the herbs do not float out. While in alpha, charge all the ingredients of the spell and put them in your bowl or pan to be heated in a low simmer. Keep the dollar bill near the stove, but do not let it catch fire. Just allow its energy to infuse the ritual. If you cannot obtain a large denomination bill, then have a quantity of small one-dollar bills to give the "feeling" of a lot of money.

Etch the candle with the word WEALTH using a pin or other pointed instrument and burn the candle over the bill, putting the bill under the candleholder or placing the quantity of bills around the candle. Let the candle burn and when you feel the potion has infused enough, let it cool, strain out the solid ingredients, and bottle. You will also now have gold (or silver) jewelry you can wear infused with the intention of wealth.

Money Oil

1 dram sunflower oil
3 drops of lemon oil
3 drops of chamomile oil
1 drop of frankincense oil
10 yellow mustard seeds
2 tonka beans

Use a double boiler and put the sunflower oil in the boiler; bring to a warm temperature. Put the mustard seeds and tonka beans into the oil to infuse. Let it cool and then add the essential oils to the mix. You can strain out the seeds and beans or keep them in the bottle. Add a few drops of Vitamin E oil to preserve the mix better, as sunflower oil tends to go rancid more quickly than other base oils, but is majickally appropriate as the base for this potion.

Paper and coin are the means by which we obtain our material goods, so place this oil not only on your body, but also on your wallet, bank account, your safety deposit box, doors of your home, and your money before you send it away to help ensure it multiplies and returns.

Money Incense

1 tablespoon of sunflower petals, crushed and dried
1 tablespoon of cloves, powdered

½ teaspoon of cinnamon, powdered

10 drops of sweet orange oil

You can burn this incense for money or carry it in a royal blue, green, or gold bag to attract the money you need. You can also sprinkle it around a money candle spell, or carry a bit in your wallet.

Money Philter

Another popular philter originally shared in *Power of the Witch* is my money philter. To make an aromatic powder that will attract all necessary things into your life, including money, food and clothing, mix the following:

1 tablespoon of yellow mustard seeds

1 tablespoon of mistletoe

1 tablespoon of safflowers

1 tablespoon of cloves

Grind the ingredients together in a mortar and pestle if you have one, adding your intention as you turn them clockwise for growth. Then add to the powder:

10 drops of sweet orange oil

10 drops of sandalwood oil

10 drops of jasmine oil

Bind the entire mixture together with resins acting as both majickal and scent fixatives, a tablespoon each of powdered frankincense and myrrh. Charge the entire mix with the words:

I charge these herbs to bring (state what you want).

You can keep this in a bowl in your home, or hang it in a blue, yellow, or gold bag somewhere in your home.

Money Candle Spell
1 green candle
1 gold candle
Money Perfume Potion or Money Oil

You can do this candle spell on a Friday or Sunday. Anoint each candle with Money Potion and anoint yourself with the potion, to attract wealth to you. Light your candle and recite this spell:

Money gold
Money green
Give me more
Than I've ever seen!

Money Drawing Spell
Money Perfume Potion
Money Incense
Money Philter
Money Oil
Birch or willow root
Parchment
Pen
Black bag

Drill a hole in the root and put a string through it so you can wear the root as a talisman. Burn your money incense and pass the root through the smoke of the bag. Sprinkle the Money Potion on the roots. Write your spell on a piece of paper and recite:

Lovely Lady of the Sun
On this Day
Wealth I have won
Fill my pockets

Silver and gold
All you can give, my purse can hold.
This root shall make the money grow
And it is so!

Touch the root to the bowl of Money Philter. Put the Money Philter into the black bag. Sprinkle the Money Oil on it. Burn the incense occasionally, and wear the potion on your wrists, forehead, and back of your neck. Carry the black bag with all the majick ingredients with you.

Fast Luck Oil
2 drams almond oil
10 drops of chamomile oil
5 drops of jasmine oil
A pinch of fennel seeds
1 pinch of rabbit fur

Use Fast Luck Oil to make things happen quickly. Take a toothpick and put it on the edge of your credit card (being careful not to drop oil on the credit card, ruining the magnetic strip) or place a small amount on your money. Wear it when you are looking for good fortune – when asking for a loan, going into a meeting, or even gambling.

Fast Luck Incense
1 tablespoon of patchouli
1 tablespoon of chamomile flowers
1 tablespoon of jasmine flower
6 drops of chamomile oil
3 drops of jasmine oil
1 pinch of rabbit fur

Burn before any situation where you need fast luck, and bathe yourself in the smoke. Only use Fast Luck Incense and Fast Luck Oil for things that are important. If you use them every day, they will not work as effectively. Use sparingly to effectively draw luck to you.

Fast Luck Mojo Bag Spell

Fast Luck Incense

Fast Luck Oil

Orange majick bag

Coin

Paper Bill ($5 or more)

Rabbit fur

Yellow mustard seeds

Parchment with the symbols of a wing, Mercury, and the Sun on it

Burn the Fast Luck Incense and touch the oil to every majickal item in the bag. Touch the oil to your wrists and forehead. Place all the items back into the bag and write your spell on the other side of the paper and place the paper into the bag.

I shall have fast luck; it will bring all goods things, money, love and health!

Symbols of a Wing, Mercury and the Sun

Candle Spell for Power and Influence
Royal blue or turquoise candle
Money Potion
Parchment with the symbol of Jupiter in blue ink

Do this spell roughly three days after the New Moon, ideally on a Thursday. Place the parchment with the Jupiter symbol beneath the candlestick holder. Carve the symbol of Jupiter into the candle with a pin. Anoint the candle with Money Potion. Recite this spell as you light the candle.

As I light this candle bright
Its spell shall bring to me
Success and money
Night after night
This spell shall sway
Then day by day
Power and Influence
Comes my way
So Mote It Be!

Moon Wealth Spell
Recite the following spell under the light of the Full Moon.

Lovely Lady of the Moon
Bring to me your wealth right soon
Fill my hands with silver and gold
All you can give
My purse can hold
For the Good of All
So Mote It Be.

Make sure the Moon is not Void of Course when doing this spell. You can find out if the Moon is Void of Course through an astrological calendar. When the Moon it is not making any of the special astrological alignments before leaving it's current Zodiac sign and moving onto the next sign. Astrologer believe the energy of the Moon is ungrounded at that time, and makes us spacy, and any lunar spells done at this time are more likely to be unsuccessful. An astrological calendar can be a handy tool for spell casters working with the Moon.

Elf King Treasure Spell
Acorn

Oak leaves

Green bag

Speak these words out loud when outside in nature, ideally in a lush green forest:

Elf King, Elf King
Bring me your treasures bright
Money glistens from your hand to mine.
Elf King, Elf King
Bring money and treasures to me that are right.
Elf King, Elf King
Crown me with your wealth so bright!

Place the acorn and leaves in the bag and carry it with you. If you don't have access to an acorn or oak leaf, you can use a picture of the acorn or oak leaf for your charm.

Faery Success Majick Herbal Mix
1 heaping tablespoon of dried moss

1 heaping tablespoon of dried fallen leaves and petals from a flower garden, ground

1 heaping tablespoon of yarrow
Tourmaline quartz
Black or green majick bag

Mix the herbs together in a bowl and ask for the faery blessings. If you don't have access to naturally growing moss you can dry yourself, it is often available at craft stores. Gather flower petals and leaves from a natural flower garden (avoiding flowers people have sent you from florists, as they are treated with too many chemicals). Carry in a majick bag with a tourmaline quartz stone for success, or scatter the mix around your home to attract the blessing of the faeries.

Good Luck Oil
1 dram of almond oil
1 dram of sunflower oil
4 drops of cinnamon oil
1 pinch of soil from where you live
Horseshoe Charm
Copper penny

We all want good luck; this potion is made with ingredients that will put the one who wears it into nature's flow of good happenings and good vibrations! Warm this potion in a double boiler to infuse the cinnamon in the oil. If you have a small horseshoe charm available to you, like those on a charm bracelet, drop it into the cooled oil. Or use other symbols of good luck, such a four-leaf clover or clover charm. You might have to go to a coin shop to get a true copper penny, as most today are zinc.

Lottery Incense
3 tablespoons of nettle leaf
1 tablespoon of chamomile
1 tablespoon of jasmine

Sprinkle of powdered cinnamon

Sprinkle of gold glitter

Pass your lottery ticket through the smoke of this blend to increase your changes of success.

Lottery Oil

2 drams of sunflower oil

10 drops of chamomile

3 drops of jasmine

Small piece of orange peel

Sprinkle of powdered cinnamon

14-caret gold jewelry

Those who do good, get good! The more you do for humankind and Mother Earth, the higher the chance you will win in the end. This potion is made with mother Nature's majick to help bring lottery success to you! Anoint your lottery ticket with it. Heat this oil in a double boiler to extract the majick of the orange and cinnamon. Dip your real gold jewelry into the oil to bring that blessing of wealth.

Money Herbal Mix

Dried rose petals

Lemon peel

Orange peel

Red clover

Fern, dried and powderedPinch of wolf fur

Sprinkle of soil from your home

Citrine stone

10 drops of Money Oil

Keep in your home to bring money to your home. The soil brings it to your home, and the wolf fur helps protect your wealth. Carry in a green majick bag to bring money to you or sprinkle on your business papers, loan applications, or job applications.

Prosperity Incense
2 tablespoons of patchouli
1 tablespoon of ground pine needles
1 tablespoon of nettle leaf
1 teaspoon of ground rose petals,
3 drops of storax oil

Since prosperity is not just money, you can burn this whenever you want blessings of prosperity in your entire life. Sprinkle it on your doorstep or carry in a gold or blue majick bag. Create after the New Moon on a Thursday, Friday, or Sunday.

Success Oil
2 drams of almond oil
8 drops of strawberry oil
6 drops of chamomile oil
4 drops of frankincense oil
1 piece of orange Peel
1 piece of lemon Peel
1 pinch of gold glitter

To be successful, we must acknowledge when we have succeeded and build upon it. Use this to aid in building upon your success and achieving your goals. Wear when you go to interviews, work, meetings, or when casting a spell.

Success Incense
3 tablespoons of frankincense
2 tablespoons of orange peel
2 tablespoons of lemon peel

1 tablespoon of strawberry leaf

1 tablespoon of chamomile flower

10 drops of frankincense oil

1 pinch of gold glitter

Burn this incense for success on all levels. It makes you feel happy and optimistic, drawing success to you.

Jupiter Oil

3 drams of jasmine oil

4 whole cloves

3 tonka beans

1 tumbled lapis stone

Harness the power of Jupiter in your spells, rituals, and daily life. Jupiter is used for success and to influence those in high places. Put it in on your chair to make yourself an influential person. Use it every Thursday, but only a drop. You don't need to smear oil on yourself or all your objects. A little will go a long way.

Jupiter Spell to Influence Others

Recite this spell on a Thursday, the day of Jupiter, to help gain the influence of a prominent person in your life. It is excellent to get the attention of an official whose approval you need. Wear the Jupiter Oil before reciting the spell.

To the Gods and Goddesses who hear my
voice, I call upon the planet Jupiter.
I draw down the royal blue light of Jupiter
So that I may influence _____
For the good of all
So Mote It Be!

Silver Money Spell
Money Herb Mix
1 clear quartz
Money Perfume Potion or Money Oil
4 cloves
3 tonka beans
1 cinnamon stick
3 silver coins
Green majick bag

Money is a necessity. Our society demands that we not only have enough to survive, but to please and entertain ourselves as well. It's true that money cannot buy happiness; however, a roof over our heads, clothing, food, and warmth in the winter are necessities.

On the waxing moon, place your silver coins out under the stars and moon. Sprinkle the herbs around the coins. Place the stone on one of the coins. Put a drop of Money Potion on your wrists, forehead, and the back of your neck. Put a drop of potion on the stone and coins. Hold the tonka beans, cloves, and cinnamon sticks in your left hand and place your right hand over them saying out loud:

By the light of the stars, by the light of the moon, riches and wealth come to me soon. So mote it be.

Place the herbs, the tonka beans, cloves, and the coin in the green bag and carry it with you always. You can make several bags to keep near you —one for your car, one for your home, and one for your workplace. They will attract money to you by the light of the stars and Moon.

Money Talisman Spell
1 citrine
1 malachite

1 gold or green candle
Money talisman on parchment
Black pen

This money talisman spell comes from the Cabot Family Book of Shadows. Perform the spell on a Sunday evening during the waxing moon. Make the Money Symbol by placing a dollar sign ($) in a circle and putting eight rays of the sun around it in black ink. On the other side, make an equilateral cross and put the symbol of the Sun, a circle with a dot in the center, at the end of each arm of the cross. Lay the stones on top of the money talisman and light the candle. Say the following charm out loud:

This majick symbol shall bring riches, wealth, and abundance to my life. I ask that this be done for the good of all. So Mote It Be!

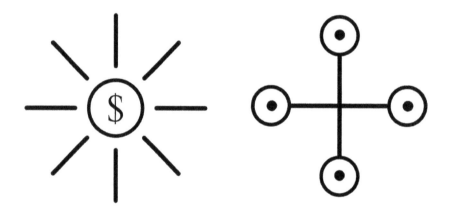

Money Talisman

Let the candle burn out. Then carry both the talisman and the stone with you for four consecutive days and nights. During the nights when you are sleeping, be sure the talisman and stone are placed to the left side of your bedside. After the four days and nights have passed, put the stone and talisman away out of sight for another four days and nights; then carry it with you again for an additional four days and nights. Store the talisman and stone in a safe place.

Successful Career Spell
3 blue candles
Jupiter Oil
Money Herbal Mix
Blue majick bag
Picture of yourself

For three consecutive nights, light one of these candles after anointing it with Jupiter Oil. Sprinkle the herbs around the candle and repeat the spell out loud.

By the power of three, success will come to me. By the power of Jupiter, I request a career to my liking that will be successful, profitable, and safe. I ask that this be correct in the eyes of the God and Goddess of All Good Things. So mote it be!

At the end of the three nights, gather the herbs and place them into a majick bag. Put the picture of yourself in the majick bag, for it's the successful career you want that matters. Keep this bag with you always. Use the potion on your wrists, forehead, and neck to bring you good luck and success.

Unexpected Prosperity Herb and Crystal Spell
Sometimes unexpected money and success is the best surprise blessing. This spell helps conjure it in ways we cannot imagine. You will need:

4 tonka beans
1 goldenseal root (or 1 tablespoon of powdered goldenseal root)

1 tablespoon of mustard seeds
3 cups of sea salt
1 clear quartz crystal
Gold majick bag
Bowl

Place the crystal in the bowl and cover it with the sea salt for twelve days to clear it of any unwanted forces. On the twelfth day, take it out and hold the crystal under running tap water to recharge its majickal force. Wash the salt down the drain. Place the crystal in the center of the bowl, surrounded by the four tonka beans and then the other ingredients. Using your Instant Alpha Trigger, charge the stone and herbs for prosperity and wealth in a manner that is for the good of all involved, harming none. Meditate with the mixture for a short time, envisioning yourself having all that you want and need. Then put all the ingredients into the gold bag and carry it with you or place it in a prominent spot in your home.

Mabon Herbal Prosperity Spell

Mabon is a time for balance and harmony as the light and darkness are equal on the Autumn Equinox. This spell brings balance to our finances, particularly when we are afraid that like the light at this time of year, our fortune is waning. Mabon majick helps keep you through the dark periods as our ancestors did through the long winters.

Mabon Oil (see below)
Mabon Prosperity Incense (see below)
1 gold or yellow candle
1 black candle
1 black pen
1 four-inch square of parchment paper for the spell
1 spice teabag with cinnamon and clove
1 four-inch square of yellow cloth, or a yellow drawstring majick bag

Gold or yellow cord

2 tablespoons of rosemary

2 tablespoons of marigold

2 tablespoons of yarrow

1 clear quartz crystal

1 citrine crystal

1 thurible (incense burner)

1 instant-light charcoal (for burning the incense)

Before casting this spell, prepare the Mabon Oil and Mabon Prosperity Incense.

Mabon Oil

1 dram of hazelnut oil

1 dram of almond oil

1 pinch of marigold flowers or leaves

1 pinch of crushed walnut shells

1 pinch of dried oak leaves

1 acorn

1 citrine stone

Mabon Prosperity Incense

1 teaspoon of marigold flowers

1 teaspoon dried oak leaves

1 teaspoon of dried fern

1 teaspoon of frankincense

1 teaspoon of myrrh

1 teaspoon of dried apple

1 teaspoon of yarrow flowers

1 teaspoon of rosemary

1 teaspoon of bittersweet

1 teaspoon of wheat

1 dram of Mabon Oil
1 teaspoon of gold glitter

Perform this spell while in a majick circle on Mabon, the Autumn Equinox. Start by charging the gold candle and saying:

I charge this candle to bring prosperity to me. I ask that this harms none and is correct for all. So Mote it be.

Charge the black candle and say:

I charge this candle to draw to me all that is safe, correct, and granted by the Gods and Goddesses.

With both candles lit, say:

This flame is the light of the God Mabon and the Mother Goddess Modron.

Light your charcoal and put it safely in the incense burner. Put a pinch of incense upon it and smell the smoke waft through your space. Put the Mabon Oil on your wrists, brow, and back of the neck. Write this spell upon the parchment paper:

I ask the Goddess Modron and the God Mabon to grant me this: prosperity in all I do, money, health, happiness. I ask for heightened psychic, spiritual, and physical balance and power. I ask this to be correct in the eyes of the God and Goddess, and for the good of all. So mote it be.

Read the spell out loud in your majick circle celebration. Thank Mabon and Modron for all things you have received, and when done, pass the spell paper through the smoke, roll it up, and tie it with the yellow cord. Charge your herbs and stones individually and place each upon the cloth square or within the majick bag. Seal the majick bag and pass it through the incense smoke.

Charge the teabag with the energy of the circle and the blessings of Mabon and Modron. Save it until the first Sunday after the Autumn Equinox, and drink it then. Before you release the circle, burn one more pinch of incense as an offering and thanks to the gods you have called. Release the circle and let the candles burn. Carry the spell and the charm with you, and wear the oil for a minimum of four days. You can also use the incense for the next four days, to magnify your spell and give thanks.

Majick Wish List

Witches are known to make wishes come true, and that includes our own wishes. Start by making a majick wish list. Meditate on the material things you need and desire. Make an initial list, and evaluate the items. Discard what is not necessary or truly not a heart's desire. Then write out a spell listing all the things you need.

I, (state your name), ask in the name of the Source, the Goddess and God, to be granted:

(List your Items)

I ask this be for the highest good, harming none. So mote it be.

Read the list out loud, charging your intentions, ideally on the Full Moon. Burn the list, or carry it on your person to remind you of its majickal power. You can also store it someplace sacred in your home, a place of majickal power, or leave it in nature in a similarly imbued area of enchantment for you.

Crystal Moon Wish List

Just like the Majick Wish List, you can further empower your dreams by creating a Crystal Moon Wish List. The Crystal Moon is the first Full Moon after your birthday. This is the most powerful time to manifest wishes for yourself. It works best for tangible desires, not intangible things like relationships or happiness. We use other majick for those goals. Make a list of items you desire, and then, like the Majick Wish List, recite them out loud, in a majick circle on the waxing Crystal Moon.

My daughter Jody had amazing results with this majick. She projected for herself a Rolex watch on her Crystal Moon list, while I was away working in England. While I had also projected for it as a sign of success, I didn't really want the watch, just the status of it as a symbol of success in our society. I had no idea that Jody wanted one too and never told her that I projected for it. Though I was generously paid for my consulting, the corporation sent a bonus, a Rolex watch! I don't wear watches due to my psychic energy interfering with their function, so happy that my majickal whim was a success, I gave the watch to Jody as a present as I knew she would like it. Little did I know that it was her wish all along!

Chapter Seven: Healing

Healing majick is a tricky subject. Most Witches believe that true healing comes from within. This is a very different concept for those who feel they are the source of healing for another. We know that we can only facilitate the healing. Even doctors and more traditional medical practitioners can facilitate conditions to improve the chances of healing. Medications can change body chemistry to promote healing and to make it difficult for foreign invaders – unhealthy bacteria, viruses, and parasites —but the body itself has to purge them. Surgery can remove diseased tissue or put bones and organs back into their proper place, but the body must rest and recuperate, integrate these changes, to fully come back to health. Anyone who thinks they are a healer is misinformed. They are not. You are simply helping the recipients heal themselves.

Whenever you do any type of healing majick, or apply your intention to herbs and food, you must always intend that it be correct and for the good of all involved. Just like with any spells, you don't want to interfere with someone's karma. What you think is for the good of all involved, and what the universe thinks, can be two different things. Sometimes we need to experience illness as a part of our karma, and using majick to force someone to be healthy without the deeper healing from within is just as harmful as any curse. That is why we don't believe true healing comes from outside of us. It cannot be forced upon us. Eventually it will reassert the illness in another form if we do not reconcile the experience within us.

Witches also know that all things have a beginning, a middle, and an end. While we can remain vital and energetic, we also know that all things must end, and sometimes illness is the way lives end. Illness and injury are a part of nature. It would be nice to think that everything is wonderful and safe all the time, but nature contains both good and ill in the natural cycles of life. It is not personal, but it is the balance of life.

When we do healing majick, we are adding energy for the person receiving the healing to use. You are creating conditions for the person to heal naturally, so they can heal themselves. The principle is the same whether your intention is physical healing or spiritual healing. The energy helps remove unwanted forces and blockages and allow the natural life force to reestablish health and blessings in the body, mind, and spirit.

LAYING ON HANDS

Laying on of hands, or in-person healing methods involving light touch, uses the energy of your aura to induce healing. Much like a Witch who charges a wand or other majickal object, you are coupling your aura, your very own light energy "packets," with the energy already existing in the object or person. Through this connection, you can project an intention and have an effect on the recipient of the intention. Charging wands, objects, and people is one of the most important skills taught in the Cabot Tradition of Witchcraft. It places the subtle light naturally found in the aura into specific configurations, which hold intent. Some find making a direct physical connection one of the most powerful ways to get results, but it is not the only way to heal.

Hands-on healing is found in many different traditions and religions. Most people are introduced to the concept through Christian ministries and remember Biblical stories of Jesus healing people through touch. However, hands-on healing has been done prior to Christianity and Judaism. You find it in many Pagan traditions. Witches and shamans of various forms have been using it for thousands of years and even new traditions of healing are using similar ideas, such as Reiki and Quantum Touch.

Although it's often called laying on of hands, technically you do not always have to touch to induce a healing response. You are extending your hands into the aura, and the aura of your hands into the body. Through this connection you can send healing in the form of visualized light and energy.

While I've experienced some pretty remarkable results, it does not mean that you will heal everyone instantly. Sometimes you do, but often it's a slow and gradual process. It all depends upon the recipient of the healing, if they truly accept the healing and are psychologically and spiritually ready to heal. It depends upon their own karma, and how the illness might be serving them. If the illness is secretly serving them in some way, they will not be able to absorb the energy and healing intention. They won't be able to heal.

Visualizing color is an important method used by Witches to heal. In the Cabot Tradition, we draw upon and build from color associations found in the teaching of Pythagoras and modern color therapy. In physical healing work, the two most common colors used are red-orange and emerald green. Red-orange, the color of an ember or burning coal, is for critical healing. While we might think every situation needing healing is critical to us personally, we don't use this technique all the time. It is only for extreme healing, advanced illness, and more severe injuries, such as broken bones. Red-orange won't heal everything. If it's the wrong color, being too intense for a situation, it won't be properly absorbed by the recipient.

Emerald green is used for basic healing. The clear green light, like a healthy green field of grass, promotes gentle growth and balance. Green is the color associated with the heart center, and near the heart center is the thymus gland, which regulates the immune system. Use green for colds and flu, for minor injuries, and for anything before it becomes critical.

For mental and emotional distress, blue is one of the safest colors, as it brings a feeling of peace and well-being. Think of the peace and clarity of a blue sky. Blue is considered a sacred color by many majickal traditions, including the Celts. Blue tattoos made from the herb woad were though to empower and protect Celtic warriors and Druids. Blue is connected with the faery realm, and what is known as "faery fire." And many consider life force, known as prana or chi, to be an electric blue, like the blue of a gas stove flame.

Pink light is also very healing, though not physically so. Pink is the color of self-esteem and self-love, which is the root of all majick. If you cannot love yourself, it is impossible to truly heal yourself. So in many cases, the most appropriate color is pink, so the recipient can feel worthy of truly healing.

All the colors have majickal qualities, but for healing, these four colors are used most often with the best results.

HEALING COLOR MAJICK

Bright Emerald Green: Heals, takes away pain, minor ailments including colds, minor cuts, bruises, first degree burns, sunburns, allergies, stubbed toe, sinus headache.

Red/Orange: For critical/life threatening problems, critical healing including diabetes, cancer, infection: some broken bones; often asthma, sometimes allergic reactions; heart, circulatory, respiratory and neurological problems. Serious viral or bacterial complications. Migraines.

Bright Pink: Self-love and self-esteem

Ice Blue: Anesthetizing, pain relief, pain reduction. Be careful using this color on backs. When the pain is gone, people tend to over-use the muscles again, resulting in further damage or injury.

Electric Blue: Total intelligence

Dazzling White: Enlightenment

Brilliant Gold: Tao, spirituality, God/Goddess

Bright Orchid: Force, the All

To heal with color, you must envision the colored light pouring through your own aura, out through your hands and into the aura of the recipient. You are invoking that energy from the universe and drawing it through your own aura to imprint it with the intention of healing, but you are not diminishing your own life force to heal. If you do it correctly, you are only tired due to the focus and concentration of your mind to hold the intention and visualization. You should not be depleted in life force.

One healing I'll never forget happened at a healing workshop I was leading at a Knights of Columbus hall. A little old lady came up to me and asked me to touch her ear, so she could hear better. She was wearing a hearing aid. I wasn't sure how effective the healing would be on deafness, but I told her I would try. I placed my hand on her ear and sent energy with the intention of healing her. The next time she came back to me, she came without her hearing aid on. She claimed it work, that I had healed her. I told her that I hadn't done it, that she had, but she wouldn't believe me.

When I was teaching in New York City, another woman approached me for healing. She was originally from Russia and was suffering with a lot of pain. Her hands were crippled with arthritis. She had great difficulty picking up anything. She asked me to touch her hands. I did, and in an unusual case of extraordinary and instant healing, immediately her hands straightened out and were perfect, just by this simple touch. It showed that she was really ready and open for healing. It amazed me, even though I was doing the touching, as I had never seen it work so quickly, so completely, before this. That was my first experience with such an instant healing.

It's easy for the recipient to idolize the healer and feel that the healer is "fixing" them rather than facilitating their own healing. In some ways, it's much scarier for most people to think they have the power to heal and that people are just helping them. It's much easier to think others can fix you, so that when you don't heal, it was someone else's fault. This type of praise and idolization is a very dangerous area to be in as a Witch and healing facilitator. We must ever be on guard for it and seek to empower people to heal, and take responsibility, for themselves.

People often get discouraged when they are practicing healing work and their work does not have the intended effect. We must remember that it is not about the healer, but about the person who is being healing. They must heal themselves, and if they are not ready, there is very little you can do to make a healing happen.

DISTANCE HEALING

Like hands-on healing, distance healing, also known as remote healing, is possible with the science and art of Witchcraft. To heal someone remotely, go into an alpha state. You envision the person who is your target. It can help to say their name, and in the case of doing work for people you don't personally know, the name, age, and city of residence of the recipient are most helpful. Repeat this information three times to draw their image and energy upon the screen of your mind. Once they are present, you can send healing light to them, much like you would if they were physically present with you. Reach out with your mind and direct a healing color to them. You can envision it as liquid color, filling their aura like paint, or like a colored screen being placed over them. Whatever image helps you imagine and call the color to the screen of your mind is okay. We often work well with creative techniques, so find a way that speaks to your own creativity. Interestingly enough, sometimes people will unconsciously pick up on the color you are sending and notice it in their vision and dreams, or start to wear it in their clothing unconsciously.

Part of my ministry is to do healing work. Every time we celebrate one of the eight Witch's sabbats in the Cabot-Kent Hermetic Temple, we bring in the red-orange light and we ask to send healing to those in need. We speak the names of those who need the healing in the ritual. All together, we envision sending out the healing light to those named, for their highest good.

We often have a healing candle as a part of our rituals. When doing healing work, you can write the name of the person down the side of the candle with a small knife or pin, right into the wax. You then fill the candle with healing energy, with the intention that the candle will magnify and continue to send the light to that person. It's a simple and effective way to send healing over a longer period of time. We don't blow out the candle, for breath carries prana, life force, and will imbalance the spell placed into the candle. When you must extinguish a candle, snuff it out with a snuffer or spoon. Do not blow it out or use wet fingers to snuff it. It imbalances the original energy of the spell candle.

Many years ago, I got a call from someone at Mass General Hospital in Boston about a construction worker whose jackhammer blew up; the resulting explosion burned the inside of his lungs. They thought he would never be healed. We performed distance healing on him, and he commented to his nurses that every time he closed his eyes, he saw a red light. Within a week, he showed a vast improvement and was able to breathe on his own again.

We worked on another woman who had collapsed and was sent to the hospital. She had collapsed several times, and they had difficulty finding out why. We sent pink light to her, for self-esteem. When consulting with her doctors, she remarked that every time she closed her eyes, her room was filled with pink light. Within a week, she was out of the hospital, and as far as we know, did not suffer from another collapse.

REFLEXOLOGY AND ACUPRESSURE

Acupressure is like acupuncture, except that it is accessible to everyone. All you need is a pencil with a rubber tip. Reflexology is best done on the hands and feet. I've found it amazingly helpful in my own healing path.

For a period in my life just before the change of life, I was getting migraines. I had gone to Needle Eye, Kentucky, with treasure hunters and had been psychically looking for treasures there. We were in the car on a hot summer day, driving near Ohio, and all of sudden, I got a pounding migraine, as if my head were splitting in half. I remember someone telling me that if you take a pencil and put pressure on your big toe, the one that hurts the most, it is the one that will cure your migraine. I pushed and turned, as I had no alternative, no medicine, on the middle of a highway in cornfields in the middle of nowhere. I took my shoe off, and one of the treasure hunters gave me a pencil. I kept pushing in on my left toe, which hurt the most. Within ten seconds, the headache started to go. By the time I pushed about twenty times, it was gone. In the past, I had taken migraine medicine and nothing touched the pain, but here, something as simple as pushing a pencil into my big toe eliminated my migraine. And I realized I needed to know more about it.

Since then I've been using the technique quite a bit. Later in life, blood tests indicated that my kidneys were getting slow, and I had a pain in my kidney, which was passing minute granules. I looked up a chart on the acupressure points for the kidney. There is a spot in the center of the hand to help send healing to your kidneys. I started doing that, in both hands. The next time I went to the doctor, the blood test indicated, to everyone's surprise, that my kidneys had gotten quite a bit better, not worse.

We have to admire ancient methods that are still around and still working for people, like acupressure and acupuncture.

Some of the charts of foot acupressure points are conflicting, as there are different systems, but here are some basics to keep in mind.

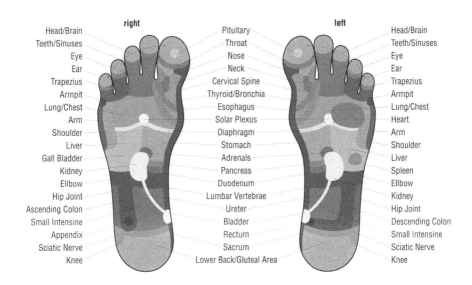

Foot Reflexology Chart

Head and Neck – the toes, particularly the big toe, relates to the head and neck. The joint closest to the foot relates to the neck. The space between the toes relates to the sinus cavities.

Spine – the inside of the foot relates to the entire spine. Massaging the inner side of the foot will help with spine and back problems.

Chest – the area across the foot containing the ball of the foot relates to the chest, including the heart, lungs and ribcage.

Waist – the center of the foot, where it is most "thin" represents the waist. If you were to draw a horizontal line bisecting the foot, the stomach area would be just above this line, with organs such as the liver near it, and below would be the intestines and lower digestive system.

Pelvis – the bottom of the foot, where the foot supports the heel, corresponds to the pelvic area.

This is just the briefest of guides to reflexology, hopefully to inspire Witches to a more in-depth study of the art and science of this fantastic healing art. For more study, I suggest *The Reflexology Manual* by Pauline Wills and *Complete Reflexology for Life* by Barbara Kunz.

Along with our energy work and stimulation through acupressure, these spells will help us on the healing path.

Healing Oil
1 dram of jojoba oil
5 drops of sweet orange oil
5 drops of lemon oil
1 teaspoon of comfrey leaves
¼ teaspoon of aloe juice
1 carnelian stone
1 clear quartz

Heat the oil in a double boiler and put in the comfrey leaves. Use fresh leaves if possible. Let it cool and then add the aloe juice, stones, and the essential oils.

Use to aid in bringing about spiritual, physical and emotional wellness. Along with anointing yourself or others, you could also use it on a charged orange candle to help promote health and healing.

Healing Incense
1 tablespoon of dried comfrey leaves

1 tablespoon of dandelion leaves

1 teaspoon of frankincense

1 teaspoon of myrrh

3 crushed almonds

1 pinch of sea salt

1 pinch of sea weed

Use this incense to bring healing blessings when burned. It does not always spell the most pleasant, but it does induce healing energy. You can also carry it in a green or orange bag for healing.

Healing Majick Herbal Mix
2 tablespoons of comfrey leaves

1 tablespoon of comfrey root

1 tablespoon of red clover

1 teaspoon of seaweed

1 teaspoon of orange peel

1 teaspoon of lemon peel

1 carnelian stone

1 quartz stone

Carry this mix in an orange, gold, or black majick bag. You could also leave it in a bowl on your nightstand to heal you when you sleep. You can make smaller bags of it, and keep one in your purse or briefcase, another in your home, and a third in your pocket, to take with you wherever you may go to speed your healing.

Faery Healing Majick Herbal Mix
1 tablespoon of pine needles

1 tablespoon of dried fern

1 tablespoon of dried moss
1 teaspoon of dried mushrooms
1 pinch of bark from a really old tree
3 pebbles from running brook
1 Botswana agate stone

Carry this mix in a majick bag to evoke the healing blessings of the faery folk. When you gather up the natural materials, you should ask permission of the faeries and make an offering to them. I like to leave small pieces of dried fruit, milk, honey, and even small replicas of furniture, like that which can be found in dollhouses.

To Banish Warts

To get rid of warts, cut a potato in half. Rub half on the warts and place the two pieces of the potato together. Bury the potato in soil. If the soil is frozen when you do this spell, you can get gardening soil and put this into a pot to release the spell. As the potato rots the warts will go away. A local plastic surgeon in the Salem, Massachusetts, area used to call on me to help children with plantar's warts, and I used this spell with great success. I usually call upon the Goddess Bridget before I do it, lighting a white candle and asking for her aid in the healing.

Ostara Earth Healing Spell

1 teaspoon of dried and crushed egg shells
1 tablespoon of honey
1 tablespoon of dried grass
1 tablespoon of dried straw
2 teaspoon of frankincense
1 teaspoon of natural clay or mud
Majick bag (pink, yellow or lavender)

Place all the charged ingredients into the bag for healing the Earth by the power of the Goddess. As you do, recite this spell:

O Goddess of our Ancestors, Ostara, bring your powers to this world and renew all that is good for nature, the animals, the land and humans, that inhabit this planet. Renew in all beings the ability to end pollution and destruction, to end disease and pain. Renew in us the power to be one with the choices you give us. So shall it be!

You can make the charm a gift when you make an Ostara basket, or you can bury it in the ground as an offering to the Earth as well. Try making a lot of them and share them with friends and family, or drop them around places in your home and surrounding area.

Beltane Health Spell
1 red candle
Healing oil
3 tablespoons of dried, crushed pink rose petals
1 tablespoon of rose hips
1 tablespoon of chamomile
1 tablespoon of comfrey leaves
1 teaspoon of honey
1 carnelian stone
1 citrine stone
1 rose quartz stone
1 lodestone
Pink majick bag

Do this spell on the Waning Moon after Beltane. Anoint your red candle with healing oil with the intention of healing. Charge all the ingredients and put them in the majick bag while reciting this:

I ask this of the Goddess and God of Beltane that health will come instead of pain and suffering: happiness, self-esteem, and a healthy body will maintain forever, for the good of all. So shall it be!

Let the candle burn and carry the majick bag with you for healing, at least until Midsummer's Eve!

Chapter Eight: Home Majick

A Witch's home should be majickal. It should reflect the enchantment of the majickal self and wishes and desires of the Witch who lives in it. Homes can be a blessing or a curse, depending on the energies you invoke into the dwelling. They can promote healing, peace, beauty, and love, but you must set the intention and neutralize anything that conflicts with your majickal goals. Everything in the home is a potential majickal tool. Look at everything through the eyes of the Witch and make your home your castle.

HOUSEHOLD FURNITURE

A home is first filled with furniture, all the functional items we need to eat, sleep and be comfortable. All your furniture can carry an intention. Most items are made of wood and metal, natural items that have their own energy and can carry a charge. Hopefully you've picked items that are not only functional but also pleasing, and that's half the majick there. But to add to the natural majick, you should neutralize and charge all of your furniture—bed, nightstands, bookcases, kitchen table, counters, dining room table, chairs, and couches. Clear and charge everything.

This is particularly true if you have antiques. Antiques carry quite a charge from their previous owners, and their energy can cause mischief and even some serious problems when allowed to run free. Sometimes energies can grow stronger in a Witch's home, including both the consciously created energies and the ones that remain on antique items and are often forgotten about. They begin to take on a life of their own, so make sure you neutralize your antiques from previous harmful energies.

A Witch's home is like a vortex of powerful energies that can magnify whatever is present, so be careful as you grow in your Craft. If items, particularly antiques, are witness to unpleasant arguments or even more serious violence, they carry those energies, and often people will feel them and be stimulated to re-enact the unpleasantness on some level. We say that we neutralize all energy that is "incorrect" for our highest good, so energies that are loving and sentimental will stay with such items. We can bring forward all good memories, such as the energies of all the celebrations, holidays, and parties. We can keep those energies and add our own power on top of it, setting the item with a very clear and specific intention.

To neutralize and clear these items, there are several methods. The easiest is to touch it with protection potion or another cleansing substance. Some people use a dilute solution of salt in water and then follow it up with just pure water or regular cleaning fluids, clearing away any salt residue. The salt will take the unwanted energies if you charge the salt and water to do so. Most Witches would follow up any physical clearing with ritual gesture of sweeping with the hands. You are sweeping out to the cosmos any incorrect and unwanted energy so that the universe can polarize it into something beneficial. Witches often use a besom, a ritual broom, to sweep out their living spaces, usually from the front door of the home out the back door. If you don't have a Witch's besom, you can certainly charge your own broom to do this clearing work. Then we charge the remaining objects, reapplying our energy into the tables, chairs, or beds. Our intention is to put the most correct energy into each item. Visualize a color of light going into the item, carrying with it your intention. Pink light, for love and self-esteem, is a general all-purpose energy for the home. It can bring a sense of self-love, goodness, safety, and harmony to those who use it. Who couldn't use a little more harmony and self-love?

Beds in particular should be used as a majickal tool. Clear and charge your bed with the intentions of comfort and peace of mind. Charge your bed for psychological balance and harmony within. Charge your pillows for good dreams. Your evenings in dreamland will be healing, bringing out a more rejuvenated and balanced majickal self.

Herbal mixtures can be placed under the pillow or mattress with intention as well, to add to the majick of your bed. We can use protection herbs under the bed to strengthen our shields and boundaries when we sleep, particularly if we feel unsafe while we sleep or suffer from nightmares. Herbs like nettles, mandrake, frankincense, myrrh, copal, and St. John's Wort are excellent for this. Those who feel safe and want to enhance their dream life can use herbs such as lavender, cinquefoil, mugwort, seaweed, and wild lettuce to stimulate majickal dreams. Lavender in general is a great overall herb for the bed, bringing rest and tranquility. It's a great all-purpose herb, whether you need more peace to feel protected, or more relaxation to release stress and dream deeply. You can also write an intention spell on parchment paper while in a majick circle, with or without herbs, and place the parchment between the mattress and box spring to manifest it.

Easy Sleep Spell
1 tablespoon of lavender
2 tablespoons of red clover
5 drops of musk oil
Blue lace agate
Bowl
2 pieces of 1 inch square cloth
Fabric glue
Lavender soap

On a Waning Moon, mix the herbs and blue lace agate in a bowl. Add the musk oil to the mix. Pass your hands over the bowl and "see" a blue light enter the herbal mix. Say out loud:

Every night when I go to bed,
my sleep will come with ease.
Sweet pictures and thoughts
will bring dreams that please.

Place the herbs on one half of the cloth. Use fabric glue around the edges and place the other cloth on top. Press the edges together so that the herbs cannot fall out. Before you go to bed, wash your face and hands with lavender soap. Place the herbal package under your pillow or on your night table next to you. As you close your eyes, "see" the herbal pillow and say to yourself:

Sweet thoughts and dreams are mine.

When you wake in the morning, go to a window or go out of doors and face east. Take a deep breath and start your day.

Have a special chair, just for you if possible. It can be a reading chair, a meditation chair, or a power chair. Use it for contemplation, education, and majick. It can be charged to help you focus. Herbs can be put under the seat cushion or sewn into the back of the chair. Resins and stones can be put beneath it. Decorate it to suit your majickal self.

Every mirror in your household should be a majick mirror. Mirrors contain great mystery to them. Most believe they are simply for primping and vanity, but the majick of mirrors lies in their ability to put you in the now. Mirrors reflect space. When we catch a glimpse of ourselves in the mirror, in our space, we are focused on being present, here and now. It's like the book from the Eastern guru Ram Dass, *Be Here Now*. We should all learn that lesson. When we are home, we are often not really home.

Our minds are off at work, with other people, at other places. We are not centered in our space. We are not settled in our own home. Mirrors help open the space and show us in it. Everyone should have a lot of mirrors for this reason. They help you slow down and "stop to smell the roses" so to speak.

Some people go as far as charging all the items in their home—clocks, lamps, televisions, computers, house plants, cooking utensils, flatware, dishes, and glasses. They charge everything. It's not that hard to do, so I think it's a good idea to infuse it all with your majick. Every time you bring something new into the home, neutralize any harmful energies and then charge it with intention. You'll be amazed and how it changes the energy of your house and helps you live life as if you are your own queen or king in the castle.

With the intention set, it is as if the items are now living majickal constructs. I think that is how Walt Disney got the image of talking and moving chairs, brooms, and furniture for his movies. Imagine the chair walking or the teapot talking to you the next time you fix an intention into an item in your household.

MAJICK IN THE BATHROOM

While it might not be the most glamorous topic, the bathroom is just as majickal as any other room in the house, and a necessary part of life. The products you use in your bathroom, for cleaning the bathroom and entire house, as well as cleaning and enhancing yourself, can be majickal. Natural ingredients in products for the bath and shower, and in our health and beauty aids, can be catalyzed with our majick and be enhanced in purpose. Natural, herbal soaps, shampoos, creams, and body washes are cleared and blessed for health and beauty.

Water itself is the source of life. Water is vitally important in our understanding of spirit. It brings life force, blessing, and clears away unwanted thoughts, energies and forces stuck to us like dirt. Cleanliness occurs on many levels. Every time you are in the shower or bathtub, you can prepare yourself majickally. Look at the astrological aspects and see it as an opportunity to do a spell on yourself, to improve yourself. Water helps us change our energy. The vast majority of our bodies is water, so learning how to work with water, how to program it with intention inside and out, transforms us.

When taking a bath, you can add crystals to the water or light candles in the bathroom charged for your intention. Oils and herbs can also be added to the water, but be careful that you are not allergic. Some herbs like cinnamon and clove, particularly in essential oil form, are caustic, so use sparingly. Nothing is worse than a chemical burn from a majickal bath. I prefer the citrus scents for prosperity workings in the bath over the spices myself. While natural musk is no longer available to Witches due to cruelty issues involved in the manufacture of the oil, I prefer musk-like blends for peace and comfort. Anything flowery will give you either a romantic or a cleansing bath. A bag of herbs over the shower-head helps keep the plant material from clogging your drain.

Though it might sounds strange, I find the use of the daikon radish, found in Eastern cooking and popularized by the healing traditions of macrobiotics, very useful in the bath. It is a mystical curative in Japanese healing culture, and when some slices are added to the bath water, it creates a powerful and rejuvenating bath water.

Majickal Bath Spells for Happiness and Harmony

1 tablespoon of rose petals
1 tablespoon of lemon balm
1 tablespoon of sweet woodruff
1 tablespoon of catnip
3 tablespoons of sea salt
1 green tourmaline

1 pink or white candle

1 muslin bag

Mix the herbs, salt, and stones together, charged for happiness, health, and self-esteem. Place the mixture in the muslin bag and either tie it to the bath tub faucet spout or float it in the bathwater, as if it were a large tea bag. Let it infuse the water with its majick. Light your candle for happiness and well-being and then enter into the bath. Let the bath waters wash away all that you don't need and fill you with blessings and majick.

Cleansing Bath Salt

1 cup of sea salt

1 cup of epsom Salt

10 drops of lavender oil

10 drops of lemon oil

5 drops of orange oil

Mix the bath salt ingredients thoroughly and seal in a jar. Make sure you charge them all for clearing and healing. When you wish to take a bath, put a tablespoon of the mix into your warm bath water and let it dissolve. This is an excellent mixture for a pre-ritual bath before a sabbat or Moon circle.

Mirrors in the bathroom are important. Not only do they put you in the "now" like other mirrors, but they help you understand your own being. While most people do not want to see themselves in the bathroom mirror, it is really good time to look at your body, to get to know it. See it as sacred, as the vehicle and house for your spirit. We realize that cleanliness has been a vitally important part of majick because in the ancient world, baths and ritual washing were a part of visiting the temple. It was both for health and safety, and to attune to the majick of the gods.

DÉCOR

The home décor is just as important as the larger items within the home. Pictures and paintings should all have meaning. They have to reflect your style, personality and your intentions. Your surroundings should be comfortable to you. You can decorate with the whole world today. You can put pictures and art reflecting the beautiful places where we feel spiritually connected. Fill your home with beauty, and you will feel beautiful. Make everything reflect the thoughts and feelings you desire, and soon you will be having those thoughts and feelings.

Use color majick when painting your home or choosing wall paper. Old homes, estates, and decorated castles tended to use bright colors— red, blue and gold. All the rooms were different colors and embellished with beautiful moldings and decorative frames. Often such estates used the color, if not always the metal, gold. Gold bring the Sun's energy— health, well-being, prosperity. Today we often chose more bland colors, and therefore have more bland lives. Witches tend to live boldly, and we use color in that way. Choose your colors appropriately. White walls often send all energy away, as they are totally reflective. No vibration is enhanced. Clear and charge the paint before you use it.

If candles are a part of your overall design, chose candle color for specific reasons, and even if you're not doing a spell, charge the candles with intention so that when they are lit, they give off an energy that is beneficial, rather than detrimental or even simply neutral. Why waste the candlelight with no intention, when it can be working for you?

Your books and knick-knacks are a reflection of who you are, what energies you are interested in establishing in your home. Books hold information. Words do not always stay inside their covers. They float upon the air and into your breath. Notice how guests are attracted to a certain book, even if they can't see the title. Make sure your books are conducive to your majickal life and a life of goodness. The same can be said about all other forms of media and art. I personally don't have any horror books on my shelves for that reason. I don't keep anything harmful, though I do keep history books. I'm inquisitive about history all over the world, and history is not all roses, but you can neutralize any harm a history book can bring into your home and retain the helpful teaching aspects.

You can also decorate your home in the décor and style of past lives that bring your comfort and empowerment. I like to surround myself in things from the Victorian era, as I have a strong past life there that is comforting to me. Using the Victorian decorations stirs good memories. Also, if you've had a past life who was a figurehead of that time, you can put a picture or piece of art of that person in your home to invite those comfortable and good past life energies into your home. For instance, I've been known to keep a picture of Queen Victoria in my own home to encourage the energies of my past life during that time period.

CRYSTALS AND OTHER OBJECTS OF POWER

Crystals are excellent items for the home. My family and I particularly favor crystal balls and have five or six crystal balls in the home. They have become points of power for us. While most people think of them as scrying devices to see the future and the past, they don't have to be. They can be used for intentions and power. Different types of minerals bring us different types of spiritual power. Clear quartz crystal is the best for all types of power. You can program it as you desire. Many completely clear crystal balls are actually lead crystal, meaning they contain the metal lead. Lead is ruled by Saturn, and while it can be helpful for protection, it is detrimental to other kinds of majick. Saturn is the planet of trials and difficulties. You might want to neutralize the lead in such a ball, charging it instead for the energy of the rainbow it reflects.

In my home, I have a lapis lazuli, a blue crystal sphere for Jupiter and success. I also have a black obsidian sphere, ruled by Pluto and charged for organization and clarity. If you do not charge an item ruled by Pluto for that intention, it can do the opposite, bringing chaos and misinformation. Pluto is a tricky planetary energy to use successfully.

Any type of crystal shape can be used throughout the house – points, polished stones, geodes, and carvings. They can be placed in the bedroom, living room, kitchen, and even in the bathroom. Here are some ideas for crystals in the home:

★ Hang crystals in the doorway for protection.

★ Place healing crystals on the nightstand to heal you when you sleep. I use carnelian for overall health while I sleep.

★ Hang prisms to bring rainbow energy into the home, with all its forces and powers. Angle them so they will hit other power points, such as altars, in the home at certain times of day. My prisms cast a rainbow on my Cernunnos altar in my living room, and my Egyptian Isis and Bast altar in my bedroom.

★ Put a large quartz point in your kitchen to fill the kitchen with healing energy to empower all meals.

★ Place crystals in the refrigerator for charging food and keeping food fresher. Quartz points do well for empowering food.

★ Place crystals in the spice rack, to catalyze the properties of the herbs that are for the highest good of the family.

★ Put an energized crystal in your water pitcher or glass, large enough not to accidentally swallow.

★ Place crystals near your pets' food bowls to help heal them. Make sure the crystals are large enough that they won't try to swallow it.

★ If you're unsure of what crystals to use in your home, you can always consult with the Witches of your local majick shop to get ideas suited to your own unique home and needs.

Smudging Incense
Pine needles and pine twigs
3 drops of frankincense oil
3 drops of myrrh oil
3 drops of benzoin oil
1 cotton string

Bundle the pine needles and twigs together with a string, creating a pine smudge bundle. Start by putting all the needles and twigs going in the same direction. Lay the string parallel with the pile of twigs, with a sufficient length of string at the end. Wrap the string around the bundle, spiraling up around the bundle, pull it tight and tie the end of the spiraling string with the length that is now bound by the spiral parallel with the bundle. It should look similar to the popular sage bundles, but with pine instead of sage Add a few drops of the oils to the bundle of pine. Let it dry. When it's fully dry, light the tip on fire like a Native American sage bundle, with a fireproof bowl or shell beneath it to catch the ashes and embers. Then let the smoke waft through your home, making sure you have opened all doors, closets, and windows. If you are in your own home, then go outside and go around your home and property three times counterclockwise. This will remove all unwanted influences and energies from the house.

House Blessing Incense
1 tablespoon pink rose petals
1 tablespoon frankincense
1 tablespoon of myrrh
1 teaspoon sunflower petals

3 drops of money oil
3 drops of protection oil
3 drops of love oil
Pink majick bag

Mix the incense together and burn to bless your home. It is particularly effective to do so after you have smudged your home; you can go around the perimeter of your home and property three times clockwise. Take the remainder of the incense and put it into a pink majick bag and hang it someplace hidden in your home, such as behind a curtain or picture frame.

King Arthur Home Harmony Spell
1 black candle
1 white candle

Light the two candles, one to attract blessings (black) and one to send out your intentions (white). Starting in the north, walk around the home in clockwise circles, as you petition the blessing of King Arthur while reciting this spell. Say out loud:

When Arthur holds
the Goddess' Hands,
Peace and Harmony
surround the Land.
From my Castle
I should never roam.
There shall be Love
and Comfort in my home.

When done with sincerity, know that you have invited the blessing of Arthur and his court into your home for harmony and protection.

Finding a New Home Spell
1 white jar candle

1 clear quartz stone

1 lodestone

Enchant the two stones by holding them in your hands and projecting the image of a new home that is ideal to you. Place them upon the candle. Likewise, charge the candle for the intention of the new home. Light the candle and let it burn. Recite the spell below. Periodically snuff it out and relight. The stones will sink into the wax. By the time the candle burns out, you will be well on your way to a new home. You can gather the stones and carry them with you while house hunting.

As the Flames
surround the Stone,
I shall find
A new Home.
So mote it be!

Peace Potion
1 dram of sweet almond oil base

5 drops of sweet orange oil

3 drops of sweet pea oil

1 drop of lavender oil

Charged all ingredients as you mix them together, to help bring love and peace into your life. Perfect for calming after a hectic day or when things around you start to get a bit out of control. This is also a great addition to aid in spell work for love and peace by using it in your majick space.

HOME ALTARS

Of course a Witch will want an altar, if not several, in the home. Altars are an important part of our practice today. Everyone wants a majickal room, a space that is dedicated to majick every day. When I lived in an old house built in 1783, I had such a majickal room to suit the majickal space. It had wide wooden plank floors, and I painted a majick circle onto the floor of my living room, nine feet in diameter. I painted it right into the wood, and I'm told the woman who lives there now appreciated not only the history of the house, but the added history of the circle I put on the floor. We used the living room mostly for majick, though I understand that not everyone can dedicate one entire room in their home for just majick.

Working Altar (courtesy of Laurie Cabot)

You can place an altar anywhere in the house, and in fact you can have one in every room of the house. Usually a Witch has a main "working" altar that is the focus of her majick. I believe an altar is necessary for a majickal focus in this day and age; even if you don't have a dedicated majick room, you can choose where to put it. Such working altars can go in the bedroom or living room as needed, and be complemented by other altars for different intentions.

All you need is a small shelf, tabletop, or other flat surface you can easily access. Many use a knickknack shelf from any craft store. Some altars are disguised, and you can't really tell they are working altars. They simply look like an arrangement of beautiful objects. You could have some framed photographs, a votive candle, a wand, a crystal, or a dish of potpourri herbs.

Many people like to have four additional altars, for the four directions in the majickal room or home. One is placed in the north, south, east and west. They can have a colored candle for the element associated with the direction, and other objects linked to the elements. You could have a mirror on all four walls, to open up the space, particularly if your majick space is small. The majick mirrors can act like portals. Some see their past lives in such majick mirrors or use them to communicate with the elemental spirits and guardians.

Different home altars can be set for specific intentions. You can have one altar to increase your prosperity. You can have another to attract or maintain love. Build altars to establish relationships with various spiritual entities, ancestors and deities.

Build an altar to the faery races. Altars to the fey invite them into your home and make them feel comfortable. I use miniature furniture on my faery altars. It's not to say they literally use the furniture, for even though some faery folk are the Little People, many are also the Big People. Setting up a "home" for the Fey is an invitation, a signal to say they are welcome and can make themselves at home. While not all would agree with my stance, as they can often be mischievous and even dangerous, the Fey are welcome in my home. I have a complete miniature dollhouse in my bedroom dedicated to them. When you send out the invitation, they will come. Believe me, strange things have happened in that dollhouse. Often the incidents are quite funny, moving things around and such. The windows, which are quite hard to open or close by human hands, will open and close "on their own." It's too small for the cats to get into, so someone is obviously going in and out of the house. My daughter Penny and I notice it all the time.

Faery Fire Oil
1 garnet
1 dram of dragon's blood oil
1 dram of almond oil
1 pinch of coriander seeds

Use this potion to bring in the power of the faery realm to aide in your majick, spells, and daily life. Particularly useful when doing fire and faery majick at the sabbat of Imbolc.

Faery Flower Oil No. 1
1 dram of elder oil
1 dram of lavender oil
1 pinch of dried rose buds

Faery Flower Oil No. 2
1 dram of almond oil
1 dram of elder oil
1 dram of lily of the valley oil
1 pinch of dried rose petals

Use Faery Flower Oil to connect with the Faery races to help in your majick.

Faery Spell
Faery wand (wand of apple, willow or hawthorn)
2 quartz crystals

Faery Flower Oil
3 votive candles

Make three circles above your head with a faery wand. Anoint yourself with a faerie oil. Say:

O Great Goddess of the Sidhe, come and abide with me. I am your daughter and keeper of the faith. In the summertime, bring to me your flowering power. Help me to tend myself so to help heal the Earth and enjoy your great beauty.

Touch your wand to the two quartz crystals and say:

I am grateful for your love and power. I have pride in my faery race. I shall grow a garden as a tool of your powers.

Use the crystals for growing a garden by placing them into the ground as you plant. Make sure at night to light a votive candle in your garden. Anoint the candles with faery oil.

Altars for specific deities are also built. They invite that god or goddess into your home and life. Such altars help establish an acquaintance, though building an altar is not a guarantee that the deity will respond. Some gods take notice, and some do not. They help you build a potential relationship, but deities are not going to do everything you ask. They are alive in their own Otherworld, with their own work, goals, and desires. They are not always available, and what we ask for is not always in their sphere of influence, or in alignment with their own work. Altars create rituals of communication. We begin by honoring the gods. Honoring them can get their attention and establish the communication. The more of a connection you have to a deity, the more likely that they will be able to hear you and can respond to you, but sometimes the response is no. We have to be ready to hear that.

While we are reestablishing our traditions, it's good to look to other cultures for inspiration and knowledge. The Voodou and Santeria traditions have rich forms of art and culture around altars for the Lwa and Orisha spirits they call upon. They also teach us that one space should be established for each, unless there is a specific relationship between two spirits, as sometimes the African spirits can become jealous of each other. Putting two altars together, or even two close together, can create disharmony with your spirits. While I haven't had any conflict like that in my home, it's good to be aware of these teachings, and when you establish communication, to ask the gods directly what they desire for offerings and rituals of honor. More will be taught about deities in **Chapter Twelve**. Right now, it might be good to just think about where you might establish altars for the gods you want to invite into your life.

Altar Incense
1 tablespoon of frankincense
1 tablespoon of myrrh
1 teaspoon of dragon's blood
1 teaspoon of Solomon's seal
1 teaspoon of cinnamon

Use this incense to cense the altar space before you dedicate it to a majickal working. If you are dedicating the altar to a specific deity or type of majick, you can add something particular for the specific altar to the base of altar incense. For example, you might add some elderflower for an altar to the Fey, or a pinch of graveyard dirt to an ancestral altar.

High Altar Oil
1/8 ounce almond oil
5 drops of frankincense oil
5 drops of myrrh oil
3 drops of styrax oil (benzoin oil)

2 drops of storax oil

3 drops of amber oil

1 drop of cinnamon oil

Pinch of sea salt

Pinch of fur from your familiar animal

Used for casting spells, anointing majickal tools and cleansing oneself before rituals. Creates the energy and aura of extreme power.

Majickal Toys

While not all adults have children's toys, some of us do. Many of us Witches are children at heart, for children are the most majickal of people. We don't lose touch with our inner child, or if we do, part of our training is to reconnect to that child-like side of things. Such toys can be very good for us to maintain our child-like majick and optimism. They can be quite healing.

I collect dolls. Dolls are like little spirits. They can be very good for you and have a rich majickal tradition. Their use is not unlike statues. We believe that statues of various gods and goddesses have power. Putting a statue in your space, even if it's not on an altar, brings the energy of that god to you. It draws in their energy to the environment where it is place. Some deities have a long-standing power. Think of the famous winged statues of Isis. Her name has been spoken for a thousand years. The image connects to a long-standing current of power and majick, so it's important to understand who and what you are connecting to with a statue.

Dolls and other toys are similar, with perhaps a lot less history. You get the ability to shape and create the energy of a doll, but in essence, they work similarly to statues. It will have the persona and purpose of the name and image you give it. It can be an ally and friend in your life. Some use statues or dolls to talk to, to take away problems and worries. In

Guatemala, there is the tradition of carrying "worry dolls." They are tiny little people in a bag. You tell them your problems, and they take the problems away. Modern doll majick can be just like that. Other dolls are used more actively in majick.

I have three shelves of majick dolls in my bedroom; each is an altar. One doll has been with me as an ally for thirty years, based upon Alice in *Through the Looking Glass*. The stories of *Alice in Wonderland* are a guiding myth for me and play an important role in my art, life, and majick.

Ritual for Awakening the Doll

When you first obtain your doll, clear and neutralize it of any unwanted energies or forces. Then hold the doll and talk to the doll. Tell it you will be empowering it with your majick. Go into a meditative state, counting down to alpha. Visualize the doll in your mind's eye as a kind and beneficial being. Give the doll the characteristics of personality and power that you want it to have. Will this doll have a specialty? How will it help you? Envision and intend it. When you feel you are done, say these intentions are "fixed" so that they cannot be changed by others or changed into something else over time. It will always be helpful and good. Say, "It will be fixed. It is done. So mote it be. So shall it be."

HOME PROTECTION

While all protection spells from **Chapter Four** can apply to the home, many specifically put things by the door for protection. Bags of herbs and stones can be hung above the door for protection. A household tool that is used specifically for protection, among other majickal intentions, is the broom.

The Witch's Broom is placed, bristles up, behind the front and back door for protection. It is an old and powerful tradition and still works. I know many Witches who use it. It not only protects, but it keeps unwanted people away from your door. Its energy simply sweeps them away.

While you can use a regular household broom, it doesn't look as good as a traditional Witch's broom. Such brooms were made of specific woods. The most traditional is a broom made with an ash handle, birch twigs and bristles, and willow to bind the bristles to the handle. Such brooms are hard to find or make. Other Witch's brooms are made from Scotch broom twigs or woven straw. You can even take a commercial broom and decorate it with paint, jewels, charms and sigils. Be creative.

If there is no place to put it behind a door, it can be hung over a doorframe for protection.

FOOD MAJICK

Our food is one of the most important ways of working majick for ourselves and for others, and we often forget that fact. Our food comes from nature, and like all things, there are natural correspondences to each ingredient that goes into our food and drink. A wise Witch will know how to use those qualities to make every meal an act of majick. While we can call it Kitchen Witchcraft today, it's part of the overall craft of the Witch, as food is a major part of our lives and sustains our life force.

The foundation of food majick is build upon the application of elemental and astrological correspondences and the correct use of intention. When you are preparing food, ask yourself, what does this item represent to me? What powers and forces is it aligned to? What am I adding to it? You then start to get an idea of what kind of majick you can do with the food before you. Think about how you would charge the food, with what intentions, and how you would present it and consciously eat it.

Along with the food itself, think about your utensils and tools. All utensils should be neutralized and charged with intention for your majick, just like any other altar tool or ritual item. Your knives, spoons, pots, pans, and everything else should be infused with majick.

With your tools in hand, both kitchen tools and ritual tools, you should create sacred space around you when preparing a majickal meal. Cast a circle around the kitchen with light. While you can use your wand, you can also use a wooden kitchen spoon as your kitchen wand. It doesn't matter if your kitchen is oddly shaped in a way that does not easily accommodate the image of a circle. The bounds of the circle can go through walls. You can visualize a circle around you, even in a square kitchen. The important thing is being in a sacred space, being between the worlds, when preparing a spell through a meal. Just as your other spells are more effective in a majick circle, your food majick will be more effective.

While in your sacred space, with your prepared tools and ingredients to be used, charge each ingredient. Just like working with crystals, herbs, or even sending healing, get into an alpha state and unite your energy and aura with the energy of the ingredient you are using. Charge it with your intention. Do this before you do anything further to the food. Do it before you chop it, cook it, or add it to anything else. Fix the intention by simply stating the energy is fixed in the food item and will not dissipate. Each ingredient might have a different intention, and together, they can have an overall purpose, so focus on the individual ingredient intentions as you prepare each ingredient, and the larger overarching intention towards the end of the process once everything has been added.

If you are preparing something with a blade, a kitchen knife, you have charged the knife to act as a focus for you majick, just like a wand. It will catalyze your thoughts and intentions as you chop and cut, so keep focused on your intention for the spell and the work of that specific ingredient. Your energy and intent will flow from you through the blade and into the food. For this reason, many Witches have a special knife that no one else in the kitchen can use, because it's a powerful majickal tool.

As you add each ingredient, the stirring is an act of majick. When you add something with intention, stir it in three times, clockwise, to blend it together and amplify its power. Even your normal stirring for a dish can add power to it. Like the knife, the spoon acts as a conduit for your energy.

The power of fire, of heat, will help ignite the spell. Just as petitions are read in a circle and burned to release their majick, or the enchanting of a candle spell begun when the wick is lit, the cooking of the food ignites the spell and begins the process. Before you put anything into the oven, make sure you've majickally prepared the food and fixed the energy. The cooking or baking will activate it, and all who ingest the food will get the benefits of the majick.

The two most popular intentions for food majick are love and healing. Love meals are a great way to share your majick and rituals with your partner, even if they are not actively involved in majick. Some consider it manipulative, but we do so much to set the stage for love in other areas—how we dress, the perfume we wear—that food majick is simply enhancing a wonderful date. When having a lover or potential love over for a meal, charge the entire atmosphere with your intention. Start with a red tablecloth, red candles, and romantic flowers, all charged. Enchant all the food for love, using herbs and spices associated with Venus and Mars. Have a little incense in the background and play appropriate music to set the mood.

Healing meals are using the majick of the food, as well as its nutritional properties, to increase healing. Much of our traditional healing majick was a basic understanding of herbalism with intention. Knowing which herbs settled the stomach, such as fennel seeds, and which ones burned out an infection, like garlic, can seem like a greater form of majick to those without the same knowledge, but the use of intention and sacred space combined with this knowledge really empowers a spell. Traditionally ingredients ruled by the Sun, for overall health, and Mercury, for improving the communication and flow in the body systems, are used in healing food majick.

A Witch friend who was having a big family dinner decided to do a little majick through her food. She had some questions about the family history, and generally folks were pretty tight lipped around her. So she did a truth spell in the entire meal. Everything she cooked was chosen to release truthful information. While you might have a vision of something strange or hilarious happening, as if it were a movie or television sitcom, it wasn't quite like that. They were simply a family sharing stories and history of what happened to them and their loved ones, but everything was truthful. By the end of the meal, they were all hysterically laughing at the tales that were revealed around that table. She got a better understanding of her family, and they all enjoyed doing it.

For more traditionalists, resources such as the classic *Culpeper's Herbal* by Nicholas Culpeper list a wide variety of foods, as well as herbs, with their astrological, if not purely majickal, virtues. The work of Scott Cunningham, including his *Magic of Food* and *Encyclopedia of Magical Herbs*, is also quite helpful in picking the appropriate associations with foods and seasoning.

Apple – Apple is a fruit tree associated with Venus, bringing love and harmony, as well as an herb of the faery realm, and the majick of Avalon. The seeds form a pentacle, making the apple a sacred symbol of the Witch. Drinking apple juice can be a form of a love potion, for self-love as well as to attract a lover that is right for you.

Carrots – Carrots are a plant of mercury, used for healing of all kinds. Carrots are rich in minerals, and like the old folk tradition, are excellent for the eyes.

Cinnamon – Use in pies, cookies, and other pastries for a great money spell. Cinnamon can be added to your coffee or tea to create a money potion to ingest. Ruled by Jupiter, it increases your status and wealth.

Clove – Cloves are another great Jupiterian herb, to bring good luck and good fortune. They are also in the traditional Yuletide pagan drink, wassail.

Juice – Fruit and vegetable juices are a way to subtly add majick of various ingredients to other dishes. Juices can be used as a base to flavor various foods naturally, and add some power to the meal. They can be used as a part of dressings for salad.

Leafy Greens – Most leafy greens, and in fact, all green plants, have associations with the planets Venus and the Earth, for love, sensuality, and grounding. Many dark greens have a high iron content, and since iron is the metal of Mars, they will carry those associations as well.

Lemon – Ruled by the Sun and Moon, lemons are a great cleanser of the body and energy and are also rich with antioxidants. They are also for success, having that lemon yellow color connected with the gold of the Sun. I use a lot of lemons in my food majick. Lemon can tenderize all meats when freshly squeezed.

Millet – Millet is ruled by the Sun and, as a grain, by the Earth. Used for overall health and well-being.

Mustard – Ruled by the Sun and Mars, mustard is used for success and well being.

Orange – Oranges are ruled by both the Sun and Mercury, making them a food of healing and success. They are very empowering.

Parsley – Parsley is ruled by Mars and is an excellent cleansing herb for the kidneys. It bring the beneficial aspects of the planet Mars.

Red Peppers – Red peppers of all kinds are used for majick involving a little spice, passion, love, and creativity.

Root Vegetables – All root vegetables help ground, center and balance. They help you be present in your body, and they ground excess and unhealthy energies. They are a great food for those who are flighty and never fully present in day-to-day life.

Strawberries – Ruled by Venus and Mars, strawberries bring love and passion, along with a sweetness that makes them particularly good for romantic majick.

Meat is a tricky subject for many Witches, due to concerns about the environment and inhumane farming practices. Some Witches are carnivores, and some are not. Some feel they must eat meat for issues of health, while others strongly believe that for health and moral reasons, it is imperative to not eat any meat. While I still choose to eat meat, my own daughter, Penny, does not.

In an interview for *The Astrarium*, an online spirituality site, Penny said:

"I feel that our plants have a higher understanding of the community, and I feel like the plant world also understands the breakdown of matter to make a larger connection to universal mind. So as much as I feel like plants feel and have souls, I also feel like their purpose is of a much wider spectrum of universal unity. I personally would be happier if nothing had to die in order for us to live, but when you look at the true order of nature, you begin to understand its components, and how water and plant life feed the universal energies through natural life cycles, like a heartbeat. They put out impulses of light waves and knowledge like a migration, and feeding the human bodies is part of that migration.

"I feel like thanking the animal and honoring them should always be done, being grateful from your heart for what you have received, and if you must eat animals, I would hope that you would grieve just the same for the loss of that live. I don't expect everyone to just stop killing animals, although it would be nice to see in my lifetime. I personally don't think there is a good enough reason to kill our animals for food at all. In my view, vegetarianism does not deny the cycle of life; in fact, I think by eating green living food, you are embracing it even closer. When you drink a glass of water, no organism died to feed you, so there can be no denial of the cycle of life."

Animals can have a very different evolutionary consciousness, and Witches need to be aware of that. Honoring the animals is one reason why many Witches will use bones and skulls in their majick, honoring the fallen spirit, though we usually find such items while wildcrafting in the woods and never harvest them. The animal fur used in our rituals is from live and shedding animals. While we would not use them today, our ancestors used human skulls for the same reason, to honor and commune with those who had fallen. Today we use skull depictions through art, statuary, and carvings, for it's is not socially acceptable to connect with our ancestors in that way.

Food can be neutralized and charged as soon as you get it home from the supermarket. Today our food comes from a thousand different places, and it travels quite far to get us. Who knows that kind of energies and intentions it has been exposed to on its travels? It's not that any of these locations are inherently bad, but we simply don't know the journey. It is far better to be safe that sorry by using our majick to clear it. In particular I always clear and charge poultry, meat, and fish. While it is wonderful to eat a fully organic diet, with any meats coming from free-range sources, it's not always possible for many of us. We live on fixed incomes and have to support our families on wages that do not always allow for it.

Make a ritual out of putting away the groceries by blessing all the food. Blessing our food has been a ritual passed on for centuries, and we've tended to forget it, or purposely not use it, thinking of "saying grace" as a Christian tradition. But Pagan cultures across the world for centuries have been giving thanks for the exchange of life for life. They give thanks to the animals, plants, and all the people who got it to the table. In today's age of fast food, no one gives thanks to the cow when going through the drive through. They try to not even think about the cow. We need to give thanks and go even further, particularly in our home. It doesn't take a lot of time or energy, and the patterns we establish today will continue in our lifetime if we set the intention of blessing and thanks.

MEDICINE AND MAJICK

Just like food, our medicines, supplements and herbs can be enchanted with energy and intention, enhancing their effect. Make a ritual not only out of your meals, but also out of your supplements and prescriptions. Whenever you get something you'll be ingesting, cleanse it of any incorrect energies as you would with any other item. Then add your intention and energy, visualizing healing light, to the item. Whatever a medicine is supposed to cure, charge it for that specific intention. Charge it to bring out all the known and unknown healing properties it has. Neutralize any unwanted side effect of the medication. Performing this ritual expands the use of all medicines. Charge all prescriptions, vitamins, minerals, and herbs.

PET MAJICK

All of our pets are majickal creatures. They are beloved members of our family and have much to teach us. I often say that I live with my cats, not the other way around. They rule the roost, keep the schedule, and generally tell us what to do and how things should be. I can't imagine my life without them.

Just as we enchant our own home, we must extend that majick to our furry and feathered family members. Do the same for your pets as you would do for yourself. Charge everything for the pet—food, food dish, water dish, litter box, color, leash, toys—with intention. Bring them healing, protection, comfort, joy, and a deeper spiritual connection with you and other members of the family.

A majickal connection to a particular pet, usually one you are more connected to spiritually than others, can be considered a familiar. A familiar is a spiritual comrade from the animal world, a partner in majick. Such animals will take an active interest in your meditation and majick practice, joining you when you go into alpha to do meditative work, or attending your majick circle rituals. They can help you do your bidding, but they often can do majick on their own. Familiars are very special creatures who often have their own agendas. Their energy is just as powerful as your own, sometimes more so, and it is quite often more pure than our human energy. You can ask them to add their majick to your spells, and often, but not always, they will help.

Cats and dogs spend a lot of time in alpha state. They are naturally majickal. That is why cats and dogs know when you are coming home. They are more receptive to psychic information, particularly to the people they are attuned with. My father had odd jobs at all hours, but our dog Domino would wait in the driveway for him, always at the appropriate time. How did he know? We knew when he went out there that Dad was on his way. Every move he made, the dog knew.

Many of us heard stories of cats who were abandoned, lost, or left behind finding their way to their owners, over terrain they have never seen. They tuned into the family. I read about one cat traveling from San Diego, in southern California to San Francisco in the northern bay area. It's about an eight-hour drive by highway. How did the cat know to do that? They must have access to non-linear information. In short, they are majick!

Animal Communication Meditation

To deepen your connection to a familiar, take the time to look into their eyes. Eye contact is unusual for an animal, but it is one of the signs that such a pet is your familiar if they will establish such eye contact with you. My beloved cat Merlin was comfortable looking you in the eye. Take time to get comfortable together, pet the animal, and then establish eye contact. Talk to them with your mind only. Make a direct mental link with your familiar.

One of the exercises you can practice to verify the connection is to wait until the animal is asleep in another room. Go into alpha level and visualize the animal. Whisper in its ear while in vision, asking it to "come here. Come here. I want to tell you something." If you are successful, the animal will awaken and come to you, often with the look of "Now what do you want?" It is a good way to effectively demonstrate your psychic connection. Just don't do it too often, or the animal will get annoyed as you are disturbing its sleep for what it sees as no good reason. The familiar doesn't need the truth verified. But it is helpful for us humans.

Just as we empower ourselves (**Chapter Eleven**), we can do the same for our pets. Whenever we groom or decorate our pets, we can add majick to the process. Bathing and nail trimming can all be enhanced by our majick, as well as the pet's collars and, with smaller animals, its little sweaters and shirts. Collars can be made into spells using the attributes of specific colors. Some people like to tie majickal items to the collar, but one should always be careful, as they can easily fall off and an animal will think it is a toy. Herbs can poison, and charm bags and stones can choke.

Don't ever disempower your pet. We might trim nails, but we never remove their claws. My furniture is scratched up, but I've chosen to have cats, and that is a possible consequence of my choice. Witches enter into relationships fully, realizing the consequences of their actions and accepting responsibility for them. I've chosen to have cats, and this is part of the reality. You can get them scratching posts. I have five, but they still sometimes use the furniture. It's not a big deal to me in the greater scheme of things. The blessings far outweigh the damage to furniture. I take care of them, and they take care of me. If you want a room with pristine furniture, lock the doors to that room.

My Familiar Oil
1/8 ounce sweet almond oil
3 drops of bergamot oil
1 drop of mugwort oil
1 pinch of lotus seeds
1 pinch of dried comfrey root
1 pinch of your familiar's fur or hair

Use this oil to both open your psychic abilities and attune to the consciousness of your familiar. You'll need to add a bit of fur or hair from the familiar you want to attune to. I know if my cats shed a whisker or lose a claw, I might add that to the oil as well. Use this to attract an animal to you to aide in your majickal workings and daily life.

Chapter Nine: Travel Spells

While Witches often prefer to be rooted at home, travel is a big part of the modern world, and it was a big part of the ancient world for us too. The Druids of Celtic society traveled between the various Celtic tribes to make pronouncements and conduct rituals. In Medieval Witchcraft, a Man in Black was a Witch who would connect various covens, traveling the land as needed, much like Merlin or Gandalf. Today our travel might not be so majickally oriented. We travel for work. We travel for vacation. We travel to visit family and friends. But if we look at travel with majickal eyes, every trip is an opportunity for enchantment and growth. You'll never see a unicorn, or your own version of the extraordinary, if you don't look for it. Most people are so unobservant. They don't look up. They don't look around. Observance is very important for a majickal person. When I would take the train from Boston to New York City, I would watch all the new scenes as we traveled through Connecticut. We would pass by the ocean, and I could count swans and cranes in the water. We'd pass through fields and forest edges, and I would look for the birds and other animals. I would try to see them all. It helps me be in the moment when I travel. It can also help to have a pen and notebook, to write down inspiration that comes as you observe. You can also spend some of your travel time in meditation, or use music and story to get you into the mood for travel.

Traveling should be a joy. The journey is part of the vacation, and it should be fun. If you look at the time as a joy, and not a chore, you can lessen any anxiety you have around travel. When you go, make sure you have the small creature comforts with you, to make the trip more pleasant.

I like to travel with a small, portable altar and ritual tools. I take with me:

Small power crystals
Miniature wand
Small pentacle peyton
Majickal jewelry and charms
Small vials of my favorite potions
Small packets of incense powders
Small candles
Matches

It can be particularly important to take the small amounts of potions, powders and stones. You might need them to do some majickal work, and even better, you can give them away to people who might need them more than you, to help empower others as you journey.

I don't believe you go on trips to spend the entire time on a guided tour. Don't do all the touristy things. Go to the local areas where people of the place and culture live day-to-day. Go to the simple places to see people and experience the energy. Go to a butcher shop. Go to a drug store. Take some time away from the tourist sites, even if it's only for one afternoon. You are not going to get a good sense of the culture and people if you don't see them where they are. You won't learn the majick of a place being stuck where everyone goes. Even when you do visit the more famous sites, explore them on your own. Tours can tire you out, and you don't need a tour to walk through the Colosseum. You can go there and experience it for yourself. And don't spend all your time just at the historic sites. Connect to the people. Connect to the food, the living music, and art.

Touch something living from nature to get a connection to the place —a tree, leaf, bark, seed, or stone. Hold it in your hands, get into an alpha state, and commune with it. Connect to the energy of the entire land through that living thing in nature. If you take such items with you, it will be a future touchstone, allowing you to easily travel the distance or even come back in time to this point. Objects you collect will take you back to the foreign lands, and you can then immerse yourself energetically into the history. Sometimes they will even connect you to your past lives.

Travel Protection

While all protection spells work whenever and wherever you go, we can take special precautions for protection when traveling. An important part of protection, and of any majick, is to focus on the ultimate end of the intention. You wish to arrive safely to your destination. So envision yourself at the place where you are going. Once you start your journey, keep your mind on the destination and arriving there safely, rather than simply getting there. You can do protection spells on your vehicle, luggage, or anything else involving travel, just like you'd do on other objects.

White Light Pentacles Around the Vehicle

Whenever I get into a new vehicle—be it someone else's car, cab, bus, boat, or plane—I hold my alpha trigger and get into a light meditative state. Then I draw white light pentacles in my mind's eye, all around in the four directions. I ask the Universe, Goddess and God, to please protect the vehicle and all upon it, and make safe travel.

Luggage Spell

If you are afraid you'll lose your luggage on a trip, place comfrey root, perhaps with hematite or a lodestone, in a white bag, and put it in your suitcase. To be doubly sure, measure out enough comfrey root for two bags. Make one with the stone and put it in the suitcase; carry the other with you as you travel. This will ensure that the two measures of root will be brought back together again. A simple spell for luggage is to charge a small quartz point for protecting and retaining your connection to the luggage, with no mishaps, and after doing so, place it in the suitcase.

Along with arriving safely, we should use our majick to project that our destination will be safe once we get there. The last time I went to Stonehenge for ceremony, we went to London for a week. We went to Islington and the open market, and while there, I got this strong psychic feeling there would be some sort of bomb scare. We left the antique market right away, and went across the street to an old tea house and sat down for a cup of tea. No sooner did we sit down, we heard the sirens and heard there was a bomb warning. Thankfully there was no bomb, and no one was hurt.

London was tumultuous at that point in history. A week before we arrived, a bomb had exploded in Nottingham. We had another adventure while taking a cab on Queen's Road; there was another bomb scare while we were going through the park. The authorities shut down the park, as they were chasing a specific car. We were stuck in the cab in the park for an hour before the police let us go. While the warnings affected us, we never saw any violence, and the actual threats were never around us, so our projection for a safe trip was good. So just because you arrive safely doesn't mean you are safe. Danger can happen while you are there, not just in the travel to and from a place. So make sure you use your majick to ensure the entire trip is safe.

Majick works best when coupled with real world action. Use some pragmatic thinking. While you are being observant on your travels, on the lookout for fun, also be vigilant and use common sense. Don't go somewhere with an unsecured pocketbook or wallet exposed. Be aware and on your guard, particularly in strange locations. Most of us walk around thinking there is no chance someone will pick our pockets or snatch our purses, but people do. Criminals target tourists in particular. There are pickpockets everywhere, particularly in large cities like London and New York. Beware people bumping you in a crowd. Always check afterwards to make sure you have everything. While we live our majick and want everyone to know majickal protection is available, it's not the "be all and end all" to life's problems, especially when you don't have common sense. Use a basic understanding of the world in conjunction with your majick. In the end, Witches laugh, bleed, and cry like everyone else, but we probably bleed and cry less than most people.

Homecoming and Places of Power

Sometimes our travel leads us home. Home isn't where we were necessarily born, or where we live now. Home is connected to our soul, to our past lives, and our current purpose in the world. I felt such a homecoming the first time I went to England. It was both a spiritual home, as my teacher Felicity was from England and taught me the majick from the Witches of Kent, and a personal home, as it was the land of my ancestors. England spoke deeply to my soul and changed me forever. Think of the places you have traveled. Have any felt like home? Did any make a connection to your soul? If not, perhaps your travels will take you there still.

For me, one of my most majickal life experiences occurred that first time I went to England. It wasn't a formal ritual or spell, but a spontaneous reconnection to my homeland. Just being on the land triggered the majick. The place where I stepped, unremarkable to look at, was more profound than any ancient site I have ever visited.

My plane arrived at Heathrow airport, and I was tired and jet lagged from the trip. Someone came to pick me up. When we arrived at the manor house in Preston-on-Stour, not far from the more famous Stratford-upon-Avon, and I stepped out of the limo, it happened. I put my foot on the ground, and all of a sudden, it felt like my feet had enormous roots and my energy was going deep into the ground beneath me. I didn't know what to make of it. I was being greeted by my host and simultaneously having this overwhelming sensation I never expected. It surpassed my later feelings in Stonehenge and Glastonbury. The most unusual thing was how unexpected it was. I didn't seek it out. I got out into the countryside, and I was struck by it. The event literally bonded my whole physical being and my entire light body, everything about me, to the land of the British Isles. Who knew that Preston-on-Stour would be the place of such a blessing?

While I was in England, I explored my majickal connection there. My majick seemed stronger, as the land simply responded to my thoughts and feelings. Anything seemed possible. I constantly tested the connection. While out on the land alone, I tried a spell known as Calling the Dragon's Breath. Within seconds, there was a cloud on the horizon that turned into the image of a huge dragon. I felt the presence of the dragon spirit, and as the Sun set, the dragon looked like it was made from fire. It was as if someone painted a dragon in the sky. Such images not present in that configuration of clouds before I started the spell.

My experiments continued with a psychic call. I had a friend who lived in the village just next to Preston. I cast the circle with the sword while walking upon the land, and then called to this friend to come immediately because I wanted to see him. I released the circle and walked back to the manor house where I was staying. No more than two seconds after I returned, he drove up.

Everything I intended in England manifested. The land was just full of life force that I could sense. Any thought I had would happen instantly. It didn't take time to manifest. I had to be very careful. I met a young man while there, named Clive, who was suffering from brain cancer. He had heard I was a Witch, and asked for my help. I agreed as long as he remained under a doctor's care as well. Healing majick is not always guaranteed. It depends on both parties, the one casting the spell and the one receiving the healing. In the end, I am not a healer. I just help facilitate the healing. I told Clive I would try, but I never had worked with someone with this type of illness. I put my hands upon his head. I cleared his energy and infused his body with healing light. A week later, he went to the doctor to check in, and they ran more tests. He soon found out that his cancer was completely gone. He returned ecstatic to tell me the healing worked.

In hindsight, seeing how well my majick worked on that trip to England, I should have taken more advantage of it to help out myself and my own life. But I didn't. I was really dumbfounded by it all. I was almost afraid of my thoughts and feelings, as they seemed so powerful there. Once I realized what was going on, I was very careful and did a lot less. Hindsight being twenty-twenty, I could have done so many things, healings and personal spells for myself and my daughters, but not doing too much was the right thing. I did what was needed. I've been back since, on a United Kingdom book tour, and it's always a majickal experience, but the amount of work I am doing on tour prevents me from having too much time for leisure and experimentation.

On my various trips I did get to visit Stonehenge and Glastonbury. I've noticed people must be careful when they visit any sacred site. Much like my whole experience on my first trip to England, people's thoughts and emotions manifest when standing upon sacred lands from the ancients. Our own personal power mixes with the inherent power of the land. Many of these places stand "between" and it's like being in a powerful majick circle, to just walk through them. I swear walking the grounds of the Glastonbury Abbey expanded my own aura to planetary proportions. No ritual was needed. I was just walking upon the grass through the ethereal landscape of the tiny village.

Sometimes we fear that such exotic locations are beyond our reach. Often they can be more affordable than you think, and with the power of majick, anything is possible. Here is a spell to help you reach any destination you desire.

Drawing Yourself to Sacred Lands

If you want to visit a sacred land, or really any place, and want to form a majickal connection to that place, you can perform a spell to link you, making your potential visit much more likely. Take off your shoes, stand upon unlined clean paper and trace both of your feet. Use majickal paper or colored paper that is not recycled with previous intentions from past writing. Orange is the color of Mercury and travel, so an orange paper would work well. Write your name in the middle of both footprints. Fold it and say and/or write the following spell:

I plant my feet in this majickal place. I connect my energy there, so that I am in two places at once. I am in my sacred place, my place of goodness, and simultaneously I am in my home as well. So mote it be.

Put it in an envelope with a feather, or package a special stone with it. Mail it to the post office of the nearest town to your sacred site with no return address. You are now connected to that town, city, or majickal place. Use that connection to open possibilities of appropriate and affordable trips to your desired place.

Sacred Soil, Stones & Dirt

Witches are well known for using the dirt and soil from a sacred or special place in majickal spells. We collect samples of the lands—dirt, soil, stones, bits of wood—to reconnect to that space in the future, or brings its majick to a talisman or potion. When holding it, or putting it upon a piece of paper and standing up on it, you can more easily connect to the place via mind travel.

Different locations have different energy. Each can be helpful in doing majick. It all depends on your relationship to the place. What do you feel from that place's energy? Is it protective? Powerful? Healing? Did you have good fortune there? Then those are the types of spells it will work best.

I have soil from the following places:

Stonehenge
Glastonbury
Cliffs of Dover, England
Findhorn, Scotland
Great Pyramid of Egypt
Egyptian Desert
Sahara Desert
Machu Pichu, Peru
Tulum, Mexico
Australia
Iceland
California
Sedona, AZ
Waikiki, HI
Philadelphia, PA
Miami, FL
Kodiak, Alaska

Helping Others Find their Happy Place

Dirt from particular places can also help others connect to these places. If you have someone in your life who is miserable living where they live, you could sprinkle some of the dirt or sand upon the doorstep of the person. It can catalyze a journey to move them someplace happy. Make sure you use dirt from someplace you associate with happiness—comfortable, safe, prosperous. You can list all the qualities you want the new place to have while holding the dirt, before you sprinkle it on their doorstep or near their feet. This spell can't force anyone to move, but encourages them to move towards happiness, wherever that might be for them. Sometimes no move occurs at all, but it simply invites the happy energy of that place into their current home. If you are dealing with a harmful neighbor, it will help change their harmful energy towards you and others into greater harmony, regardless of whether they stay or leave.

Sometimes Witches will gather other natural items from places they travel, and it can be difficult to get them back home. I had a plastic bag full of acorns for my friend Ian when traveling overseas. Acorns naturally can make one invisible, in the sense that people do not notice or recognize you. I used the acorns' majick to move them through customs without a question or concern. I put my bag with the acorns right upon the counter, and the customs agent didn't even look in my bag. Invisibility, particularly if you are well known, can be an excellent skill to have when you are traveling and want to be left alone.

Under the Tuscan Sun Spell
To Move to a Happy Place of Beauty

1 sunflower or several sunflower petals
2 sunflower seeds
1 yellow or gold candle
Parchment paper
Black ink and pen
1 citrine stone

Send a letter or email to the area or town in which you wish to move and ask the Chamber of Commerce of City hall to send you information about their town. Tell them you wish to move there.

On a piece of paper, trace your footprints. Place them in an envelope with one sunflower petal and send it to the post office of the town where you wish to move. When you mail your footprint, do not put a return address on the envelope.

Place your candle in a holder and sit in a place to do your spell. Sprinkle sunflower petals and the three seeds at the base of the candle. On parchment paper, write this spell:

Sunlight bright and brings cool
Starlight nights and peaceful moons
This is where I belong
A happy life without strife
A place of beauty!

Spell To Move Your Home

When you have decided what country, city, state, or village you wish to live in, then you can project for that move to happen with this spell. You will need:

1 brown candle

1 yellow candle

1 royal blue candle

New Home Incense

Incense burner

Charcoal

Parchment

Black pen

Envelope

Stamps

Map of where you want to live

Post Office address of the place where you want to live

First obtain a map of the area, and if possible, a picture of the general area. On a Thursday after the New Moon, place your candles on a table. Place your incense burner in front of the candles. Light the candle and the charcoal. Sprinkle incense on the burning charcoal and let the majick smoke rise.

Place the map in front of you. Visualize a beautiful home and your opening the door with a key and walking into your new home. Place your left hand on the map while you visualize.

Write on a piece of parchment paper with a black pen the following:

This is my home, the home of beauty and love. I shall be safe, happy, and spiritually complete in this beautiful place. So Shall It Be.

Put the spell within the envelope and put the address on the envelope. Do not put a return address. Put the stamp on it while the incense is smoking, then pass the letter through the majick smoke.

Put all three candles on the map. Let the candles burn for one hour, then snuff them out. Snuff out the incense charcoal if still smoldering and then bring your letter to the post office and mail it. If you have access to some of the soil from where you wish to move, sprinkle it over the doorstep where you live now so you step on the land where you wish to live.

When it arrives in the place you have chosen, the majick begins. Your letter has placed your energy in your new hometown. Of course you need to look in real estate properties in that location to truly find a place. But the spell has prepared the way. Pack your belongings because you are moving soon!

Sell Your Home Incense

1 tablespoon of patchouli

1 tablespoon of spearmint

1 tablespoon of sunflower petals

8 drops of apple oil

Gold or copper glitter

Burning this incense, particularly burning the incense outside of the front of your home, will lift your intention upon the winds, and the air will bring in the right buyer to find your home and make an offer.

MAJICKAL WATERS

Like gathering soil from sacred sites, Witches will gather water from majickal sites and from other less well-known sites that still contain power. Water is the lifeblood of the Earth. Water imprints the vibration of place. Using such water in majick is a way to direct energy to that place, and since essentially all water is connected, sharing water in majick connects many different places together.

Wells, springs, and rivers are considered to have their own spirits. Sometimes water spirits were known as nymphs in the Greek traditions. Such places were sites of healing and inspiration. The sacred wells of Glastonbury are very important sites in the Cabot Tradition, as well as most majickal traditions with a connection to Arthurian lore. The Red Well of the Chalice Gardens is infused with iron, and is considered a very feminine power of healing and love. The White Well, across the street, is saturated with calcium deposits, and regarded as a more masculine power, though both have properties of healing. In Ireland, the sacred well associated with Bridget, known as Brid in ancient times, is also a source of healing and inspiration.

Waters can be gathered from streams, rivers, lakes, and the seas, and can be used in majick much like soil from sacred sites can be used. Seawater in particular is used to anoint the edges of an altar to sanctify it with the powers of life, as all life is drawn first from the sea. Waters can be mixed and diluted with local spring water, with salt added to create waters to asperge sacred space before rituals. Then your space will have connections across the world, and your healing work and majick will reverberate out into the entire world.

Water Blessing Spell
Water from five special places in separate bottles
1 clear quartz crystal
1 large glass container

Before you begin, decide on what kind of blessing you want to infuse upon these waters. The blessing can relate to any intention or wish that you have.

Three days before the Full Moon, starting during the day while the Sun is out, mix the waters together in the glass container. Charge the clear quartz with your blessing and drop it into the water, to infuse the water with your intention. Speak your blessing upon the water, whispering it above the water nine times. Leave the water out in the moonlight, and then in the sunlight. On the second night, repeat your blessing again nine times. Again, leave it out all night and all day. On the third night, the night of the Full Moon, whisper your blessing nine more times and leave it out all night. Retrieve the bottle before the sun rises; it is now infused with three days of sunlight and three days of moonlight. Pour this water out whenever you want to bless something with your intention. You can add it to bath water for yourself, sprinkle it around you, or pour it out where you wish the blessing to manifest.

Chapter Ten: Psychic Power

All people are psychic, no matter what they might believe. To be psychic is to listen to your psyche, which according the Greeks is really a part of your soul. Everybody has the potential to be psychic, to use their intuitive gifts. Many people, however, close themselves off to that possibility.

Everyone processes energy and can interpret that information. Many people simply do so unconsciously, but people can train themselves to consciously read the energy of a situation or person and interpret it. Everybody's energy body, or aura, carries information about the past, present and future. To be psychic simply means you can drop into an alpha brain wave state intentionally and allow that information to come through your awareness and be used.

Being psychic is a natural thing. Anyone can do it. Some are born doing it. They don't understand the mechanism, but cannot imagine being any other way. They simply do it. Most consider it a gift. While some Witches are naturally psychic, many are not. They enhance their potential, whether they have a natural gift or not, by learning the mechanism, and with practice, gaining control. Unless there is serious physical brain impairment to cognitive function, one can learn the basic mechanisms to use psychic abilities.

One of my students had a powerful experiencing proving not that she was psychic, specifically, but that everyone has the potential, even those who seem to be disconnected from everything else. This student was taking Witchcraft One in the Adult Education Center and got there each night by bus. It was late afternoon in the winter, and she was having some doubts whether she should be taking the class and studying Witchcraft. She found herself gazing at her own reflection in the bus window, and thought of herself as a little girl, when she carried her teddy bear with her wherever she went. It was that little girl who first thought of herself as a Witch, but now as an adult, she was doubting it, and wondering if a class in Witchcraft was really a good idea.

On the bus was a very drunk man acting somewhat belligerently with people on the bus. He staggered over to her, looked right at her and said, "Don't you know that all little girls who hold their teddy bear in front of the mirror are Witches?" And then he staggered off the bus. She was shocked, but it made the possibility of majick and psychic powers as an adult suddenly real for her. Here was this man essentially reading her mind, her energy, with such a specific image. Perhaps due to the drinking, he was in a state of mind that could pick up on the energy, and she was probably the most focused and powerful mind concentrating on that bus, so he was drawn to her.

Many people who are naturally psychic often self-medicate with alcohol and drugs, hoping to shut down the thoughts, feelings, and visions associated with psychic abilities, though many times, it has the opposite effect. It can open you up to more information, but you cannot control the filters to discern what is real, what is symbol to be interpreted, and what is nonsense.

Majickal training, and specifically Witchcraft, helps us learn what our psychic abilities are and how best to control them through the use of disciplined meditation and the science of alpha. Controlling your ability to enter and leave an alpha state, or a brainwave range of seven to fourteen cycles per second, is the key. Those who understand how to do this have the key to the secret doorway of majick and mystery that in ages past, only sorcerers, shamans and Witches could access. Today, we know through the science of Witchcraft that this is possible for anyone who desires it. There is a little bit of Witch, a little bit of a psychic, in us all, even if we don't think so ourselves.

PSYCHIC SENSES

Psychic abilities come in many different shapes and levels. They are often described by their parallel physical senses—sight, hearing, touch, taste, and smell all have their psychic equivalents. Psychic sight is often known as clairvoyance, meaning clear vision. Psychic hearing is clairaudience, or clear hearing. Clairsentience is possibly the most powerful of all, though least understood. The term means clear knowing, and it's for those who receive information by simply knowing about it, without having to put it into pictures or words. Those who have the gift of clairsentience as their psychic channel often say things like, "I don't know why. I just know it." For some it starts purely as the classic "gut" feeling, but can expand in a detailed, non-linear knowledge about people, places and events.

Psychometry is a form of psychic touch. By touching objects, your energy mingles with it. Similar to healing or charging an object, your aura co-mingles with another aura, usually that of an object, but rather than placing an intention into it, you are allowing information to come to you and interpreting that information. While the mechanism for it is touch, the information can come through the usual channels of clairvoyance, clairaudience, or clairsentience. Touching the object is just the trigger for the process, and it forms the link to the specific target you want to read.

Psychometry works best on objects that have a history. You can pick up psychically on the information of the object's history itself or the energy of the owner and past owners. While it can sometimes be difficult to sort though the different layers of energetic history, matching particular impressions to particular owners and times, it can also be an extremely accurate method of connecting. In one psychic reading session,

I was asked by a woman to do psychometry on a watch. I immediately saw her boyfriend, who was married, and I saw that she was married too, and that they were having an affair. I told her what I saw, and she took the watch out of my hand, said that it was enough, and promptly left the reading.

Less well-known psychic senses include psychic forms of smell and taste. The information coming through these channels can be difficult to interpret. Psychics with these talents will experience a particular odor or taste and interpret the experience in terms of psychic information. In the old time Spiritualist séances, it was common to psychically "smell" roses when good spirits were manifesting. Less pleasant odors were present when less than helpful spirits made their presence known. The smell of roses was often coupled with a high pitch tingling bell coming through the clairaudience channels. Some healers will smell or taste particularly things to indicate various levels of health or illness. Fresh bread might indicate robust health, while the scent of gasoline could indicate cancer. Each psychic with these skills has to build up their own list of interpretations over time and experience, to determine what each of the signals means. Though quite possible psychic talents, most people's initial psychic experiences occur through intuitive knowing, inner voice, or inner vision, not psychic smells or taste.

Several occult techniques can help increase psychic ability. I've found that doing anything in a majick circle ritual increases psychic ability, clears your reception, and focuses the work you are doing. Scent can trigger psychic ability, particularly the smoke of incense. Various combinations can be created, though single plants are also effective. Many use sage, but it does nothing for me personally. Sage is more clearing and healing, and not so psychic in my experience. Mugwort is an excellent incense for psychic awakening. Traditionally combinations of mugwort and wormwood were burned together. Mugwort opens the senses, while wormwood helps call the spirits to communicate with you. Frankincense and myrrh are also used together. Frankincense uplifts and expands our mind while myrrh can help purify and focus. They both help induce a natural trance state. Storax is a favorite of mine as an incense for psychic ability and cleansing. Sandalwood is a gentle scent to open a Witch's vision.

If scent is not your cup of tea, stones are another excellent aid to clear and magnify energy. Quartz points or spheres are excellent to help us develop psychic power, and they can be used as scrying devices. Moonstone is a wonderful mineral to develop intuition. Blue Lace Agate helps clear and calm down people who are nervous about their intuition and impressions.

Any stones, oils, or herbs ruled by the Moon would be beneficial to developing intuition, instinct, and psychic ability, no matter what the channel.

Power of the Witch Oil
1 dram of almond oil
5 drops of ambergris oil
4 drops of musk oil
3 drops of frankincense oil
2 drops of patchouli oil
1 pinch of copal

Anoint yourself with this oil to enhance your physic ability.

Power of the Witch Incense
3 tablespoons of white willow bark
2 tablespoons of patchouli leaves
1 tablespoon of oak-moss
1 tablespoon of frankincense
5 drops of Power of the Witch Oil

Fibers from an old majickal cloak, chopped fine
Bristles from your besom, chopped fine.

Burn this incense to enhance your psychic and majickal power.

Witch's Sight Incense
1 tablespoon of benzoin powder
3 tablespoons of mugwort
2 tablespoons of lavender
1 teaspoon of eyebright
1 teaspoon of rowan leaves
13 drops of gardenia oil
3 drops of honeysuckle oil

Burn to open your third eye and improve your divinations and psychic readings.

Rainbow Colors of Alpha Spell
1 red candle
1 orange candle
1 yellow candle
1 green candle
1 blue candle
1 purple candle
1 lavender candle
Power of the Witch Oil
Power of the Witch Incense

Use this ritual to bring in the rainbow colors we used to reach alpha state in the Cabot Tradition. Anoint each candle with Power of the Witch Oil. Burn Power of the Witch incense in your ritual space. Have the candles lined up, in the order of the rainbow, from right to left. Light each one, starting with the red candle to your right, with the words:

With the power of alpha, I become more and more psychic everyday.

Then light the orange candle and repeat the same incantation. Continue moving right to left with the yellow, green, blue, purple, and lavender candles, reciting the majickal phrase seven times in total. Let the candle burn down if you can. If not, snuff them, and when you relight them again, repeat the phrase for each candle, continuing the process of snuffing and relighting until all the candles burn completely. Once the spell is complete, notice any increases in your intuition and psychic abilities. You will find you will be able to bring in more light energy and more psychic information than you could before this spell.

Mermaid Spell for Psychic Vision
1 red apple

Go to the seashore with your red apple, ideally with the Waxing Moon in sight. Recite this spell and make an offering of the apple, a faery fruit, to the mermaids of the sea.

Moonlight dances on the waters as the tides rise.
Crystal clear psychic vision is the mermaid's prize.
Her psychic power is a gift to you.
You shall use it and be wise.

If she accepts your offering, the mermaid spirit will increase your psychic powers by granting clear visions to you. But it is up to you to grow the wisdom to understand and interpret your visions.

Eye of the Cat Potion
1 cup of water
1 tablespoon of sea salt
½ teaspoon of catnip
1 cat's eye stone

Place all the ingredients in a small pan and warm the potion for fifteen minutes. If you would like to have your potion have a beautiful aroma, add a scented oil you like or your favorite perfume. Remove the potion from the stove and let it cool, then pour it into a bottle or jar. Used for psychic sight and cat-like intuition.

Cat Spell to Become Powerful & Psychic

If you wish to be powerful, it is an advantage to know what people are really thinking. You will want to "see" what is in people's minds when you wish. You will need:

1 mirror
1 picture of Bast, the Egyptian cat goddess
1 Eye of the Cat Potion
1 cat's eye stone
1 white candle and candleholder

Sit in a quiet place on a waxing moon. Light your white candle. Touch the candle with your Eye of the Cat Potion and say:

Flame so bright,
Help me to see into the dark.
Help me to see
What is right.
Bring Witch's Sight!

Place your picture of Bast and the mirror behind your candle and look beyond the candle flame and look into the mirror. Anoint your wrists, forehead, and the back of your neck with this potion. Hold the cat's eye stone in your left hand and say:

Bast, Goddess of power,
With your eye of wisdom

Help me to see into the minds of others and set me free
Free to succeed in all that I do.
I shall live my psychic life with integrity, love and care.
I shall use my psychic power to help others and the world.

Place the picture of Bast under your pillow at night and carry your cat's eye stone.

MOONS OF THE YEAR

While the Full Moon influences our psychic vision, each Moon of the year has its own characteristics and qualities, attuned with the cycles of nature. Their potions can help attune us to the lunar power as it passes from Full Moon to Full Moon throughout the year. They are simple water-based infusions that can be made upon your stove, simply using hot water to extract the herbal properties, like making a tea. Strain out the materials, add the salt, and bottle to use anytime. Add any glitter when the potion has cooled and been bottled and make sure to shake it up before each use. Anoint yourself with the potion on your brow, your third eye, before or during the Full Moon ritual. It will empower your majick. You can also wear the potion as the Full Moon approaches and as it wanes, to keep yourself in harmony with the Moon's cycle.

Seed Moon
Full Moon in Libra

When the Sun is in Aries, at the end of March and the start of April, the Full Moon will be in the opposite sign of Libra. The Seed Moon is the moon near the Vernal Equinox, Ostara, when the Moon's pull helps germinate the seeds and activate the bulbs and roots so the green world can return. It is a time for long-term plans, for planting seeds of future intentions.

Seed Moon Potion

2 cups of spring water

3 tablespoons of sea salt

13 sunflower seeds

1 teaspoon of frankincense

7 apple twigs

Pinch of rose petals

Gold glitter

Yellow or gold ribbon to decorate the potion bottle.

Hare Moon

Full Moon in Scorpio

When the Sun is in Taurus, at the end of April and the first part of May, the Full Moon will be in the opposite sign of Scorpio. While the Seed Moon before was about the fertility of the plants and seeds, the Hare Moon is associated more with the fertility of the animals, named after the totem of the Hare, long associated with Witchcraft, fertility, and shape-shifting. The Hare Moon is usually near Beltane, and Buddhists call this Moon Wesak and celebrate Buddha's birthday on it.

Hare Moon Potion

2 cups of spring water

3 tablespoons of sea salt

1 teaspoon of myrrh

1 rose quartz stone

1 clear quartz stone

1 pinch of rabbit fur

Pink, green and yellow ribbons to decorate the potion bottle.

Rose Moon
Full Moon in Sagittarius

When the Sun is in Gemini, at the end of May and the first part of June, the full Moon will be in the opposite sign of Sagittarius. We call this the Rose Moon as many flowers are in full bloom at this time, and depending on where you live, often the rose is one of them. It is a time for things to be blooming, for a sense of wonder to be in the air and the mysteries of the gods to be afoot.

Rose Moon Potion
2 cups of spring water
3 tablespoons of sea salt
1 teaspoon of rose petals
1 rose quartz stone
1 pinch of dragon's blood
Red glitter
Red and pink ribbons to decorate the potion bottle.

Mead Moon
Full Moon in Capricorn

When the Sun is in Cancer, at the tail end of June and into July, the full Moon will be in the opposite sign of Capricorn. Cancer and Capricorn, Mother and Father, Goddess and God, come together at this time. The unions of couples in May, near Beltane, are celebrated with mead or a honey wine, giving rise to the concept of the honeymoon or mead moon. At this time we celebrate the sweetness and abundance of life. It is usually the Full Moon nearest to the Summer Solstice.

Mead Moon Potion
2 cups of spring water
3 tablespoons of sea salt

1 teaspoon of local honey

1 teaspoon of frankincense

1 citrine stone

1- 3 freshwater pearls

1 clear quartz

9 corn kernels

Green glitter

Yellow and green Ribbons to decorate the potion bottle

Wort Moon
Full Moon in Aquarius

The Wort Moon celebrates the abundance of healing and medicinal plants known as worts, such as the fiery St. John's Wort or mugwort. It occurs when the Sun is in Leo, at the end of July and through much of August, and the Full Moon of this time, near the harvest of Lughnassadh, is in Aquarius.

Wort Moon Potion

2 cups of spring Water

3 tablespoons of sea salt

1 teaspoon of mugwort

1 teaspoon of myrrh

1 teaspoon of rowan berries

1 clear quartz stone

Gold leaf flakes

Yellow and blue ribbons to decorate the potion bottle.

Harvest Moon
Full Moon in Pisces

The Harvest Moon usually occurs between the first harvest, Lughnassadh, which is of grains, and the next harvest, Mabon, which is of fruits. The Moon is full in Pisces, for the Sun is in the sign of Virgo, the corn maiden. This can be a time for allowing your manifestations, your seeds from the Seed Moon, to bear out and harvest the results.

Harvest Moon Potion
2 cups of spring water

3 tablespoons of sea salt

4 acorns

10 apple twigs

1 tablespoon of dried leaves

Gold glitter

Orange and yellow ribbons to decorate the potion bottle

Blood Moon
Full Moon in Aries

One of the most ominous sounding Moons is the Blood Moon, associated near the "meat" harvest of Samhain, when animals were traditionally slaughtered and salted. This Full Moon occurs in Aries, the sign associated with the color red and bloodshed. It occurs when the Sun is in Libra, which includes the end of September and the first three weeks of October. It is a time for release, offerings to the spirits, and seeing the consequences of our actions.

Blood Moon Potion
2 cups of spring water

3 tablespoons of sea salt

5 sticks of applewood

1 crow feather

1 teaspoon of myrrh

1 teaspoon of dragon's blood

1 piece of bone
Red ribbon to decorate the potion bottle

Snow Moon
Full Moon in Taurus

While ideally the Snow Moon is the moon nearest to the First Snow, in this system of naming it astrologically, it is the Full Moon in Taurus, when the Sun is in Scorpio in late October and into much of November. It is a powerful Moon for manifesting our dreams and finding the stillness of our inner self.

Snow Moon Potion
2 cups of spring water (use melted snow if possible)
3 tablespoons of sea salt
1 clear quartz crystal stone
1 howlite stone
Grass from Glastonbury or another sacred site
Silver glitter
Silver and white ribbons to decorate the Potion Bottle

Oak Moon
Full Moon in Gemini

The Oak Moon occurs near the Winter Solstice, when the Oak King is reborn and takes sway after the Holly King's rule of the waning half of the year. The Full Moon occupies Gemini, while the Sun is in Sagittarius, from the last third of November through December to the Winter Solstice. The Oak Moon is a time for strength and seeking guidance for the future.

Oak Moon Potion

2 cups of spring water (use melted snow if possible)

3 tablespoons of sea salt

1 teaspoon of oak leaves

3 acorns

1 teaspoon of pine needles

1 teaspoon of holly leaves

1 teaspoon of frankincense

1 clear quartz stone

Green and red ribbons to decorate the potion bottle

Wolf Moon

Full Moon in Cancer

Opposite to the Mead Moon is the Wolf Moon, which occurs after the solstice, when life can feel its bleakest in the dead of winter. While the light is growing, we still feel the pull of the dark and cold. The Sun is in Capricorn, the sign of the Father, while the Full Moon at this time will be in Cancer, the promise of the return of the Mother and springtime. The Wolf spirit guides, guards, and teaches us in the dark months.

Wolf Moon Potion

2 cups of spring water (use melted snow if possible)

3 tablespoons of sea salt

1 hematite stone

1 pinch of wolf fur

1 teaspoon of myrrh

Silver or gray Ribbon to decorate the potion bottle

Storm Moon

Full moon in Leo

The Storm Moon is the Full Moon in Leo, while the Sun is in Aquarius, nearest to the feast of Imbolc. It is a time of potential change and chaos. The last storms of the winter season occur, and in warmer climates, rather than snowstorms, they are tremendous rainstorms.

Storm Moon Potion
2 cups of spring water (rainwater from a thunderstorm if possible)
3 tablespoons of sea salt
1 teaspoon of storax
Wood struck by lightning
1 lapis lazuli stone
1 clear quartz stone
Blue glitter
Black and blue ribbons to decorate the potion bottle

Crow Moon
Full Moon in Virgo

The last of our twelve Moons usually occurs right before the Vernal Equinox, when the Sun is in Pisces in February and March. The Crow Moon is a time of mystery and majick, of endings and the potential of new beginnings. It is a great time to get psychic insight into the coming growing season, or to do majick for unusual and strange things that would not normally work at other times in the year.

Crow Moon Potion
2 cups of spring water
3 tablespoons of sea salt
1 teaspoon of dragon's blood
1 crow feather or black feather
1 white feather
1 clear quartz stone

Clear glitter
White and black ribbons to decorate the potion bottle

DIVINATION

Divination is the application of psychic ability through a system of symbols. Today divination usually refers to things like Tarot cards, runes, and I-Ching coins. It can also include more fluid forms of divination that do not require fixed symbols or drawing lots, such as gazing into a crystal ball or using ink in water. Such acts are known as scrying. The images formed during scrying become a focus for our psychic sight. We project our perception of the screen of our mind out into the object and interpret the shapes and images we see. Sometimes the images are formed strictly in our psychic vision, as when we gaze through a clear pure crystal ball or into a fire. Other times the shapes are formed by the fluidity of our point of focus. Tea leaf reading is such a form of divination. You swish the tea around and when you tip it out, you look at the leaves that are stuck to the inside of the cup and interpret the images based on what things they mimic. A "Y" can mean yes to your question, while an "N" can mean no. A ring can indicate a marriage or commitment. A star can foretell success or fame. The same method is used in Victorian lace readings, cloud gazing, or scrying in incense.

More archaic forms of divination, still used by some, include reading bones either by throwing them down on a cloth and interpreting their pattern, or burning bones or shells in fire and interpreting the cracks. Practitioners of geomancy interpreted the pattern of holes made when asking a questions and randomly poking the ground or a box of sand. The most complex and least-accepted form of divination is the reading of omens through the entrails of a sacrificed animal, but the simplest and most common form of divinatory advice is flipping a coin. Heads means yes, and tails means no.

Feather omens, based on finding a feather naturally on your path as you walk out in the world, can be a powerful form of message. Look back to **Chapter Three** on different kinds of bird feathers and what they can mean majickally. The colors of the feathers will also influence their meaning, even if you don't know the type of bird feather it is. Gray and white feathers are always good news. You are getting some sort of blessing on your path. Brown feathers are about friendship. Black feathers deal with majick and justice. White feathers alone can be good news, or to keep your eyes open for a deeper spiritual message.

When I was having financial difficulties with the Internal Revenue Service, I found a little gray and white feather on my shop's doorstep. I didn't pick it up. After three days of rain and wind, it was still there and I realized that perhaps the feather was a message for me, and that I should be open to some good news. I went into the shop and found out that the IRS was forgiving my debt to them.

Divination's basic philosophy is that all things are connected, and while we can often be blind to patterns that are all around us, we can use these tools and systems to see the patterns around us reflected. It is a fulfillment of the age-old Hermetic teaching "As above, so below." We often go to someone else when we really have difficulty, as someone not involved in the situation is more likely to see the patterns without bias and give us an honest account with no ulterior motive, conscious or not. Witches and wise women are famous for giving counsel through divination.

SPIRIT COMMUNICATION

A big part of psychic ability is talking to the Otherworld. Through this ability, we can speak to the spirits of the deceased, the faeries, and the gods themselves. We can receive information and lessons from these spirits while in an alpha state, and they will often give us direct information we could not possibly receive through linear channels. It's important to realize that not all spirits are here to teach and help you, but spirits, like people, can often give us helpful information.

While there are many types of spirits, the ones most commonly called upon in Witchcraft today are the ancestors, the faeries, and the deities. These are the most in alignment with our path and spiritual tradition. Previously, in **Chapter Two**, we spoke about the spirits who aid us in majick, listing them as faeries, elves, gnomes, dwarves, dragons, animals, ancestors, ancient Witches, heroes, and deities. While all are helpful in majick, not all of them tend to show up in psychic readings for direct messages and information.

Animal spirits have a presence to them, and psychics can often pick up on them, but, being animals, they are not the most talkative of spirits, though there can be times when both spirit animals and deceased pets can get a message across to a psychic.

More commonly, messages come from direct ancestors, loved ones from this life who have passed on, but who are present still with us and can offer comfort and counsel to us. When you look at the overall history of practices labeled today as Witchcraft, some of them going back to the ancient world, the concept of speaking with the dead was strongly entwined with them. Those who naturally gravitate to the psychic often have experiences in communicating with the dead, sometimes spontaneously without specific intention. Beyond those beloved dead are the dead of our tradition, the ancient Witches who guide us from afar. They can communicate with practitioners of our Craft and help draw those who would walk the path of the Witch to the right practices, groups, and teachers.

People are often afraid that the dead will come to haunt them, and while haunting is a possibility, it is usually not from our loved ones. Spirits, including our loved ones, can reach out to communicate and might do so through a knock on the door, flickering lights, a phone call with no one there, or even the feeling of being touched, but they do not have the capacity to do you harm. Hauntings have really nothing to do with people who have crossed to the other side.

It appears that once you are truly crossed over and settled, in death you are at a higher intelligence, and you can look back at your life and understand from this new perspective outside of space and time. You understand what was a karmic lesson and what your part was in it, like a part in a movie or play. The dead are usually not sad or worried about anything, but they do express concern for their loved ones left in the world and try to explain their role.

Once, an older woman came in with her adult son, who was about forty years old, for a psychic reading. They wanted me to bring through their father. They didn't say that openly, but that was their intention. And he came through. The one thing his spirit kept saying to me, to his son through me, was that he was a terrible father and mean to his wife, but he wanted his son to know now that he could have taken him to many baseball games instead of just that one, and he did regret that. The spirit of the father was not sad, he understood why, but he wanted his son to understand that now he regretted it, and with this information, possibly feel different about his relationship with his father. The son confirmed that the father only took him to one baseball game as a child, and felt better knowing how his father now felt from the other side. It was a healing experience for them both.

Another mediumship reading came when a woman came into my shop just as I was closing early. One of the priestesses in our tradition, Willow was dying from cancer, though I didn't know how seriously ill she was at the time, but this woman caught me while I was trying to hurriedly close my shop, insisting she needed a reading. I agreed and grabbed my tarot cards. She told me to put the cards away that she simply wanted to know if her son, who had died a week previous, was okay. I got into an alpha state and described him to her as he came through. He came through immediately, and she confirmed my impressions. He was fine, but I know that sounded trite to her. She just couldn't take that he was fine and be done with it. He described a few things to affirm that he really was fine, and then I saw him thrusting a sword at me. I was confused, but told her what I perceived. She said he was buried with a sword and that it was his prized possession. It was his great grandfather's, and he treasured it. He told me that he felt like he was the Highlander from the movie of the same name, and he was going to live forever now. Though we are sometimes apt to censor ourselves when doing psychic readings, thinking we are being silly and the message cannot possibly be what we are getting, I know better. I relayed the message just as I heard it. I know if something comes through, I should speak it. She gasped in shock, as it was the last film they saw together. He smiled and then faded away. That bit of information was the confirmation she needed to truly know that we connected and that he was okay. The confirmation was not only meaningful for her, but for me as well. It was an intense reading that taught me how powerfully profound things are for those on the border of life and death.

When we realized it was Willow's time, I helped her cross over to the Otherworld. I could describe the Otherworld, the breeze on my face, the light. Even with the lung cancer, she started to breathe calmly and then peacefully left us to go to the Otherworld. She initially fought it, but once we began talking about the Otherworld, she was able to let go, but it was only because of this young man's spirit. I could do this for my friend only because he showed me how real it was.

Speaking to the Dead Incense
3 tablespoons of comfrey leaf
2 tablespoons of myrrh
2 tablespoons of mullein leaf
1 tablespoon of black copal

1 tablespoon of tobacco leaves
1 teaspoon of yew needles
1 pinch of coffee
1 pinch of graveyard dirt

Speaking to the Dead Oil
1 dram of almond oil
10 drops of myrrh oil
5 drops of storax oil
3 drops of rosemary oil
1 drop of peppermint oil
1 pinch of Black Sea salt
1 pinch of graveyard dirt

Between the Worlds
Black Candle
Speaking to the Dead Incense
Speaking to the Dead Oil

Between the worlds is a veil. To beckon loved ones to speak with you, first you must wait until you see the veil. It appears as a mist or fog to the human eye. Sit quietly in a darkened room. Burn Speak to the Dead Incense. Anoint your black candle with Speak to the Dead Oil. Write the name of the person you would like to speak with on the parchment paper and place the paper under the candle. Light your candle and sprinkle a little bit of the loose incense around the base of the candle. Gaze into the flame of the candle and say aloud:

I ask that the doors of the Summerland be opened and that all good spirits may walk into my world. I shall be truly blessed to speak and hear my beloved ones and friends in Avalon. God and Goddess, bless me and bless my loved ones.

Conjure Incense
3 tablespoons of mullein leaf

2 tablespoons of jasmine flowers

1 tablespoon of garden sage leaf

1 tablespoon of dittany of Crete

12 drops of pine oil

3 drops of amber Oil

½ teaspoon of copper glitter

Conjure incense can help us conjure and manifest the presence of spirits more strongly in our rituals. It can be used to commune with the dead, but also helps manifest all sorts of spirits, from elementals and angels to the gods and goddesses. If you are outdoors with enough ventilation, you can burn quite a bit of it and see them take form and shape in the smoke.

Faeries can mean specific forms of elder nature spirits, but for our purposes here, includes what is commonly thought of as faeries and elves, gnomes, dwarves, and all elemental spirits. Water spirits such as nymphs, tree spirits known as dryads, and all manner of plant and land spirits can broadly be classified as faery beings. Some would even classify dragon spirits, as a union of all the elements and personifications of the deep earth powers, in this category. The dragons express fire as their fiery breath, air through their wings, earth through their deep caves and love of treasure, and water through their serpentine energy. Nature and faery spirits most often seek to communicate when the balance between the human world and the faery world has been disrupted. Like the ancient Witches, they are more likely to communicate with the majickally inclined rather than showing up for a chat during a psychic reading for someone who simply seeks questions about their life.

Faerie Sight Herbal Mix
1 tablespoon of chamomile
1 tablespoon of St. John's wort
1 tablespoon of lemon verbena

Carry in a green bag to enable you to see faeries.

Lastly are our deities and heroes. Some are ancient ancestors who have assumed mythic proportions. Others are manifestations of the great powers of nature, such as the Sun, Moon, Earth, and stars. Most dwell in their own realm, with their own purposes and agendas, but are available to the practitioner who knows how to reach out to them. Deity majick is covered in detail in **Chapter Twelve**.

PSYCHIC TRAVEL

Psychic travel refers to the arts of travel without our body, and can include astral travel, mind travel and time travel. It's a type of travel not often talked about outside of esoteric circles, though it's something we all experience from time to time.

Astral travel is the process of projecting your entire energy packet, your aura, on your journey. It's a more complete experience than some other forms of psychic travel, as it can give you a full sensory experience, as if you were truly in a location without your body (hence the often-used name, out-of-body travel). While you are projecting your aura away from your body, you are still connected to your body. Your body is not "empty." Popular mythology says there is a silver thread connecting your spirit to your body, but that's not real in my experience.

Astral travel is the source of bilocation stories. You are not physically in two places at once, but some project such a powerful astral double that other can perceive it, even if they are only remotely psychic, and believe it to be a real physical person, not a spirit double.

While full body projection is possible, and some feel it is very important to learn to control consciously, I don't believe it's necessary for all Witches to learn. There are other techniques that can yield the same practical results, such as mind travel. While it can be practiced, others experience it spontaneously. We naturally experience it unconsciously when we reach delta level of brainwaves, though not everybody always reaches delta in the sleep state. Have you ever experienced waking up, but you can't quite open your eyes or move? Your aura has not come back completely.

Mind travel is different from the more popular astral travel. It is akin to what is known today as remote viewing. It's a form of mental projection occurring over distance, but it is the same mechanism as when we mentally connect to a tool or herb to catalyze its power in our spells. If I am working a healing case with someone who is physically in Australia while I'm in Salem, Massachusetts, I would connect to them energetically, mentally, through their light. I might see them on the screen of my mind, but whether I perceive them as coming to my screen, or me going to their location, I can choose to look around where they are and get a sense of the people, furniture, and structures.

When in an alpha state, you simply ask your mind to travel to a specific person or place. You need some identifying feature for it – the name of the person, the address of the location, or simply an awareness of where the location is without a street address. But you need something to connect you to the place.

Mind Travel

Hold the intention of your destination in mind. Count yourself down into an alpha level and intend that your mind, your perceptions, go to the destination target. Allow your perception to come to you. What do you see? What do you feel? However you get your psychic impressions, it will come to you. Look at everything. When you are done, intend to return your awareness. Count up and write down what you saw, or draw a map. Notate it in any way that is clear and verifiable. If you cannot visit the location, obtain pictures and maps and see if your perceptions match the location. In time and with practice, most Witches can be very adept at this kind of psychic work. An ideal target is a retail store you know about, but have never visited.

You can attempt to use your mind travel skills to have a true astral travel experience, but being very conscious can make it difficult. I find my most powerful astral experiences occur when I'm in my sleep. While I travel through dreams, I meet new people and see new places.

My daughter Penny has vivid astral travel experiences while she sleeps. She recalls one very vivid and disturbing travel where she saw someone somewhere in the world commit suicide. It was a vivid as sitting down with me, but she visited astrally with a black woman speaking about how a man took her baby. She said very clearly, "I've got to hit those wires." She then experienced the woman ending her own life through the electrical wires. Was Penny's conversation with her conversation an observation through another's eyes, or was she speaking to her spirit? Astral travel can take you to random places, and we don't always know the purpose of our visits.

It's best to program yourself, waking and in dreams, for pleasant and safe journeys. If you run into violent situations, you can use your majick to project protection and try to stop the violence.

Good Dreams Incense
3 tablespoons of jasmine flowers
4 tablespoons of lavender flowers
2 tablespoons of mugwort
1 tablespoon of eyebright
1 tablespoon of oak-moss
1 tablespoon of benzoin powder
10 drops of musk oil

Burn this incense before going to bed, filling your bedroom with the smoke. Make sure to extinguish it and all remaining charcoal and embers before actually going to sleep. Try burning it in a cauldron, and then placing the lid on the cauldron before bed.

Dream Candle Spell
Black candle
Light blue candle
2 pieces of parchment
Black pen

Write on one piece of the parchment with a black pen, asking for the removal of violence, horror, stress, and anxiety from your dream state. If there is anything specific worrying you, include that as well. Place it under the blue candle. On the other parchment slip, write your intention to dream and connect with all that is good, all that is educational, for the highest good harming none. Place it under the black candle. Light both candles and recite this spell:

Shimmering candle,
With your divine light.
Reveal my future
In my dreams tonight!

With clarity of dreams, you will have peace, healing, and possibly a glimpse of your own future.

Faery Dream Majick Herbal Mix
1 tablespoon of white willow bark
3 tablespoons of lavender
2 tablespoons of rose petals
1 tablespoon of red clover
1 tablespoon of dried mushrooms
5 drops of mugwort oil
3 drops of sweet pea oil

Carry in a pink or blue majick bag to evoke the power of the faeries in your dreams.

My own experiences with time travel were not altogether pleasant. They simply seemed to happen to me, and I couldn't control them. I don't want to say it was dangerous, but it didn't feel totally safe. I experienced a profound shift of dimensions while exiting a train from Boston into Penn Station in New York City. I entered a time realm, and I'm lucky I came back. We don't really know how it works. There might be wiser Witches than I who know how to control it safely, but I don't recommend it.

Safer forms of time travel involve traveling in your own past, or in the past of your own soul through past life regression.

Past Life Spiral Spell
Paper spiral talisman
Black candle
Herbal mix of mugwort, jasmine flowers, and benzoin
Black majick bag
Blank journal for past life recall

Spiral back to your past lives. Regression is not only an awakening for our creative experiences from our past selves, it is also part of a healing process to acknowledge our fears and to recognize our courage, talents, and qualities. Place the spiral talisman in front of you along with the lighted candle. Hold both of your palms upright and say aloud:

I now draw to me the pictures and knowledge of my past lives; I wish to see only the most productive, successful, and romantic times.

Sprinkle a small bit of the herbal mix around the candle. Lie down and place the spiral on your forehead. Visualize a rainbow of colors. Lie quiet and relax. Allow yourself to "see" your past life as if it were a movie in your mind's eye. After you have "seen" and "heard" your past life, open your eyes. Place the rest of the herbs and the talisman in the majick bag.

Write down all you can remember and all you have experienced. Search for photographs and pictures that express your experience and glue them in a blank book. Begin your own past lives journal. Continue to write in your journal and compare situations in your past lives with the experiences found in this life.

Spiral Talisman

Chapter Eleven: The Majick of Empowerment

Empowerment is the key to majick and Witchcraft. To truly embrace being a Witch, you must embrace your own power and the responsibilities that go along with it. People are afraid of even saying the word "power." We're conditioned to think that power is bad, when it is actually a necessary part of a successful life. Many believe that seeking power is not spiritual, but those without personal power are not effective in the world. People are afraid of what others might think when the word "power" is used, but the problem occurs when only power is sought. Seeking power in terms of self-empowerment, power over self, and the ability to create the life you intend rather than power over another is all part of the majickal path.

Self-empowerment is not self-aggrandizing. It is about living above your perceived limits and having no limitations other than the highest good of any given situation. When we practice the spirit of majick, we have to take our feelings about power to a higher level, releasing all the limiting conditioning we've accepted over the years about our value, self-worth, and ability to create change. At the heart of majickal empowerment is self-esteem and self-love. With it, we can develop a confidence that grows both our majick and our daily life.

Sovereignty—the ability to reign over your own self and your life—is a foundation stone for the practice of Witchcraft. We are the ones putting a crown upon our own heads and pulling it down tight. We must put ourselves on our own throne. We must also balance this power with humility, consideration, and compassion. Those in a true position of power, like the kings and queens of old and the successful people of all kinds today, including presidents and CEOs, know how to find that balance. Sadly the ideal and the reality often fall short, but Witches strive for the ideal.

While those with power can be in a position to "lord it over" others, when we gain power on any level, we must always keep ourselves vigilant to use it in the most correct way, a balanced way. We must also conquer the fear of claiming our power. Don't be afraid of putting yourself in the position of the boss, whether as the CEO of a corporation or the president of an organization. If you are called to it, then carefully assume the power. When in such positions, envision yourself like the sacred kings and queens of old. Wield power as a sacred priest or priestess would, because in essence, you are a sacred mediator of such power, regardless of the position or title.

Even without a recognized title, office, or position, you are potentially a person of power. Anyone can be. You simply have to claim it. It all depends on your desire, your majickal projections, and your ability to feel and envision your highest personal power, because your highest personal power can be manifested. We have to deal with many layers of societal and familial programming that tells us we can't do this. A lot of structures are put around us to tell us we are not rich enough, pretty enough, thin enough, strong enough, and these structures can knock us down. We need to examine the foundations of those structures and look beyond them. For any complaint, you can find someone who overcame it. If you have been told you are too fat to be powerful, effective, or happy, look at Henry VIII. History is filled with exceptional people, and the only thing separating you from them is the drive to empower yourself. Any one factor has nothing to do with your ability to achieve your goals and find happiness.

I have a good friend who is a nurse and has eight children, all boys. As they were growing up. each of the boys wanted to be something different or expressed very different personality traits and interests. They were each unique. One wanted to be a firefighter like his father. Another wanted to be a designer. Another painted his toenails and played with Barbie dolls. Their parents encouraged each of them to find their own blessings and explore their own desires. Each is empowered to be his own person. Their mother, too, had to find ways to empower herself while raising a family of eight boys. Her own majick spell was to get a tiara; when she puts it on her head, empowering herself to take time off for herself, it's a signal to her boys and her husband that it is not the time to bother her. They scatter and give her some space, respecting this ritual. The tiara, a type of crown, indicates she is charge of herself at that moment, and they understand. She's a clever woman to devise this ritual. In many ways, we need to learn how to put on our own crowns, even if they are invisible. We need to live our lives from this place of personal empowerment.

Sovereignty Mirror Bath Spell

To invoke the blessings of the Goddess Sovereignty into your life, use this spell. You will need:

Hand Mirror

Eyeliner or lipstick to temporarily write on the mirror

Ritual blade (athame or other knife with a blunt edge or a silver butter knife or letter opener)

7 candles with the colors of the rainbow – red, orange, yellow, green, blue, deep purple and violet

Write the spell upon the mirror in eyeliner or lipstick, with the colors black and red both sacred to this ancient goddess of the land.

I am Sovereign.
I have the courage of all Goddesses.
The Witch lives within me.
The blade of light, truth, and power belongs to me.

Light the candles. Get into the bath and relax for a bit. Read the spell aloud and meditate upon its meaning as you gaze into the mirror. Look into your own eyes and know these words are true. Put the mirror down and pick up the blade. Raise it above the water, like the sword Excalibur rising out of the lake. Move the blade until the reflected light strikes you, igniting you with the power of the Witch. Know that you are changed and never give away or compromise your light, truth, or power again.

MAJICK AND POWER

Nothing happens one hundred percent of the time, be it medicine, politics, mechanics, anything. Nothing is one hundred percent certain. There are always exceptions, preventing something from coming to be, and that is for a good reason, even if we don't know what the reason is. This law of the universe is the Principle of Cause and Effect. There is a reason, but we cannot always perceive it.

Likewise, no one's majick is effective one hundred percent of the time. Don't put yourself in a position to make yourself or others think that your majick always works in every circumstance. It can feel that way, particularly when you begin with some success, but no one is invincible in their spellcasting. Don't make the mistake of thinking that you are somehow less powerful or defeated when a spell does not work. If you really know your majick, you don't have to believe that you are one hundred percent effective, because you'll know that you hold the intention of what you do is correct and for the good of all involved. Far better for a spell that is incorrect and harmful—even if you didn't know it consciously—to fail rather than come true and cause harm. If you do something that is against the greater good, if you do something harmful intentionally or not, you will have to live with the consequences of it. That is why we put the intention "correct and for the good of all involved" in all of our spells.

You are a part of the universe, and you must understand your majick will work in the times that it is "supposed" to work. Your desires, your urges, and your intention are a part of the overall patterns of the universe.

People try to put time limits on their majick. Sometimes you can, and sometimes you can't. There is nothing wrong with trying, but do not think that you are almighty, dictating how everything will unfold in every detail. If you were, the world would be under your thumb and you'd be Goddess or God. But you are not. Don't confuse control with empowerment. Empowerment helps you realize that you are a partner with the divine in your majick. Often the universe, Goddess, and God know how best to unfold things, creating situations much better than what we could imagine or control ourselves.

Sometimes it is our self-identity that causes us to want us to express ourselves in seemingly bold or powerful, yet ultimately unhealthy, ways. Many come to majick and Witchcraft wanting to hold knowledge and power over others. That is not our way. When we do so, it is really our current self-created identity that is feeling vulnerable, that feels it is in jeopardy. Such actions mean we are not comfortable with who we are. Exercises in self-esteem, such as the Majick Mirror, are so important as the first steps of empowerment. Those who are the most controlling are usually the most angry or fearful, and those are the ones without that self-esteem and self-love. They are trying to project their own low feelings onto someone else. In reality, they want love more than anything else and are constantly bidding for attention to have someone else replace these awful inner feelings, not consciously realizing that no one else can change these feelings. You must start with yourself, and you can then be open to love from others. You will then recognize your own qualities and gifts, build a stronger identity that can lead to personal empowerment. This is the secret to true power. Recognizing the need for a healthy self-identity is the first step.

Some people wait for someone else to identify them, to recognize them and tell them who they are, what they should do and what they shouldn't do. Usually it starts with our parents and then continues in school, religion, marriage, work, and friendships. Witches practice our craft to reforge our identity, to choose who we want to be, and to take responsibility for ourselves and our own happiness. The Majick Mirror is a step in the process of self-creation.

Majick Mirror Exercise

The Majick Mirror is an exercise of gazing at yourself in the reflection of a majick mirror, a mirror that has been charged to manifest your intention. It helps increase self-love and self-esteem by combining the majick of the mirror with affirmation exercises.

While gazing into the mirror, recite aloud affirmations, beneficial phrases to reprogram your consciousness to help heal and grow. This will help you develop your relationship with yourself and with others in your life. With a strong sense of self and healthy relationships, your own intuition, perception, and power will grow. All of your abilities as a Witch develop, making you grow wise and more confident.

Sit or stand quietly before a mirror and hold your Instant Alpha Trigger. Look into the mirror and gaze at yourself. Say to yourself:

I love myself.

I empower myself with confidence.

I am gaining better control of my thoughts, words, and actions.

I better understand all forms and flows of energy both inside and outside of my body.

I'm getting smarter and wiser, and more intelligent.

I improve my psychic ability every day.

I understand that thoughts and words are powerful, and are forms of action; I'm responsible for all of my own actions.

I will always use energy in a correct manner for the good of all.

Every time I go into alpha, all my bodily functions improve: my eyesight, my hearing, and my vision.

Every day in every way I'm feeling better, I am better, I'm getting better.

I'm becoming more of a genius every day.

You can envision yourself surrounded and filled with pink light as you do this, and can repeat the affirmations as you do. I suggest doing each one three times. You can also add to the traditional affirmations with the following:

I am powerful.

I am the Queen/King of my own life.

I am a Goddess/God.

I am fulfilling my full potential.

When you are done, give yourself total health clearance. Place your right hand up over the top of your head, palm downward at the crown chakra. Pull your hand downward in front of your face, in front of your heart and your solar plexus, then push outward with your palm away from you, and say:

I am giving myself total health clearance. I am healing myself.

When done, gently release your Instant Alpha Trigger and release your gaze from the mirror.

Self Esteem Oil

1 dram of almond oil

5 drops of rose oil

7 drops of lilac oil

6 sunflower seeds

1 citrine stone

Wear this oil when you want to feel a greater sense of self-esteem and self-empowerment. It uplifts your sense of self.

Self-Esteem Dream Pillow

An excellent method to have healing majickal dreams is to create a dream pillow. This formula can be adapted for other intentions, but is designed to help you gain confidence and self-esteem as you grow on your majickal path. You can use all of these herbs, but it is only necessary to choose three of them for your Self-Esteem Pillow. You can also add a few drops of Self-Esteem Oil.

Rose petals

Savory

Damiana

Mugwort

Agrimony

Rowan

Angelica root

Celandine

Star anise

Anise seed

Horehound

Peppermint
Red clover
2 Squares of Fabric (suggested size, one square foot each)
Cotton filling

Sew the squares of fabric on three sides, allowing an opening for the herbs and cotton. You can bless each stitch with the enchantment "Every stitch shall bring to me, perfect sleep and harmony." Charge all of the herbs for healthy, happy, and productive dreams and place them into the pillow, along with the cotton from a craft store, intermixing the herbs with it. When you have a nice fluffy pillow, sew up the last side and lay with it when you sleep. Keep a dream journal on your nightstand to see if you can record and capture your dreams and understand what they might mean to you.

Dragon's Blood Oil
1 ounce almond oil
1 teaspoon of powdered dragon's blood resin

Dragon's blood oil is used for protection, empowerment, and really any majickal intention. Dragon's blood helps you collect your thoughts and will, and catalyzes all majick. You can use just a drop in any spell, or put it on yourself and your tools before doing any majick.

Witch's Spell Box
Decorated wooden box
Rowan berries
Parchment
Black ribbon
Pen

Rowan berries add extra power to any spell. To empower a spell with the majick of the Rowan tree, you can write your spell as you normally would, but do not burn it. Tie it with a ribbon and place it within the box, along with the rowan berries. Do not open the box till your spell comes to fruition. Be careful what you wish for... you might just get it, as Rowan majick is quite powerful.

A WITCH'S BREATH

In martial arts, you learn to breathe in a certain way to bring the chi, the light of the universe, into your body. Breath connects you to the universe. The power is imprinted upon the life force, and when you exhale, you are exhaling your intention. If you focus that breath upon a single intention, you can make it more powerful. In our Celtic mythology, there were nine maidens warming a pearl-rimmed cauldron in the Underworld with their breath, indicating the power of the breath, as the nine maidens are associated with the nine Ladies of the Lake and the nine Witches of Gloucester.

The use of breath is an age-old tradition. You must practice inhaling the energy, being aware of it. Breathe in through the nose and out through the mouth. You can practice it when walking or running, or any other form of exercise. When using your breath for majick, sit down and breathe deep. Inhale to the count of nine, drawing it into your lungs, holding it to the count of ten, and then breathing out to the count of ten. You can start at the count of five and slowly build up until you get to the count of ten. Don't stand up right away, as it will make you lightheaded. Just breathe normally for a while. When you are ready to empower a spell, go into alpha, start breathing, and then focus on your projection upon the inhale and exhale your intention to the universe.

You can use the following incantation to empower your intention upon any crystal.

A Witch's Breath will ignite her spells...
Whisper on a crystal

Blow upon the cauldron's steam
Whistle to the Wind
It is so.

Stirring the Cauldron

Cauldron

Spoon

Candle

Crystal

The incantation can also be used to evoke the power of the nine maidens by doing majick through the stirring of a cauldron. Fill your cauldron with sacred water, such as the Blessing Water from **Chapter Nine**, or storm water, melted snow water, or even water left under the Full Moon, the classic Moon water. Light your candle with your intention. Pass the stone quickly through its flame. Infuse the stone with your intention and breath, and then drop it into the cauldron. Begin to stir. If your spell is to manifest, stir clockwise. If it is to remove something, stir counterclockwise. Use the Witch's Breath to empower the water and stone. You can also use this incantation:

Flame that Boils
The Cauldron
Spin the Spoon
Have the Spell
I cast come to
Me Soon!

Pour the water out wherever you want the spell to take effect.

OPTIMISM, PESSIMISM & BALANCE

For true empowerment, we need to find balance. Once we begin to recreate our identity and choose who we want to be, we then need to find balance between all things. As humans, we naturally have hopes and fears interwoven with our intentions and dreams. We need to discern what truly is before we can project our majickal intention for the future. You can only begin a journey by knowing where you are right now.

Everything is possible, and hopeful optimism helps us manifest what might at first seem unattainable. It is a tool in our majickal toolbox. Many of us have setbacks before success, and part of our practice is learning to learn from those setbacks. Certain talents can be innate, such as many creative abilities. But you still have to work hard to develop those skills and apply them in appropriate ways to be successful. Most actors, musicians, and artists are often knocked down again and again before achieving success. Those who can keep hope outlast those who give up on their dreams. I love the story of comedian Jay Leno living in car for six months in Los Angeles until he got his first professional job. You have to be prepared for the rejection, though when you experience it, naturally it feeds your pessimistic side. If you feel called to do something in your majickal heart, then you cannot give up on your dreams. You have to stay focused and realize that anything is possible. Perhaps the person who is saying "no" is not the final authority. Perhaps there is another way. When I took my first book to an agent, I was told, "No one would ever want to read this." I had to say, "I think you are wrong." Since then thousands of people have read it, making Power of the Witch a classic in the world of Witchcraft. I later ran into that agent at the Ritz Carlton during an event featuring Frank Sinatra. By that point I was well known, and all he could do was look at me a little sheepishly, as he knew he'd been wrong and had missed out on something special.

The balance between optimism and pessimism is a difficult space for me to be in, personally. One I get an idea in my head, it's already happening as far as I'm concerned. That's only a problem when it turns out that it is not happening. Sometimes the timing is wrong, no matter how much we might think otherwise. Some projects and goals need to be put on the back burner. They cannot manifest now. They need time to grow or develop. Like seeds, all things germinate and grow in their own time. Some seeds don't grow at all. Part of our balance is learning to discern what is waiting to germinate, what has already sprouted and needs our attention, and what might never germinate. Some seeds that we have given up on surprise us when we are not looking, and suddenly we have a flower. But if we only look at that pot, our other flowers can wilt due to neglect. Sometimes you have to work with what you currently have, rather than what you are hoping to have. This is part of the lesson of balance. Balance helps us keep going. Every failure is a step to success. Failure can teach us how not to do something, encouraging us to find a new balance and a new method.

If you focus too much on one thing and don't keep your eye on all the others, you are going to have some major problems, and that will distract from your empowerment. Failing at something that could have been successful if you had not made an error of judgment can sap your enthusiasm for future pursuits. If you have a great urge to do something, but you leave everything else behind and it doesn't work out, you will feel less effective, and that will influence your self-esteem. Find the balance between what is and what you are hoping to create. Certainly project for the future, but don't neglect the present.

In America, everyone seems to be striving for a model of perfect success, measured by a huge house with a stainless steel kitchen with granite countertops, a pool in the backyard, and two or three cars. If you don't get that, it can be easy to feel like a failure. Some people will get that. Perhaps that is their karma. But until that happens, can you be happy with what you have? The majickal path shows us we are not entitled to anything in the material world, anything at all. You are born into a place and time and must make use of what you have. If you are reading this, you have probably had the luck, the karma, of being born in a place where you have many basic needs fulfilled. If you have a job, a roof over your head, and food on your table, you are doing much better than most of the world. If you have heat in the winter, clean water, and appropriate clothes, you are very lucky. Don't take it for granted. Can you enjoy the simple things? Can you enjoy your life, the sunshine when the sun comes out, or the cool breeze on a hot day? Balance is about being in the moment, even if we are putting energy towards manifestations in the future. Can you enjoy the moment?

All unfolds at its proper pace. Our majick helps to simply shape it and put us in the right place at the right time, doing the right thing to align our intentions with the unfolding universe. Even when we don't believe it at the time, majick has taught me that everything really does happen within the seemingly correct time for us. I know personally that I've projected for manifestations of things, working very hard and adding a lot of energy to it, thinking it was supposed to happen "right now" or in some specific time frame. Then fifteen years later, the exact things I thought I wanted to happen would happen. They did come, just as I projected, but not when I thought they would. A great example would be obtaining our federal legal recognition for what is now known as the Cabot-Kent Hermetic Temple. I thought we would get our 501c3 status in the 1970s, but it didn't come together until the 2000s. It took time to get the right people and right circumstances together, even though I assumed I had everything in place earlier.

As I get older, I understand one of the secrets is learning to do the work, but then sit back. I'm learning to sit back on my heels and not fret. I'm not going to worry. I plan, use my majick to project for my goals, and I work towards those goals, but I let it unfold naturally. That is what is most important, doing the work in harmony with your intention. Follow up your spells with real world action. Getting upset that something is not occurring fast enough will simply negate and neutralize the work you've already put into it. When you get upset, it's like you become Charlie Chaplin in one of his slapstick movies. He drops his hat on the floor and reaches down to get it, only to kick it further away. He waddles over to pick it up, and kicks it further down away from him. Getting upset just kicks your goal further away from your reach. Relax and let it unfold. Let it come in its own time.

If Witches and magicians were able to do things in the time span we desire, this world would become immediately magnificent. We'd have a wonderful world. The air would be clean. The water would be clear. We would do it all instantly. Yet we live in a world governed by time and natural law. There are consequences to our actions that unfold over time, and likewise, the solutions must unfold over time. Majick helps the process along.

Balance and Serenity Spell

This spell helps us find balance in times when we are having difficulty finding the balance and the peace we seek as Witches. You will need:

1 pale blue candle

Self-esteem Oil

Parchment paper

Prepare your sacred space. Cast a circle. Write this spell on parchment and anoint your candle with Self-esteem Oil.

Forever is my life to be Balance and Serenity.
Work and play shall Come my Way
Pleasure, Peace and Beauty can
Be brought to my Life's plan.
So mote it be!

Start your Witch's Breath deep breathing and empower the spell with your breath, with your chi. Recite this spell and burn it, scattering the ashes once you have released your circle. Let the candle burn and you will find yourself coming back into balance.

Self Love and Charm Candle Spell
Bright pink candle
Picture of yourself
Favorite perfume
Something you treasure, such as a special piece of jewelry

Cast a circle. Anoint the candle with your favorite perfume or cologne. Light the candle and place your photo and treasure next to the candle. Recite this spell to gain a greater self of charm and self-love.

Candle of Divine Light
Fill me with Love and Charm!

Let the candle burn, and when done, carry or wear your treasured item to feel the effect of this spell.

Mighty Witch Spell
Silver buckle
Black candle
Witch's robes
Picture of yourself in your Witch robes

Dress in all black or in your Witch's robes. Find a silver buckle. Light a black candle. Place your own picture next to the candle. Hold the buckle and conjure a picture in your mind of the Ancient Witches that have gone before you. They will put their power into your buckle. They will be your secret coven. Recite this spell:

The one for whom this candles flames
Shall be a Mighty Witch
Mighty Witches from the Past
Mighty Witches from the Now
Ancient Wisdom know my name!
Know that I shall drink the flame of power!
My name is Witch!
So mote it be.

After you charge your majickal buckle, sleep with it for one night. Wear it secretly in your daily life for your connection to the Ancient Witches, and in your majickal work as a part of your majickal clothing and robes. You can tie it on a ribbon and wear it as a charm when wearing robes or cloaks if a belt would not be appropriate.

Ancestral Power Spell
Black candle
White candle
Speak to the Dead Incense

Light your black and white candle and burn your incense. Recite this spell:

The Light of my ancestor shall glow
My spirit power will grow
Hour by Hour

Lie down and do a meditation envisioning the universe. See the sky above you. Levitate your astral self into the sky. Go beyond the sky into the solar system, and then into the universe. Feel yourself connected to all the stars, just as all our ancestors are connected to the stars. Feel how we all come from start stuff, just as the scientist Carl Sagan said. That is a huge part of our ancestry. Take that empowerment from the universe, that energy, back with you, as you feel yourself floating back down to your body. When done, let your incense and candles burn out.

POWER WITH OTHERS

People come to visit Witches, believing them to be all-powerful. This is one of the shortcomings of people coming to see us for help. They don't understand the unfolding of time and believe that all is possible instantly. I blame Walt Disney and all his stories, popularizing the idea of majick working instantly. Because of these public perceptions, if your spell doesn't work instantly, with movie theatric special effects, then you are a phony and majick is not real. Very few people are interesting in the spirit of majick when they seek a Witch's help. They have no idea of what goes into casting a spell, or how they traditionally manifest. Well-educated, empowered Witches often have a success rate of our spells working nine out of ten times, even if the effect is delayed sometimes.

Our model of power is not power over others, but power with others, to create natural, win-win situations. Sadly we get asked to do curses, to put spells over or on people, without regard to the highest good and harming none. Part of empowerment is empowering others. A Witch doesn't think selfishly about herself only. If we are seeking balance, we are seeking to help educate and empower others. While not everyone will be a Witch, nor should they, many can benefit from the healing and empowerment of Witchcraft. If you do act selfishly or harm others, and even if you succeed in a stated goal with these methods, the universe will harm you back to restore balance. When you harm other people and the community at large, you detract from the goodness of the world. Ultimately you are not really helping yourself in the end, as we are all connected. To hurt another unnecessarily is to hurt yourself. While there are always people who will be offended at the things you do, to purposely disregard the effect you have on others is ultimately self-defeating and disempowering. Seemingly successful selfishness proves ineffective in the long run. We must depend upon other things and other people in this world if we are all to survive and be successful.

Witches use their power to help heal the Earth. Part of this work is the practical understanding of environmentalism, conservation, and stewardship. Small and large actions build up; even learning to not waste water when you wash your face or brush your teeth is an important part of this awareness. Other times, Witches put majickal actions into effect, projecting for the future of the Earth where nature is preserved and pollution is diminished. Learning to think of the fate of the entire world—not just ourselves and individual people, but all people, as well as the animals, plants, water, air and the whole environment—is a necessary stage of our evolution. How do your actions affect the entire planet?

Get Over It! Incense
2 tablespoons of witch hazel
1 tablespoon of myrrh
1 tablespoon of dragon's blood resin
6 drops of frankincense oil

This incense helps us use our self-esteem to get beyond things that bother us and focus upon our own lives, not our failures. It helps keep us balanced when we think something hasn't gone right.

Go Away Incense
1 tablespoon coffee grounds, dried
1 tablespoon of frankincense resin
1 teaspoon of High John the Conqueror root
1 teaspoon of coriander
5 bay leaves
1 pinch of mandrake

10 drops of protection oil
Pinch of dirt someplace away from your home or property

Go Away Incense helps us move out of the way of people who are harmful for us, and move those people into a better place for them as well. Coffee can help us find the right place for us. Burn the incense, and speak the name of the person you wish to remove from your life into the smoke.

Stop Gossip Incense
1 tablespoon of elderflower or elderberries
1 tablespoon of slippery elm
1 teaspoon of clove
1 teaspoon of ginger

Burn this to stop malicious talk about you and your loved ones. It helps those who would talk ill about you to focus upon their own work and issues.

Stop Gossip Spell
Burn the Stop Gossip Incense and recite the following spell:

On this day,
All gossip goes away.
What Gossip Comes to me,
I neutralize three times three.
So Shall It Be!

Win In Court Incense
1 tablespoon of bay leaf
1 tablespoon of mustard seeds
1 tablespoon of chamomile

Burn this in any legal ritual to bring success.

Win In Court Charm

Win In Court Incense

1 whole bay leaf

Black felt-tip marker

Write the words "Win" and, if possible, the judge's name upon the bay leaf, using the marker. Burn Win in Court Incense and pass the whole bay leaf in the smoke, while you recite this spell three times:

The light shall
Rise and begin
To sort that I
May win in court
So Mote It Be!

Put the bay leaf in your left shoe when you go to court, and you will be victorious!

MAJICKALLY DECORATING YOURSELF

Image is an important aspect of self-esteem and empowerment. That's not to say that it's only what's on the outside that counts, but feeling good about your self-image can start by choosing to wear the things that make you feel empowered. You are taking control over the most obvious aspect of self-image. Making changes to your outer image can produce internal shifts, just as internal shifts can change how people perceive you in the outer world, even if you do nothing different at all. Confidence changes the way we stand, walk, and talk. Putting on particular adornments can help us produce those changes inside. Those who come to Witchcraft often decorate themselves in subtle and not so subtle ways to embrace their inner Witch and flow with their majick power in every moment.

Clothing, jewelry, and make-up are effective ways to use the power of color, light, and nature to alter your energy. When well-crafted, they change the atmosphere of your own self, not only for you, but creating an atmosphere of majick for anyone who encounters you. You can create a signature, an energy that helps identify you. It all starts with intention.

Some people hold the intention of not wanting to be identified. They simply want to blend in. They want to hold no signature. While that can be useful in certain circumstances, to be able to move as if invisible, if you do it all the time, it does not lend to your self-esteem. All it can take is doing one thing different from whatever you ordinarily do. It helps empower you.

There is majick in make-up. It was originally considered a majickal art, using herbs and minerals to paint the body. I've always outlined my eyes. The way you paint your face prepares you for the world. It draws attention to you as a part of your signature. Hair is another important part of image. While I'm a natural blonde, I've died my hair black, leaving parts of it blond to assume the image of the Witch. Black draws power and light to our crown chakra. Tradition tells us that redheads are the most powerful Witches. I'm not sure I agree, but red is an empowering color. Red is the color of life force. If you want to draw on that energy in your life, dye your hair red. For others, blond is the bright and most striking color. Blonds do get a lot of attention in our society. In the end, it doesn't matter what color hair you have, as long as it empowers you, as long as you feel beautiful and stylish and confident with it.

I've always admired the Egyptian styles and culture. I know it is a deep part of me, ever since I was a little girl. Black kohl eyes, what they now simply call smudging the eyes, paired with the jet black hair empowers me. One can look at the recent run of pop stars and models to see that the fashion of outlining your eyes in black is back in style. They say the eyes are the windows to the soul, and if you want people to look at your eyes, you have to draw their attention.

Along with the hair and eyes, color majick can be invoked through the use our nails. Colored nail polish can draw to us certain forces. I use blue nail polish to bring the power of success and Jupiter to me.

While many men won't feel as comfortable with changes in hair color, or the use of majick through nails and make-up, clothing is something we all use to create our signature image. Many Witches wear black because on the physical plane, black absorbs all colors, all light, so it draws the blessings of all planets and powers to you. When you are wearing white, you are reflecting all colors and unable to absorb them. Different traditions put different emphasis on absorbing or reflecting.

If you know your astrological birth chart, what is called your natal chart, you can draw in the best colors specific to you and your own energies. Those with more advanced astrological knowledge can look to see how the current alignment of planets for the day aspects their own birth chart and choose clothing colors for the day. On my own Twitter social media account, I look at the general favorable color of the day for all and message about it. Before Twitter, I was doing it on the radio. Sometimes the color is influenced by the planetary day of the week. Other times it is based upon the planets making powerful alignments on that day. Wearing the favorable color of the day helps you and empowers you to be in alignment with the forces of that day. I get a lot of feedback from folks who feel it has really helped them.

Along with clothing, jewelry helps empower a Witch. Each aspect of jewelry is ruled by majickal forces. The metal aligns with a planetary power, as well as any stones or other colors used in the jewelry. Look at your majickal correspondences to see what influences you are inviting in your life and make sure you cleanse and charge your jewelry with your majickal intentions. In general, if you have a lot of psychic energy, you won't need to wear silver. You should instead wear more gold for physical strength and health. If you are unsure about your psychic talents, wear silver to boost them. I personally like wearing both, for both the Goddess and the God. I have a pentacle that is silver on one side and gold on the other for balance.

Jewelry doesn't have to be expensive to be effective. As long as the item reflects and refracts light, it can do majick. You don't have to go broke getting expensive stones. A raw quality stone, or a synthetic such as chromium dioxide or cubic zirconium can work too.

KINETIC TESTING

Also known as applied kinesiology, kinetic testing is a method to test your body's resistance or acceptance of a substance. In my second degree Witchcraft classes, we test students to see if silver or gold is a better metal for jewelry. To perform it, it's best to have two people—a tester and a subject. Gather up a small amount of gold jewelry and another small amount of silver jewelry. You can also so this for other metals, but start with the gold and silver. The subject being tested should close her eyes, and the tester should place one of the small piles in their receptive hand. If you are right-handed, then your left hand is receptive. The hand with the jewelry can be held to the heart or solar plexus. The dominant arm, your right if you are right-handed, should be extended outward to the side of the body, parallel with the floor. On the count of three from the tester, the subject is to hold the dominant arm out rigid, while the tester applies downward pressure on the arm. The subject attempts to resist as much as possible.

If the arm holds rigid in the first few moments, that metal is correct. If the arm immediately fails and they cannot resist, or if there is a noticeable difference, then the metal is incorrect. Repeat with the second metal, without revealing yet which metal is which. Usually most people respond strongly to one of the two metals, and weaker on the other ,though some people are balanced for both, but might find that copper shows weakness. The concept is that things that are good for us strengthen us, while things that are bad for us weaken us. It can be used for metals in jewelry, but also with herbs, vitamins, or anything else.

The results can be shocking for many people. It's a great demonstration for skeptics to the power of majick, vibration, and light. While doing a lecture in New Hampshire where many of the attendees were doctors and their wives, I was demonstrating the technique. I had a skeptic doctor come up to prove me wrong. He was strong and well-balanced, and it was hard to move his arm with either gold or silver. Bu my daughter Jodie was in the front row and gave us a pack of cigarettes. I put them in his hand, and immediately his arm fell with slight pressure. He was shocked and a little embarrassed, but he seemed more open-minded by the end of the lecture.

All other accessories and items can be used in majick, from our belts and shoes to handbags and wallets. Decide on the image that is both true to who you are and what you want to project out into the world, who you want to be. Use everything at your disposal to craft the majickal self-image that will help you transform the atmosphere of your life. In the right atmosphere, anything is possible.

THE WITCH'S ROBES

While I offer suggestions on clothing power colors for everyone based on the astrology of the day, anyone who has visited with me knows I am always wearing the long black robes of the Witch. One of the few things we know in our history is the wearing of long black robes for our people. Whether every Witch did it or not, I don't know, but I feel it's a strong connection to the ancient Witches of our past.

I made a vow to the God and Goddess so that I would always be visible in public, as when I came out as a Witch, there really were no public Witches. There were a few authors at the time, but I feel that each community's Witch should be visible and available as a part of our work in the world. Much like the Catholic priest or nun who is easily identifiable, I feel Witches need that recognition on sight. I was very naïve at the time. I didn't expect all the things that would come to me, both good and bad, from the simple decision to wear a black robe publicly. I haven't broken my vow. I wear them always. I have public robes, home robes, gardening robes, evening robes, and formal ceremonial robes. I even have a painting craft robe when I'm working on messy projects.

Many years ago I gave a lecture at the Old Town Hall on women's spirituality. Women from all walks of life came. We talked about the Goddess in history, the Goddess within, and compared the image of the Witch as priestess to other religious archetypes for women. I asked, by a show of hands, how many women in the room are nuns? Five women raised their hands. They were in jeans and simple shirts. I expressed my concern, not that there were nuns in the group. I thought that was great. I was concerned they were not proudly wearing their robes and habits, that people couldn't see them. People didn't know they were there. People need to see them to be able to go to them for help. My wearing the robes was important for the same reason. I believe you shouldn't give into pressure.

When I walk the streets of Salem, I'm both applauded and vilified because of the way I dress. Many have assumed that because I was a Witch, I was bad luck to have around and would put a curse on them. We need to break people of these stereotypes by confronting them. It's not that we couldn't do those things. Anyone can send bad energy to harm another. We consciously choose to do the opposite, to do no harm. But it's a choice. We must take responsibility, and in the end, it's not our place to judge. Many people come to the Witch because they don't feel they can trust mainstream public and religious authorities. They can come with a lot of judgments and recriminations. For those people who fear other avenues of help, we are the safer option.

While I have religious reasons for wearing the robes—to advance my work as a High Priestess of the Craft—there are also esoteric reasons to wear the Witch's robe. Most Witches and magicians wear robes for ceremony, even if they have not taken a vow to wear the robes full time. As you know, black absorbs light energy, and wearing a full-length black robe brings more majickal energy to you. It's even more powerful with a hood drawing that light to your crown chakra as well. We often accent our robes with another color—a sash or scarf representing the appropriate power color or the sign the Moon is in when performing a ritual. We also use color accents for the seasonal sabbat rituals, as each sabbat has traditional colors associated with it.

Samhain	Black and Orange
Yule	Red and Green
Imbolc	Orange, White, Pale Blue, Lavender, Magenta
Ostara	Red, White, Black, Pastels
Beltane	Green, Red, and White
Litha	Gold, Yellow, Green, Brown
Lughnassadh	Gold, Green, Gray, Black
Mabon	Orange, Bronze, Gold, Red, Green, Black, Wine, Purple

Give thought to your own majickal garb. Wearing a robe for ritual will set a tone in your mind and create the proper atmosphere to help induce a deeper majickal awareness. Like everything else, the robe is just a tool. It helps, but you are the source of your majick. Some traditions, like the Cabot Tradition, have specific ceremonial garb you obtain when you train and initiate into those traditions. Our black robes are decorated with the

Royal Stuart tartan on the left shoulder, and High Priestesses and High Priests wear a braided cord of white, red and black. Solitary and eclectic Witches can design their own majickal garb.

If you haven't taken a vow to wear majickal garb in your everyday life, the act of putting it on only for ritual trains your mind to enter into a majickal state. Just as the scent of incense and oil can be a memory trigger, the look and feel of a particular article of clothing, piece of jewelry, or other accessory can trigger a new awareness. Removing it is then a signal that your majickal experience is over and helps you ground back to normal, waking consciousness.

Seasonal Sabbat Oils

Along with seasonal clothes, Witches can attune to the power of the Turning Wheel by using sabbat oils not only in ceremonies, but also as part of their daily empowerment rituals. Make these oils near the sabbats, and they can last you for a few years, growing in power as they age. Gently warm the carrier almond oil and infuse a few pinches of the dry herbs, then add the essential oils once you have let the oil cool and strained out the solid plant matter.

Samhain Oil
4 drams of almond oil
2 drams of lavender oil

Infuse rue, tansy, rosemary, caraway, white willow bark, garlic, birch bark, and yew.

Yule Oil
4 drams of almond oil
2 drams of pine oil

Infuse cloves, cinnamon, nutmeg, pine bark, elderflower and dragon's blood.

Imbolc Oil
2 drams of almond oil
1 dram of dragon's blood infused oil
Crushed garnet
1 drop of honey
1 drop of milk

Infuse heather, wheat, rose hips, chamomile, and storax.

Ostara Oil
2 drams of almond oil
1 dram of jasmine oil
1 dram of lily of the valley oil
Pinch of eggshell
Pinch of rabbit fur

Infuse jonquil flowers, crocus flowers, sunflower seeds, clover, and willow bark.

Beltane Oil
1 dram of almond oil
2 drams of dragon's blood oil
1 dram of rue oil
½ dram of rose oil
1 clear quartz crystal
Drop of honey

Infuse oak bark, yarrow, mint, rosemary, rue, broom flowers, rose nettles, nettle, blessed thistle, and strawberry leaves.

Litha Oil
2 drams of almond oil

1 dram of lavender oil

1 dram of rose oil

1 dram of grape-seed oil

1 dram of musk oil

Pinch of sea salt

Infuse sage, mint, basil, chive, parsley, iris, heather, hyssop, rue, thyme, fennel, fern, St. John's wort, and Irish moss.

Lughnassadh Oil
1 dram of almond oil

1 dram of olive oil

2 drams of heliotrope oil

1 dram of hazelnut oil

1 dram of fir oil

1 moss agate

Blue jay feathers

Infuse nasturtium, clover, yarrow, heliotrope flowers, rose petal, comfrey root, elderflower, sunflower seeds, corn, oat, wheat, goldenrod, garlic, and pine.

Mabon Oil
2 drams of almond oil

1 dram of hazel nut oil

1 pinch of dried oak leaves

1 acorn

1 teaspoon of sea salt

2 marigold leaves

1 drop of storax oil

1 cat's eye stone

Infuse sunflowers, yarrow, marigold, mistletoe, rose hips, wheat, oats, oak, apple, rue, myrrh, and storax.

Blue Moon Oil

1 dram of almond oil

9 drops of lilac oil

5 drops of jasmine oil

Pinch of mugwort

Pinch of myrrh resin

1 moonstone

Blue lace gate, blue quartz, or aqua aura quartz

The 13th moon of the solar year is the Blue Moon, when two full Moons appear in a calendar month, which is the counting of the Witches' coven and Witches' power, but which happens only occasionally. Using this daily will bring things to you more than once in a Blue Moon.

Sacred Oak Oil

1 ounce of grape-seed oil or sunflower oil

Oak leaves (broken into pieces or dried and powdered)

One acorn

Pinch of sea salt

Simmer the oil on a low heat and then later charge in a majick circle. Use to anoint candles and other majickal objects to evoke the wisdom of the oak and the Druids. Samhain is an ideal time to both make and use Sacred Oak Oil.

Mermaid Oil #1
2 drams of hazelnut oil
1 seashell
1 pinch of seaweed
1 pinch of sea salt
1 ocean pebble

Mermaid Oil #2
2 drams of almond oil
2 drams of hazelnut oil
Large pinch of Irish moss
¼ teaspoon of sea salt
1 seashell

Bring the beauty and grace of the mermaid to you. Wear this oil and gaze into water, be it the water of a bowl, your bath, a pool, lake, or better yet, the ocean You can recite this poem to call upon the Mermaid's power as you anoint yourself with the oil.

The blue wave feathers white
her green hair lays spread on the water bright.
Mist, not meant to drink,
sprinkled with starlight falls from the link
of her shelled arm.

Mermaid Salt
2 cups of sea salt
1 tablespoon of seaweed
10 drops of Mermaid Oil (1 or 2)

Use in bath to connect to the Mermaid spirits.

Dragon's Mist Oil

1 dram of heather oil

1 dram of oak moss oil

1 dram of pine oil

3 drams of witch hazel extract

1 sprig of broom, chopped fine

1 piece of Irish moss, chopped fine

2 pinches of vervain

½ teaspoon of sea salt

Anoint yourself with the Dragon's Mist Oil and recite this poem to attune to the spiritual forces of the dragon spirit of the ancient lands. For some, mist will literally rise up and surround you, letting you truly know the dragon's presence is with you.

Wind among the bough did sigh,
and the dragon's wings did move
across the Midnight sky.
Trails of mist on Earth so long,
And the dragon's breath did prove
Merlin did not lie.

Ritual Incense

1 tablespoon of frankincense

1 tablespoon of myrrh

1 tablespoon of copal

1 tablespoon of benzoin

1 tablespoon of storax

Burn in any sacred space or when casting a majick circle.

Smudging Incense
1 tablespoon of frankincense
1 tablespoon of pine needles
1 tablespoon of garden sage
Rose twigs/stems
Apple twigs

Make a bundle with the rose and apple twigs in the center. Wrap the pine and garden sage around it, and slip the frankincense inside the greens. Wrap tight with a cotton thread, creating a bundle like a Native American sage bundle. Make sure to only burn in a flameproof vessel, dish, or shell.

Weight Loss Incense
1 tablespoon of dandelion root
1 tablespoon of parsley
1 tablespoon of chickweed

Burn this in beauty and health spells to help lose weight and come to your ideal weight and health, or you can carry it with you in a white majick bag.

Wishing Star Incense
3 tablespoons of red clover
3 tablespoons of chickweed
2 tablespoons of rose petals
1 tablespoon of St. John's wort
10 drops of lily of the valley oil
7 drops of musk oil
1 piece of silver

Burn at night when making wishes upon the stars on a spring or summer night. Speak or think your wish as the incense carries your intention upward towards the stars. Carry a portion of the incense in a black or silver bag to return it to you.

Witch's Lightning Incense
1 pinch of lightning-struck oak
1 tablespoon of pine resin
1 tablespoon of frankincense
1 tablespoon of myrrh
1 tablespoon of apple wood
Pinch of rabbit fur

Burn this is a ritual to empower any spell and speed up any majick. Makes things manifest lightning fast!

Witch's Lightning Oil
1 dram of almond oil
10 drops of myrrh oil
10 drops of sweet orange oil
5 drops of oak-moss oil
5 drops of apple oil
3 drops of pine oil
Pinch of lightning-struck oak
Pinch of wood betony
Pinch of rabbit fur
Piece of sterling silver

Use this to speed up your spells, bring about success and strength with this beautifully scented potion created with powdered oak from a tree struck by lightning.

Spell for Mystery

This spell has people see you as mysterious and powerful. Look into a mirror and recite:

May my eyes become the eyes of a cat, seeing into the darkness of people's minds.

Spell to Have Your Voice and Message Heard
Orange feathers

There are times when no one listens to us or what we have to say. Use orange feathers, for Mercury, to launch your message to make sure you will be heard. Ideally do this when the wind is blowing, or from a high spot, be it the top of a hill or the top of a building. Hold the feathers in your right hand. Speak your message, what you want someone to hear in your life. With a strong breath, blow upon the feathers and release them to the wind.

To Do Well in School
2 tablespoons of eyebright
1 tablespoons of scullcap
1 agate stone
Glass bowl

Charge the herbs and the stone and put them in a small clear glass bowl. Place the bowl on the desk or table where you do your homework. Cross your first two fingers on both hands, the index and middle fingers. Place both hands with fingers crossed over the bowl and say:

"I will retain all information."

Proceed with your homework as usual.

Seven Lights Potion
½ cup of sunflower oil
3 teaspoons of rose petals
3 drops of heliotrope oil
8 drops of sweet orange oil
8 drops of musk oil

To be used in A Spell to Take Away Sorrow, or generally when you want to bring light into your life and a good attitude into your mind.

A Spell to Take Away Sorrow
This spell will help take away sorrow and emotional pain and bring a happy future. You will need:

Black ribbon, 2 ½ feet long
White ribbon, 2 ½ feet long
1 bottle of Seven Lights Potion
2 white candles and candleholders

Sit in a special place where you can see nature outdoors. Touch the candles with the potion. Hold each candle in your hands and close your eyes. Imagine a rainbow forming in the sky over where you are. Light the candles and hold the black ribbon. Envision all your sorrow as you tie nine knots into the ribbon. Touch the knotted ribbon with the potion.

Untie the nine knots in the black ribbon; as you untie each knot, say "Sadness and sorrow go away; only happiness can stay." Once you have untied all the knots, touch the white ribbon with the Seven Lights Potion and begin to tie nine knots. As you tie the nine new knots, say these words:

Light of Love
Light of Hope
Light of Harmony

Light of Peace
Light of Laughter
Light of Happiness
Light of Care
Light of Power
Light of Moving Forward

Touch your wrist, forehead, and the back of your neck with the potion. Snuff out your candles and hang the white ribbon where you can see it every day.

Old Witch Spell
1 black candle
1 piece of parchment
Mixture of rue, rosemary, rose petals, frankincense, and myrrh
1 match
1 ash pot
1 black majick bag

On a New Moon, place these majick herbs around the candle. Light the candle and say:

Alive and well and with this glamour spell,
No one shall know my age.

Write your name upon the parchment paper and place it under your candle. Let the candle burn for five minutes. Remove the parchment paper and put the edge of the paper into the flame. Make sure you have a pot to place the burning paper into. When the paper is burned, place the ashes into the majick bag with a pinch of herbs. On the following evening, light the candle again and place some herbs around the base. Say aloud:

Beauty, glamour, and youth stay with me.
So mote it be.

Let the candle burn out. Place the herbs in your majick bag and hide it in your home. Never blow out a candle with your breath.

Whistle Up the Wind
Parchment

Pen

Feathers

Herbs

Whistle

Send your spells on the air to manifest. Meditate on a spell you wish to do, think clearly about your intentions. Write your spell on parchment or unlined paper. Carry your spell, herbs, feathers and whistle to a beach, hill, or open land, like a park. Clear your mind. Stand and face south. Blow your majick whistle three times, then wait for the wind to rise. You may repeat blowing the whistle until the wind comes. Then speak your spell out loud, and let the spell float on the wind. Let your feathers and herbs fly into the wind. Thank the wind and air. Your spell is done for the good of all, harming none.

Welsh Spell to Raise the Wind
Tie three knots in a cord or thread when there is wind. When there is a need for wind again, untie one knot.

Broken Pot Spell
Buy a clay garden pot. On the side of it, take a black marker and write whatever habit or situation you are trying to get rid of. Take it outdoors and find a place where there are large rocks. Speak out loud, reading the words about what you wish to rid yourself of. Then throw the pot into the

rocks, or if large rocks are not available, put the pot down and then throw rocks upon it to smash it. As the pot smashes, so shall your bad habit be banished. Walk away from the shards, letting them crumble over time. Don't return to that spot.

Samhain New Year Spell
Recite this majick spell on Samhain, while in your celebratory circle

I speak for all that hear me, as High Priest/ess, sovereign of my majickal time. I stand in Avalon, our sacred space. I ask the God and Goddess to grant us: A bright and prosperous New Year; wisdom of my ancestors to be used in a correct way; that my spirit be filled with gratitude for our Lord and Lady; that I heal myself, the world, and all in it great and small; that Mother Earth be healed, the air clean, the water pure, and the Earth rich. I ask for clarity and harmony for all. So mote it be!

Black Cat Spell for Fame, Fortune, and Happiness
On a Waning Moon, wear black clothing from head to toe. You will need:

1 black candle and candleholder
1 black cat or the picture of a black cat (the black cat must be your own and the cat must be loved, fed, and cared for)
Cat fur (black cat fur is ideal; brush your cat to obtain it. The fur must always come from a live, shedding, happy cat)
1 large mirror
Catnip
1 black majick bag

Find a quiet private room. Place the mirror on the floor and prop it up against the wall. On a table nearby, place your candle. Sprinkle the catnip around the base of the candleholder. Place the majick bag next to the candle. Light the candle. Hold the cat fur in your hand and get down on the floor, facing the mirror. Crawl towards the mirror like a cat stalking its prey. Make a purring sound. As you come near the mirror, say out loud:

Fame, Fortune, and Happiness is my game. All this shall I catch as I speak my name.

Crawl closer to your mirror, then reach out and touch the mirror and say:

I have the cloak of the black cat, and I will be prowling, stalking, and reaching my prey – fame, fortune, and happiness. So shall it be.

Go back to your candle. While purring, place the cat fur and cat nip in the black bag. Place the mirror in a place where you can peer into it every day to renew the spell. Carry the bag with you at all times and then bathe in the spotlight!

Transformation Spell

Another spell first revealed in *A Witch in Every Woman* is this spell of transformation. Many times we feel stuck and have difficulty transforming ourselves or our lives. While written originally to empower women, it can be adapted by male Witches who also need transformation.

Three black feathers (ideally from a crow)
Black ribbon
White ribbon
Red ribbon
White candle and candleholder

Charge your white candle for transformation and light it to illuminate your working. Take the three dark feathers and tie them together with the three ribbons. Hold the ribbons and feathers together in your left hand and recite this enchantment:

I see the beauty of my agelessness
I am walking the path of all Goddesses hold my head high.
I am Queen
I am giver of Earth, Air, Fire, and Water.
Flowers bloom at my feet.
Upon my crown are branches of trees.
The stars shine upon the leaves and sprinkle into my hair.
A ring of stars marks my way to the Land of Women.

Hang the feathers in your home to continually invite the power of transformation into your life. When you feel the time is right to release the spell, scatter the feathers and the ribbons to the winds, letting them go, yet you could frame and recite the words of the spell to ever remind you of your beauty amid transformation.

Chalice Spell
1 chalice
Spring water
1 black candle
1 white candle
1 small dish
A clipping of your hair
Athame
Altar oil
Parchment paper
Black ink and pen

This spell is to insure everlasting life. Set the altar with a black candle to the left and a white candle to the right. Place the chalice between the candles, and the small dish to the left with your hair in it. Anoint yourself with the altar oil. Write the chalice spell on parchment in black ink.

Holy chalice, you hold the divine secret of and are the source of everlasting life. You hold the waters of life. Iska-ba, bless me as I drink your majick so that my spirit lives forever and that I may sit at the table with our gods and goddesses, the ancestors and ancient ones.

Cast your circle. Pour the spring water into the chalice and charge it with the athame. Stir with the athame in the chalice three times clockwise and say:

"I stir the waters of life. Iska-ba."

Read the spell aloud after lighting the black, then white, candles. Hold the chalice up over the altar and say:

"A libation to the gods, goddesses, and ancient ones."

Drink almost all the majick spring water, but leave a small amount to pour over the clippings of your hair in the small dish. Pour the libation over the hair.

Release your circle. Keep the dish with the chalice water and your hair in a sacred place in your home. When the water has naturally evaporated, place the charged hair in a majick bag and keep it in a sacred place.

Chapter Twelve: Deity Majick

Some spells and intentions are fueled primarily by the personal power of the Witch or magician. Others rely on the vibration and light energy of their correspondences. The herbs, oils, stones, and shells help fuel the majick, by being in alignment with the intention. Other spells are deity driven. They connect us to a deity, either through a mental or spoken invitation or through appropriate majickal correspondences.

Sometimes when we refer to "deity," we mean the universe manifested as a divine intelligence. In the most basic way, Cabot Witches call this the Divine Mind. The Principle of Mentalism tells us we are all thoughts within the Divine Mind. Our basic nature is divine thought. We are created from these divine thoughts, and when we use our thoughts, we too create. The Principle of Polarity and Principle of Gender divide this Divine Mind into female and male, into what we call Goddess and God. They are the divine feminine and divine masculine of the universe. Many Witches call the Goddess our Lady, and the God our Lord, to indicate their vastness, beyond our current human understanding. They are truly the infinite powers of the universe.

Many people erroneously think that Witchcraft is focused exclusively on the feminine. While we seek to restore the respect of the divine feminine, and while many do find their way to the Witch's path through the Goddess, the importance of the God's power and spirit is equal to that of the Goddess. There is a balance of life force. We humans are a blend of male and female energies, beyond our physical gender. We must try to achieve the unique balance that is right for each of us. Balance helps us stay in harmony with ourselves, with each other, and with the universe.

Only with this balance can we ascend to higher knowledge and a better life. Only with this balance can we gain the understanding to flow with the life force on Earth. This is imperative to the survival of all beings on the planet. Many religions have tried to teach this; unfortunately, however, it seems to fall upon deaf ears.

In our myths, when the Lord and Lady are in good graces with each other, the land and all upon it live well. Tales of sacred kingship and queenship are not only about the people, but their relationship with the Goddess and God to bring blessings upon the land. The kings and queens are priests and priestesses, not unlike the pharaohs of ancient Egypt, ruling both politically and in many ways, religiously. When things are well between king and queen, things are well between Lord and Lady, and the kingdom flourishes.

Our path is the path of life and acknowledges both this female and male force in all majickal workings. Technically we can see all spells as divine, for we all a part of the Divine Mind. We all are a part of the Goddess and God. In our history, the Goddess and God change face and names with each tribe in Europe. The face of the God is seen most easily in the Green Man, but also in the Sun and in many animal forms. The face of the Goddess is seen in the planet itself, but also in the Moon, the stars, and the flowers. Localized forms of divinity, from every tree and hill, then gain names and forms as goddesses and gods.

Triple Goddess Incense
1 tablespoon of white sandalwood
1 tablespoon of red sandalwood
1 tablespoon of myrrh
1 tablespoon of jasmine flowers
1 tablespoon of red rose petals
1 tablespoon of patchouli
3 drops of myrrh oil

3 drops of jasmine oil

3 drops of rose oil

This incense is used to call in all aspects of the Goddess. If you have three specific goddess names to call upon the goddess, you can call upon them. This will help you understand the three phases of the Goddess as the maiden, mother, and crone, as well as the goddess of the sky, earth, and underworld. This incense is good for helping with any emotional problems, bringing balance, clarity, and power. If you have anxiety or stress, this Triple Goddess Incense can help you. You might be unaware of the subtle changes using this incense, but keep track of your work in the majickal journal. It is particularly powerful if you are wearing items of clothing or jewelry with the colors of white, red, and black.

Triple Goddess Altar (courtesy of Omen – Salem, MA)

Call of the Goddess Oil
1 dram of almond oil
10 drops of lotus oil
5 drops of benzoin
3 drops of rose
3 drops of pomegranate oil
1 pinch of sea salt
Small rose quartz stone
Skeleton key

Use to connect to any goddess, particularly to get the Goddess' attention. Mix the ingredients together stirring with the skeleton key. You can later use that key upon a chain or cord as a way to open the gates to the Goddess in your life and protect yourself from harm by calling upon her.

Horned God Altar (courtesy of Hex – Salem, MA)

Horned God Incense
2 tablespoons of white oak bark
2 tablespoons of patchouli leaves

1 tablespoon of black copal

1 tablespoon of myrrh

1 tablespoon of nettle

1 tablespoon of vetiver

1 teaspoon of oat straw

1 pinch of powdered antler

10 drops of patchouli oil

7 drops of vetiver oil

Burn this incense to connect with the horned and hoofed God of Witches. Through working with the Witch Father God, we learn to break any past Christian conditioning. It's important to learn that the Horned God has nothing to do with the Christian Devil. He is a god of life and death, but not of evil. He is a god of nature.

Sun God Oil

1 dram of almond oil

6 drops of sunflower oil

6 drops of corn oil

6 drops of frankincense oil

2 drops of pine oil

1 drop of lemon oil

Crushed pyrite

Piece of gold jewelry

Wear to attune to the powers of the Sun God, including success, health, and happiness. This can be an excellent oil to lift depression and bring light into your life.

To bring balance to masculine and feminine energies, you can burn both the Triple Goddess and Horned God Incenses, each in a separate thurible. You can also wear the Call to the Goddess Oil on your left wrist, and the Sun God Oil on your right wrist.

Beyond these primal expressions of God and Goddess, there are other manifestations of divinities. These are the gods of ancient pagan myth. Figures from our ancestry, and from the realm of what we now call the Fey or faeries, are recognized as gods. Figures such as Lugh from Irish myth are considered gods, and others, like Merlin and King Arthur, are now recognized as gods in many traditions. Over time, history becomes legend and is then transformed into myth, and the figures take on more godlike, mythic importance.

Some spells and rituals are done to call upon one of these specific figures, to aid in our majick, to teach us, and to heal and inspire. These gods are alive in the Otherworld, in the realm beyond the veil. They are not dead spirits, but our living ancestors from ancient times transformed to a new level. In such times, cultures lived with majick as an everyday reality. It was ingrained in everything they did, so they are often much more adept at using majickal skills and techniques than we are today. But just because they are considered gods today, it doesn't mean they always used their majick correctly in their own lives. Hints of these tales and their lives come to us through myths. They teach us not only about the gods, but important lessons about our human lives.

One can look to the tale of Rhiannon to see a tale of both deception and self-deception. Her majick was used in a very odd way. We might ask why she didn't do better, but that is very easy for us to say, looking through the distorted lens of myth from our modern era. At that time she was human too, with the same failings and problems we have today. Now when we call upon her, she can help us around areas of deception and self-deception. She knows more about deception and can aid you in getting clarity. When I fear I'm being deceived or fooling myself, I call upon Rhiannon.

Likewise we see more personal difficulty in the tale of Blodeuwedd. After her deception and betrayal, the god Gwydion, who was the uncle to Lleu, the husband she betrayed, turned her into an owl as punishment, though I'm not sure that would be punishment for me. In some ways, she got her freedom after being created and controlled by others. Even though her fate was more deserved than the punishments heaped upon Rhiannon, we can still learn from it. And we must remember that by the time a myth gets to us, we have no idea what the original form and teaching was. Sometimes we can ask the gods themselves to show us their first stories

While Rhiannon's area of expertise was perhaps born out of pain, each god does seem to have a specialty, a forte. They can not only help you by using their special talents, but also help you learn the same talents. Some gods are warriors. Some gods are wizards and Witches. Others bring love. Many bring healing. Each has an area, or several areas, of expertise. In many ways, the gods mediate that power of the divine mind and help us learn from it because they learned about it in their own lives and myths.

Being in the Otherworld, a mystical realm that exists simultaneously with our own physical universe and which makes up a part of the cosmos, gods are outside of what we know as space and time. From their vantage point, majick can work much more quickly and directly. The Otherworld is considered the template, the perfect pattern of our world. When they make changes in their world for us, corresponding changes occur in our lives. This is the strength of their majick, and one of the key reasons why gods can help you manifest powerful and long-lasting changes.

One of the primary factors to work successful deity majick is to have a relationship with the goddess or god you plan on calling. Like people, they will most likely not answer you if they don't know who you are. There is no rule that a god has to answer a human, and they are less inclined to if they don't know you. Unlike the concept of God in other religions, personal deities don't have to be there all the time. They are alive with their own existence in the Otherworld beyond us and are open to relationships with humans who honor and respect them. That honor makes them more apt to respond, but it's not guaranteed. When not communing with us, they have other things to do that are most likely beyond our linear comprehension, but they have their own lives, challenges, and tasks to attend to, just as we do.

Part of building a relationship with them is to avoid going to them only when you have a problem and then never speaking to them when things are good. If you only see them when you are in dire straits, like most people, they are not going to want to see you. A relationship is about the good times and the bad. Friends whom you spend time with are more likely to be there in tough times if you've built a relationship with them and not taken them for granted. Gods are like that too. They are not at your beck and call.

Some things you can do to develop a relationship with the gods:

Learn Their Myths

Each of the deities we know about has a story, a mythology that tells us about them. One of the best ways to honor the gods is to learn their stories, not what we think their stories are. There are a lot of books out there, some with good information and some with less-than-accurate information. When possible, go to a direct translation of the myths that have survived. If possible, learn more about the parent culture where the deity hails, especially their language. Saying a few words to a deity in their native tongue, or at least an approximation, goes a long way to connect with their energy. As you establish communication with the deity, you might find that they will share how their myth applies to your life now.

Build An Altar

Build a special altar for the deity you want to work with and get to know. Many Witches build an altar to the deity they call upon the most, to honor and respect them. Spend time regularly, if not daily, at the altar. Many statues of the gods are available today. If you can't get a statue, frame a picture of the deity. Photos of traditional statues and art are easily available online. Use candles in colors associated with the god. Use stones or crystals, particularly if you can obtain one from a land associated with that deity. Find other symbols and items that seem to resonate with the deity. They will guide you when traditional lore is not available. Say a prayer and speak to them. Don't expect the gods to respond with profound message and contact every day, but make a daily effort forge a strong link between you.

Make Offerings

While it seems superstitious to some, making offerings to the gods and spirits is a time-honored tradition. Historic records often show us what our ancestors used to honor the gods by giving it to them in ritual. Today we use offerings such as candles and incense, or we pour a glass of water, wine, beer, or liquor. Cakes and bread are common as well. These are similar to the gifts offered to the faeries. It shows that you are spending time preparing something that resonates with that deity, and the energy put into the offering helps you connect on a deeper level. Offerings should be disposed of regularly, either buried in the ground, left at the edge of nature, or respectfully thrown out if you are living in an urban environment where the other two options are not available. You should never eat or drink any items once they have been put out on the altar, for they no longer belong to you.

Make Deity Art

Making paintings, drawings, statues, chants, songs, and dances to honor the gods is an alternative form of offering. You are offering your art to connect deeper with their energies. Such art can be a mix between researching their characteristics and symbols and letting them guide your intuition, developing a personal view of that deity in the process.

Speak Their Names

To get a god's attention, speak their name three times out loud. Names are words of power. Light energy travels with sound as well as thoughts. Your voice lends power to your majick. Say the god's name three times and try to hold an image of the deity in your mind's eye. Imagine how they would look, based on ancient artwork and their stories.

Converse with the Gods

Don't go to the gods with only problems. Speak to them about your own life on a regular basis. When you do have a problem, rather than telling them what you want them to do for you, get into a meditative state and ask them for advice, and then heed that advice. Sometimes they will give you practical advice, provide a spell to do, or offer to take a problem off your hands and take care of it from their vantage point in the Otherworld.

Invoking

Invoking the deities is asking them to speak through you, or to teach and work through you. An advanced technique in the Craft is allowing a god with whom you have a strong relationship to come through you and guide your words, actions, and energy. Invocation goes beyond just asking them to help or to be present with you; it is asking them to be inside you. It is not possession, at least not in the way most people think of possession, but it is an act of deep divine communion. Good ritualists, healers, and teachers often find ways to let the gods speak through them with invocation. Their energy becomes a part of you, and you become more like them, absorbing their traits and abilities more easily. When the invocation is done, you are left changed for the better.

I hear some people say a spell is like a prayer. Well, I don't see the comparison. Witches know that they can project their own energy and majick to manifest their intention. We don't always call upon our gods and goddesses to help us. In fact, I was taught that I must try all I know psychically, physically, and majickally before I call on a god or goddess. Also our gods and goddesses do not always answer. This is why we work hard to create a relationship with a god or goddess that we relate to. Knowing the history of each god and goddess will guide you to the ones to develop a relationship with. Each deity has a story of how they dealt with their trials and tribulations.

Once you have decided the goddess and god you feel close to, make a special altar for them. Honor them with crystals, candles, potions, and their favorite things from their story and culture. Be sure to stand in front of the altar and call their name and talk to them. Do not talk only about what you need or want. Do not talk only about your troubles. Ask questions to give you more wisdom. Praise the gods so you will feel their presence. Hear their voices and be sure to write down what you hear or feel. Keep a Book of Shadows specifically for your work with the gods.

While the Witchcraft I teach is European, and the Cabot Tradition focused on the gods of the Celts, including the Irish, Welsh, Scottish, and the native British legends and myths such as those of Arthur and Camelot, you can borrow from other cultures. You must have a thorough understanding of how majick works and a respect for those cultures. If your ancestry is from another culture, it can be quite effective to call upon deities and spirits from your birth culture. As long as you do so with respect and the intention of harming none, you can borrow from other cultures. Many feel a call to the Voodou pantheon of Lwa spirits. You don't have to be Haitian or even African to call upon them once you know what you are doing. Others are attracted to the practices of Ceremonial Majick and call upon Hebraic, Latin, and Arabic spirits and god-forms.

While historically many of these cultures used majick to harm others, modern Witches today do not seek to do harm with any majick, borrowed or otherwise. This requires a familiarity with the culture, spirits, gods, symbols, and intentions of whatever spells you are adapting. The trick is finding things you can use that you are ethically comfortable using, that suit this age and time.

When you read some of the classic ancient spells of Egyptian or Ceremonial traditions, you'd think all they ever did was harm. One of the first Egyptian spells I ever researched ended up being a curse upon an enemy to live one thousand years with severe diarrhea. It's quite sad really, all that energy wasted on hurting each other. Therefore you want to make sure any spell you are borrowing is not harmful. Keep it within your own majickal culture and personal laws. As you explore, you might find other deities you resonate with, such as Diana or Adonis. Sometimes they will call out to you, and you can develop a relationship with them. One of the goddesses I have a strong relationship with outside of the Celtic pantheon is Isis.

Isis Altar (courtesy of Laurie Cabot – Salem, MA)

Isis

Isis is one of the oldest and most powerful goddesses of the ancient Egyptian religion. Sister and wife to the god Osiris, she resurrected him when he was dismembered by his brother Set. Their son Horus later succeeded his father as the ruler of Egypt. Her name means "throne," identifying her as the true source of power for the pharaohs of Egypt. The flooding of the Nile River was said to be the tears she shed for her husband. Known as Aset in the Egyptian tongue and Isis to the Greeks, she is know as the mistress of majick and the great goddess of a thousand names. While originally Egyptian, her worship was exported to many other countries and cultures. It is said her name was spoken in so many places over and over that it is now like a mantra, creating the energy of her being and blessing.

The first time I called upon Isis, I never really understood what her lesson or message for me was. I called on her and asked to be able to see her, to be able to understand her better. When I did, she appeared as a tiny speck on the screen of my mind. Then she started to move towards me. The closer she got, the bigger she got, as if she started way in the distance upon the horizon. By the time she reached me, she was so tall that I was the size of her toe. She was a giant. It was overwhelming to me. I didn't know what it meant then. Now, having a greater understanding of the gods and the universe, I have a better idea of how vast she is. Trying to understand her in such a cosmic scope was no small task. We, in our limited human existence, are growing towards the Divine Mind, just as the gods are. There is so much more beyond our understanding, an infinity beyond all that we know. The gods have grown beyond our human understanding, and they can help us in this transition as they too grow.

Isis teaches me that we can go beyond our human limitations and become one with universal light, because universal light is present all around us. While I think we can be one with the universe while incarnated, we certainly can go even further when we shed our mortal body and have learned enough to end our incarnation cycle all together. As an ancient Egyptian ancestral power, Isis—like the ancient adepts and avatars in other cultures—is able to manifest whatever she needs, making herself the mistress of majick. Miracles of resurrection and miraculous conceptions are attributed to her work.

Our current humanity doesn't have the framework to understand and recognize this level of majick. We have been programmed to believe it is impossible. But once we understand and truly embed the process within ourselves, we'll be able to manifest whatever we need. While I understand the concepts, it doesn't mean I've fully integrated these lessons into my life and can use it anytime. I'm here, like all of us, on a journey, limited by our time, place, and consciousness. Ancestors like Isis knew this kind of majick, living it truly in all areas of life. And contact with them helps us regain it.

Isis Oil

1 dram of almond oil

10 drops of rose oil

5 drops of amber oil

5 drops of styrax oil

3 drops of lotus oil

Isis herself guided me in the making of this potion, helping me find one of the oldest fixatives known in ancient Egyptian perfumes, styrax (benzoin). When you wear this potion, you attune to this powerful goddess and bring her to your side.

Danu

Danu is the mother goddess of the Irish gods, who are known as the Tuatha de Danu, or Children of Danu. Danu has very few myths written about her, seemingly like a more cosmic goddess, though some relate her to the planet Earth, the waters of the ocean, or the vast cosmic ocean. Scholars believe her name might originate with the Danube River. She has a cognate in Welsh mythology with the Welsh mother goddess Don.

We see her as the Great Mother, along with the god Dagda as the Father God. She can be called upon for help with any and all forms of majick, being a source of all things. Many petition spells can call upon the Goddess and God in general, or Danu and Dagda.

Danu Altar (courtesy of Omen – Salem, MA)

Danu Oil Potion
1 dram of almond oil
12 drops of dragon's blood
10 drops of rose oil
1 small clear quartz crystal
Rose petals

Mix rose petals and a small quartz crystal in the vial of mixed oils, all charged in honor of Danu.

Danu Unicorn Horn Protection

2 gold candles
1 chalice
Spring water
Holly sprig
Holly crown
Gold ring
Danu Oil
Spiral wand of wood or horn
Athame
Picture of a unicorn
Parchment
Pen

King Edward's "Unicorn" horn is still in Buckingham Palace in England. He used it to prevent himself from being poisoned. We know the unicorn to be the protector of women. The holly tree thorns are a symbol of the unicorn, and it is said owning a sprig of horned holly is the same as owning a unicorn horn.

Write this spell on parchment paper:

Danu Mother Goddess
We bring the flame and the Holly to our sacred circle.
The flame to return the Sun to Mother Earth
and the Holly to protect the Earth.
The blessed Unicorn resides in the Holy that lies on our altar.
The cauldron flame brings the power and return of the Sun's life,
giving majick to all that attend this ritual.
At this time, I hold the Golden Ring

and wear the Crown of the Holly King.
The Golden Ring is the ring of the Sun, never ending. Never undone.
Danu, Mother of our kind, the Sidhe
Conjure the majick so that we will be revived and renewed in our majick
power to tend the Earth and our needs.
We are your faerie children.
Bless us, Mother, from darkness and fear,
once again with the turning of the year.
So shall it be.

Cast your circle with a wand. Anoint yourself and the candles with Danu Oil. Light the gold candles. Place the unicorn picture at the base of the candles. Place the chalice with water in the center of the altar. Charge the waters of life with the athame. Place the holly crown upon your head and put the gold ring on the altar where you can reach it. Position the spell where you can read it on the altar, while holding the ring and holly.

Read the spell, holding the holly sprig and ring. Snuff the candles. Hold the chalice up over the altar and say, "A libation to Danu, the unicorn, and the Holly King." Place your thumb into the blessed waters and to your lips three times and say, "Iska-ba, the waters of life." Release your circle.

Put the gold ring on your finger and place the holly sprig in your home. Keep the crown in a sacred place in your home. You can relight the candles to extend the spell, but be sure to not blow out the candles with your breath. Snuff them out each time you are done until you've burned them all the way.

Dagda

Dagda is one of the most powerful of the Tuatha de Danu, known as the All Father and protector of the tribe of gods. He is described as a giant, with a club that kills its targets with the first strike and resurrects them with the second. His harp changes the seasons with its music, and his majick cauldron never goes empty.

Dagda Spell
1 brown candle
Small iron cauldron
Assortment of grain and vegetable seeds

The Dagda's cauldron is the vessel of abundance, manifesting food. On the Waxing Moon, light your candle in honor of the Dagda. Take the cauldron and cleanse and charge it. Charge the seeds for abundance and food in your household. Fill the cauldron with the seeds and make a talisman for the household to make sure no one goes hungry in the home.

The Morrighan
The Morrighan is an Irish triple goddess, known as a goddess of war, sexuality, and sorcery. Her three aspects are referred to in various texts as Anu, Badb, and Macha, or the goddesses Badb, Macha and Nemain. She has many totems, but is particularly associated with crows and ravens, so black feathers make an appropriate symbol to connect with her. I also associate the poisonous plant henbane with her.

This triple goddess helps teach you about strategy and overcoming your enemies. Your enemies can be your circumstances, specific people, and most importantly, things within you that are self-defeating. She transforms us through the battle and can teach us powerful majick to be better warriors in our daily lives.

Morrighan Altar (courtesy of Omen – Salem, MA)

Macha

One of the most well-known and beloved manifestations of the triple goddess Morrighan, Macha is also associated with crows and ravens, as well as horses. In particular, her myths are about the proper treatment of people, women in particular, and she punishes those who have harmed women or gone against the natural laws of the land. When she took physical form in Ireland and was pregnant with twins, due to the boasting of her husband about her majickal nature, she was forced by the King of Ulster to race against his fastest horses. If she failed, her husband would die. He boasted that his wife was swifter than the king's horses, knowing her majickal nature. She won the race, gave birth to twins upon the spot, and cursed the men of Ulster to feel the pains of childbirth in their time of greatest need. Later, in the era of the hero Cú Cuchulain, the curse came true and the men could not fight due to the pain.

Macha, along with the Morrighan, is called upon in majick to bring evil-doers to justice, to stop those who commit crimes. When we call upon her, we do not tell her what we want to happen, but we simply ask her for justice. Black feathers correspond to this majick.

Macha Philter

1 tablespoon of pine needles
1 tablespoon of rosemary
1 tablespoon of sunflower petals
1 tablespoon of sage
1 tablespoon of apple leaves
2 dried mushrooms
3 drops of Sacred Oak Oil

Use this majickal philter to honor the goddess Macha and her totem, the crow. At Samhain, you can carry this philter with you in an orange or black majick bag as a charm to deepen your relationship with her.

Macha Oil

2 drams of grape-seed oil

1 dram of hemlock cone oil

1 dram of pine oil

2 dried mushrooms

1 crow feather

Do not put this oil upon your skin, but use it to anoint talismans and objects to attune to Macha.

Macha Samhain Blessings

I place into this chalice
the power and majick to bring
prosperity and health to all who do good works,
And for those people who do not do good...
They shall receive what they deserve.
The Goddess Macha shall drink this spell
And protect the goodness that shall manifest
for all who hear my voice.
Our new year brings blessings to mind, body, and spirit
to those who heal themselves and the world.
So Shall it be!

Lugh/Lleu

This Celtic God of light has many manifestations. To the Irish, he is Lugh Lámhfhada, Lugh of the Long Arm. His spear is associated with the power of light and lightning and is one of the four sacred gifts of the Irish gods, along with the sword, stone, and cauldron. In his journey he became skilled in many different talents and entered the home of the gods, the realm of Tara, due to his many skills. Eventually he became high king of the Tuatha de Dannan. Though more of a lightning god, in the modern neopagan revival, he has become associated more and more not just with light, but also with the Sun and with the harvest gathering. The first harvest sabbat, known in the Irish traditions as Lughnassadh, actually celebrates the funeral feast of his foster mother, not the king himself. She, as a giantess, cleared all of Ireland of field-stones, so the fields could be planted, leading to the actual harvest.

Though pronounced a bit differently in old Welsh, his cognate across the Irish Sea is Lleu Llaw Gyffes, meaning "Bright One with the Skillful Hand (or Strong Hand)". While Lugh is usually pronounced like the modern name Lou, many say Lleu the same way, though technically it is more akin to the world "lay" but with the tip of your tongue to the back of your top teeth, almost spitting out of both sides of your mouth.

His tale is found in the myth cycle of *The Mabinogi*, detailing his unusual birth by the goddess Arianrhod, along with his brother Dylan the sea god. He was adopted by his uncle Gwydion and cursed three times by his mother. Gwydion helps him overcome the three curses, though the last curse, to never have a wife from any of the races currently upon the Earth, resulted in a newly formed, yet ultimately treacherous bride in the flower maiden Blodeuwedd. Gwydion comes to his rescue again and curses Blodeuwedd, turning her into an owl, a bird shunned by the other birds and feared by many.

While both Lugh and Lleu derive from an older Proto-Celtic deity (whose name, meaning, and origin Celtic scholars still debate), today we call upon him as the god of light. We use open flame to call him. He can help us gain personal and political power and use our power for the good of our community. Based upon Lleu's marriage, we tend to never call upon him for love or marriage spells and advice. While many don't like to hear the word "politics" or any of its many forms, it plays a vital role in our communications and community building with all the people around us, whether we like it or not. In any culture, you need to be aware of the political arena you live in; otherwise you are just a pawn in the game.

Lugh/Lleu helps us make the most appropriate choices to use our power wisely.

Cauldron Fire of Lugh
Small iron cauldron with lid (used to burn incense)
High-proof rubbing alcohol
Epsom salts
3 drops of frankincense essential oil
3 drops of orange essential oil
3 drops of ginger essential oil
3 drops of rosemary essential oil

One of the ways we honor Lugh in our sabbat rituals, particularly at Lughnassadh, is to have a small iron cauldron with a lid. The small cauldrons used for incense are ideal, for the larger the cauldron, the taller the flame, and this can be dangerous indoors. We usually put the smaller cauldron inside of a larger cauldron, to contain the smaller cauldron in case there is any spill or accident.

Fill that cauldron halfway with Epsom salts, or if you have no Epsom salts, table salt will work. Cover the salt and fill the rest of the cauldron three-fourths full with high-proof rubbing alcohol. You can add drops of solar or fire-oriented essential oils. If you don't have the oils, you can use a pinch of the herbs themselves, but it will not be as aromatic. Cover the cauldron until you are ready to use it.

When you invoke Lugh to your circle of celebration, start by uncovering the small cauldron. Light a match and toss it into the small cauldron, setting the alcohol on fire. It will burn, releasing the scent of the oils, while the flame dances around the cauldron mouth. It's a dramatic, powerful, and effective way to work with this god of light. Feel his presence in the light and fire.

Brid/Bridget

Bridget, known as Brid in the ancient days and transformed into St. Bridget by the Christians, was actually the daughter of the Dagda. Myth suggests that he had three daughters, all of them named Bridget. She is a triple goddess, but she is not the maiden, mother, and crone. She is the goddess of poetry, the goddess of healing, and the goddess of smith-craft. Her priestesses kept the fires of her holy shrine going in Kildare, and now the nuns there keep the fires burning. Many healing wells are also sacred to her.

To me, she is one of the most maiden-like goddesses. She is not a mother figure. Call upon her for healing. She is a great herbalist, a woman of the home and the hearth fire. She can help you heal and support your family through great cooking. She can help with any issues around family and home. Flame and all fire are her allies, along with sacred waters. To build her an altar, make or obtain a Bridget's cross of straw or wheat. Surround it with three red candles. That can draw her attention and energy to you.

Brid's Oil

2 drams of almond oil or olive oil

20 drops of sage oil

10 drops of dragon's blood oil

1 crushed garnet

Use this oil for the three areas sacred to Brid—writing, healing, and creativity. If you are a writer, poet or musician, she can help you. If you are practicing any of the healing arts, from the majickal to the more medical, call upon Brid. If you want to manifest an idea into form, like the blacksmith shaping metal, use this oil and call upon Brid.

Brid Altar (courtesy of Omen – Salem, MA)

Protection Candle Spell with the Goddess Brid

3 black candles

3 brass candleholders

3 heaping tablespoons of vervain

Get into your majickal space. Pick up each candle and repeat out loud:

By the power of the Triple Goddess Brid, this candle will bring the light to protect my home, family, friends, animals, coven and me. So mote it be!

Place the three candles in their candleholders and put them close together. Sprinkle the vervain in three interlocking rings around each of the candles. Light the candles, and sit for a moment staring into the candle flame.

Three Rings

Envision the Goddess Brid placing three rings of light around all that you want to protect. Release your circle. Let the candles burn. Never blow out the candle. Use a snuffer or a spoon to extinguish the candles as needed, and relight and burn again until the candles are gone.

Brid Career Spell

I call the power of Brid to bring to me (name yourself) the knowledge that I need to have for a career that is successful. I ask to be granted the awareness, ability and enthusiasm to bring my career to fruition and success. I ask this for the good of all. So shall it be!

Recite this spell upon the Waxing Moon to change your career path. Brid, the goddess of many skills, will help you.

Bridget's Psychic Fire Circle

Bridget's sacred fire can inspire you, warm you, and energize you. Her priestesses are known as "keepers of the flame" and with this ritual, you can share in the fire majick of this sacred goddess.

Red stone – ruby or garnet

3 black candles

3 white candles

3 red candles

Create a circle of candles around you, alternating colors white, red and black. Light the candles in a clockwise direction and sit in the center with your red stone. The candles and their fire represent the goddess herself, and the stone, her psychic flame. Get into a meditative state and hold the stone to your solar plexus, just under the rib cage. Feel the flame feeding the stone, and the stone bringing the energy of Bridget into your body. Recite the spell of Bridget:

This is my psychic flame within.
This will spur the fire of my psychic abilities.
I carry this stone as a symbol of your strength within me.
I am the Keeper of Flame.
Every time I relight a candle I rekindle my psychic ability.
I know my psychic sense guides me, protects me, heals me, and showers me
with love and self esteem.
I always use my psychic ability for the good of all people.
As a Witch, I never do harm or return harm.
I neutralize and bind all evil thoughts, actions, and deeds
And let the outcome be the Force of the Great Goddess Bridget.

Extinguish the candles, but you can relight them in the circle, or one by one, to rekindle the flame. Carry the stone close to you and touch it to rekindle the psychic flame within you.

Nuada

Nuada was the elder king of the Irish Tuatha de Dannan, ruling before Lugh. He carried the sacred sword, one of the four gifts of the Tuatha, along with the spear, stone, and cauldron. He ruled wisely during many troubled times, but due to the laws of the gods, the king must be perfect. He lost a hand in battle and had to step down as king for a time. Later he returned when his hand was replaced with a majickal silver one. Then his majickal physicians replaced it with a flesh and blood hand.

Much like Lugh, Nuada is a great leader, knowing when to act and when to step aside to let others act. He can teach you these valuable lessons. To call him, use the image of a silver hand. If you have a charm with an arm or fist, that will help call him, particularly if it is made from silver or can be coated in silver. Many charms, particularly from the Portuguese traditions, use the image of a fist, and you can find such charms to connect to Nuada. You can also paint a glove silver as a token offering to him. Silver candles can be placed upon his altar.

Ceridwen

Ceridwen is the goddess who is the mother of all bards, for she gave majickal birth to the bard Taliesin. In her tale, she had two children, a beautiful daughter named Creirwy and an equally ugly son named Afagddu. Ceridwen is a sorceress, and wanting to help her son with majick, she decided to brew the potion of inspiration, known as *greal*, in her cauldron. She makes a servant boy named Gwion stir, while an old blind man tends the fire. The potion is remarkably complex and requires many ingredients, gathered at specific times. She travels gaining all the ingredients, leaving the two in the hut to tend to the brew. When almost done, the cauldron overheats, and three drops come out of the cauldron, burning Gwion on the thumb, which he sucks, drinking in all the potion's power. He instantly knows all the stories, songs, and spells; he also knows that Ceridwen will kill him for this mistake. He escapes, but she chases him through a fantastic journey of a variety of animal shapes. Finally, he hides, transforming into a grain of wheat, and she, as a black hen, eats him. Majickally she is pregnant with his seed and gives birth to him nine months later. That new child becomes the bard Taliesin.

Ceridwen is a great Witch, a sorceress without peer. She can teach us the art of shapeshifting, herbal majick, and the mysteries of the cauldron. While I think all gods can shapeshift, she excels at it. She also keeps the cauldron of knowledge and inspiration, so she can grant inspiration to you. One has to be careful with Ceridwen. She can be tricky, and she had a temper on her. Some call upon her to help with issues of anger, since she knows them so well. She also helps us find the beauty in what appears to others as ugliness.

Ceridwen Altar (courtesy of Omen – Salem, MA)

On an altar of Ceridwen, a cauldron is the best item. Her totemic animals are the sow, as well as the four she shape-shifted into: a greyhound, an otter, an eagle, and a black hen. Any symbols or images of these animals are also helpful to connect to her.

Ceridwen Oil
2 drams of almond oil
20 drops of hazelnut oil
Hazelnut shell
5 grains of wheat

Using this potion to gain inspiration from the Goddess cauldron and to have the enchantress guide you on the path.

Ceridwen and Celi Spell
Silver candle
Gold candle
Sun potion
Moon potion
Gold and silver jewelry

Speak this spell outdoors at daybreak, sunset, midnight, and at the rising of the Moon. Anoint the silver candle with the Moon potion and the gold candle with the Sun potion. Wear a balance of gold and silver jewelry.

Ceridwen, Goddess, Creatrix,
All the phases of the Moon have come
And still more to come.
By the light of the Moon,
I shall dance, sing and praise your power.
Celi, God of Light and the rising and setting of the Sun.

Ceridwen, Celi, give us the light of the day and night.
May we see the sunrise and set upon our greatness,
And may the Moon wax and wane
Upon our fulfillment of a prosperous life.
So Shall it be!

Celi is another name for the god of the Sun and the light, sometimes paired with Ceridwen. Few myths survive associated with this God, though his name is found in the controversial work known as *The Barddas of Iolo Morganwg.* You can commune with Celi by calling upon him while watching the Sun rise, particularly if you are doing waxing style majick with him, and you can call upon him to diminish things when the Sun is setting.

Taliesin

From the tale of Ceridwen, the young boy who was Gwion is put into a leather satchel by the enchantress and cast upon the waters to float away. He was found on Beltane by a man fishing for salmon, who opens the sack and finds the bright-eyed Gwion, explaining how his new name's meaning of "bright and shining brow" possibly referred to his third eye. The child begins to speak eloquently, claiming "bright and shining brow," or Taliesin, as his name. He goes on to be a great bard and magician, later serving in the court of King Arthur and a companion to Merlin.

Taliesin helps us with poetry, storytelling, and majick through verse and song. He is the consummate bard. I called upon him once and asked to hear one of his spells from ages ago. I got into a very deep trance, placing a bull's horn filled with aromatic herbs upon my chest as I laid down in the bed. In vision I saw him on the edge of the woods by a meadow. He came towards me, repeating stanza after stanza of poem. It was a love spell. I was mesmerized by it as he got closer and closer. I told myself I had to wake up and remember what he was saying, but he entranced me. When I woke, this is what I remembered:

I am the soft breeze that moves your golden hair
I am the cool wind that brings color to your face.
I am the spindle that weaves the clothes you wear.
I am the fingers that sew the trim of lace
that crown your beauty,
that warm your heart.
I am the songbird that sings your love,
that sounds your beauty,
and beats your heart.
I am the moonlight that showers your sleep,
that deepens your beauty,
that rests your heart.
I am the starlight that illumines your dreams.
Love is all that is seems.

This spell came directly from Taliesin. He was giving me what I asked for, but I didn't realize that it was really a love poem for me. As a child, I did have golden hair. It was a very profound experience that I didn't truly understand until it was over, but I share with you what I was able to record.

He can teach you just about any kind of spell you need, not just love spells. Be sure to have a pen and paper ready to record it when you awaken.

Musical instruments, particularly anything Celtic, would be sacred to him when building an altar. His totems from his journey are the rabbit, salmon, bird, and wheat. He was also responsible for the death of two horses, as the remaining potion of greal became poison, cracked the cauldron, and poisoned the water and two horses coincidently or karmically belonging to the family of Elphin, the man who later rescues him. Because of this, he can also be associated with horses.

Arianrhod

Arianrhod is the Welsh goddess of the starry sky. Though some consider her pale whiteness to indicate she is a Moon goddess as well, her castle is said to be revolving in the stars. Her brother is Gwydion the magician, and their uncle is the magician king Math. She gives birth to two unusual sons, Dylan and Lleu. Her actions seem unusual for most of us humans, as she immediately lets Dylan jump into the sea, and she abandons Lleu to her brother, who raises him. It is implied that their birth casts aspersions on her virginity, and perhaps Gwydion is the father, and this is why she wants nothing to do with them, and in particular, makes Lleu's life difficult. She curses him three times. First to never have a name unless she names him, and she vows not to name him. Gwydion tricks her into naming him using a majickal disguise. She curses him to never bear arms unless she arms him, and vows to never arm him. Not being able to bear arms as a man in Celtic society was quite a curse. Again, Gwydion tricks her with a disguise. She then curses him to never have a wife of any of the races upon the Earth. No easy out with that curse, so Gwydion and Math create a bride for him from flowers. While it's easy to see the cursing Witch in her tale, many think it is really a tale of initiation and transformation. Similar to the Morrighan, she tests those who are hers, whether children, lovers, or students. There are later tales of the bard Taliesin being imprisoned in her revolving castle, but learning to see everything from the starry vantage point. Arianrhod can be the harsh teacher, but she can empower you to conquer the adversities of life and find creative solutions to your problems. She helps connect you to the heavens and stars, and their special celestial majick.

Arianrhod Oil

2 drams of almond oil

½ teaspoon of dragon's blood resin

1 dram of apple oil

2 drops of storax oil

1 pinch of mugwort

Use this oil to connect with the Goddess Arianrhod. She can help us see the lesson in the harsh situations of our lives. She can also help us connect to the Moon and starry realms.

Arianrhod Spell

3 paper stars

Arianrhod Oil

Three stars are a symbol of the sky goddess Arianrhod. Before you cast this spell, take one star in your hands and call upon the goddess to help you make up with your lover. Anoint it with the oil. Place that star in your pocket or purse. Hold the second star in your hand, anoint it with oil, and ask the goddess to stay with you until the spell is done. Place this star in your home where you sleep. On a starry night, hold the third star in your hands, anoint it with oil, and speak this spell out loud.

Falling star
in streaking path
bring your light
to destroy all wrath.
Shed your light,
send your beam
bring my love
this pleasant dream.
For the good of all, harming none.

As you throw the star into the night sky, envision your lover dreaming of you both together and happily loving each other.

Rhiannon

Rhiannon is a Welsh goddess whose tale is found in the Mabinogion. She is the mother of Pryderi. His name means "trouble," and much of her story includes the troubles she gets into and how she gets out of these problems. Her totems are birds and horses. While she is best known through the Fleetwood Mac song sung by Stevie Nicks, the song has little to do with her actual myths. I find her a figure for empowerment, as she can help us avoid making the same kinds of mistakes she did.

Rhiannon Bath and Potion Ritual

Use this when you want to call upon the powers of Rhiannon and ask for the blessings to learn from her past so that you are not forced to repeat it. It is an excellent spell to help remove chaos or unnecessary and unwanted drama in your life. I first wrote about this spell in my book, *The Witch in Every Woman*.

1 chalice – silver or glass

1 cup of apple juice

3 powdered hazelnuts

1 piece of clean oak bark or 1 teaspoon of powdered oak bark

Before creating this potion, it is essential to take a cleansing bath. Make a majickal bath of sea salt, dulce (seaweed), lavender flowers, and hazelnut powder. You can place them in a linen bag to prevent them from clogging your drain. Light white and lavender candles anointed with the potion as a part of your bath ritual. This is a time to let go of all suffering and doubt. Know that you deserve the best that life has to offer, and your life has no need of manipulation, deceit, lies, dangers, plots, and ill words.

You neutralize them and let them go. As you get into the bath, call upon Rhiannon:

O gracious lady Rhiannon
You have suffered so that I may not,
You have endured the pain and sorrow that no woman deserves
With your majickal expertise and power
Your most beautiful spirit shelters me from deceit.

Once your cleansing bath and attunement to Rhiannon is complete, go and make your potion to work with the energy of Rhiannon further. Charge all the ingredients in Rhiannon's name and put it on a low simmer. At the first sign of bubbles boiling within the juice, turn off the heat and let it cool. If your oak bark is one piece, you can keep it as a charm to continue your work with Rhiannon. Pour the strained potion into your chalice. Call her name three times, thinking about the kind of help and blessing you are seeking from her. Thank her for empowering you, and drink the potion with long, slow sips, savoring every drop. Whatever remains is an offering to be poured out upon the green Earth.

Merlin

Merlin, or Myrrdin in Welsh, is the magician of King Arthur's court in the days of Camelot. He is also considered a Druid and wizard, a walker between the worlds connecting mortals with the realm of Avalon and the Lady of the Lake. While seen as a scholarly wizard today, his older myths portray him more like a prophet or bard, and a wild man of the woods. Quite possibly there was more than one Merlin. Legend tells us he moved the stones of Stonehenge from Ireland to where they stand in England today. He gave prophecies about the world from his glass tower and was ultimately imprisoned away, some say in a cave, others a tree or in his tower itself.

I have a strong relationship with Merlin. When I call upon him, I feel he's always interested. Unlike some of the other gods and spirits, he is more apt to communicate with you often. He does like to talk, and he's most definitely a trickster. If you are a majickal person, study the art and science of majick; he is eager to teach. He'll put you through the paces and give you tricks you don't realize. He gives you things you need but don't ask for, and often don't want. You have to be careful when you work with Merlin, as you never know what you are getting.

When you say his name to call upon him, you can mind travel to his cave, Merlin's Cave, in Tintagel, England. It's one of the places very much connected to his energy. I see him less the wizard and more a man of the forest, dressed in animal furs. At times he has the brown hair of the woodsman, and other times the white hair of the wise man. He can shift his shape. Upon his altar, or in spells to call him, use things from the forest, particularly apple and oak. Wands of wood are great links to the magician. The triskele symbol is also a good way to connect to his energy. Mushrooms are a great offering for him, as his totem is the pig as well as the falcon. Use the titles Wild Man, Wise Man, Man of the Forest. While he likes to talk, you often have to flatter him to bring him forward. And then you have to be ready for him. It's best to have a question in mind, or to ask him to teach you something specific once you have him. He doesn't like to be summoned for frivolous reasons, and if you do, he might not come again, though that is true of most gods and spirits. He is an excellent teacher of potions and mixtures and can give your formulas to use. Automatic writing with him is an excellent way to obtain a formula or spell. Ask him to write one for you. I've had great success with it. He can also help you develop your abilities as a seer and psychic. He is a guardian of sacred places and all of nature. He helps me learn many things.

Triskele

Merlin Incense
2 tablespoons of white oak bark
3 crushed acorns or 1 teaspoon of acorn flour
1 tablespoon of oak leaves
Peel of 1 dried apple
5 drops of musk oil
5 drops of fir oil

Burn to evoke the power of majick and the mysteries of Merlin. This scent helps you increase your psychic ability and majickal strength.

Merlin Oil
1 dram of hazelnut oil
1 dram of fir oil
1 pebble from a location sacred to Merlin, such as Tintagel (Merlin's Cave) or Dinas Emrys (Merlin's First Prophecy)
1 sprig of oak, lightning-struck if possible

Wear this oil to connect with the magician of Camelot, as well as to add power to your majickal workings.

Merlin Samhain Honoring Ritual
The chill of the October wind sometimes changes overnight to hot and summer-like, a time known as Indian Summer. I prefer the chill and the falling of colored leaves and the departure of the Sun. Most doorways are decorated with mums, pumpkins, and cornstalks, making way for the October night of majick. During this time the veil between our world and the world of our ancestors is open. On Witches' New Year, Witches of the Cabot Tradition dress in costumes depicting our spell for the coming year. We dress as we want to become, wearing this costume so all the community can project what you wish to become. They can see you in that role.

Then comes the harvest. In older times, it was a meat harvest. Today it is pumpkin pie, baked apples, applesauce, and apple butter, and the remaining last vegetables of summer. Even Dunkin' Donuts coffee shops serve pumpkin-flavored coffee and pumpkin muffins. It seems modern society often has a deep memory of what the fall brings.

In modern times New Year is January 1st—most people dress up in their finest clothes and celebrate together, showing their wealthy by dining out and drinking champagne, actually casting the same spell we Witches do on Samhain.

We do not display violent or horror-provoking costumes. We do, however, often honor our ancestors and loved ones past by wearing a skull motif. The skull is the House of our Spirit, not a symbol of horror.

More and more this fall, Merlin has been in my mind and of course synchronicity comes into play as Christopher Penczak brings to me a stone from Merlin's Land in Wales. The book, *The Quest for Merlin,* by Nikolai Tolstoy has been given to me and know it is a third sign that Merlin is opening the door to his world. I would be foolish if I did not take these messages to heart.

So I started my communication with Merlin. Here is an honoring spell I have done to let him know the respect and awe I have for the Man of the Woods. This wild man has the craft of prophecy. My spell is to ask Merlin to lend his psychic gift to me.

Oak wand

3 apples

1 boar's tooth (on a string or in a pouch to wear around your neck)

Pinch of wolf's hair

Stag antlers

Apple juice

Chalice

Bird feathers

Stand outdoors near a wooded area. Fill your chalice with apple juice and set it on the ground. Wear the boar's tooth around your neck. Place the apples and wolf fur around your chalice. Place the antlers in front of the chalice. Hold the feathers in your left hand. Hold your wand in your right hand. Cast a circle around yourself and your majickal tools.

Blow the feathers into the air and say aloud:

Good People of the Old Ones
Come to this Marked Place
And help me with my majick.

Pick up the chalice and say:

Merlin, this it to honor you.
This drink of the sacred apple shall bring your voice to mind.
Grant me that voice of prophecy and the wisdom of the wild woods.
Show to me the power of the stag.
I offer these sacred apples to feed your spirit.
You are no longer touched by the hostile king of the Christians
You are safe now.

Drink the apple juice. Save a little and pour it onto the Earth. Hold the antlers over your head and say:

Merlin, you are blessed to me.
Please guide me.
Make me wise.

Thank the Fae for helping you. Blessed be.

Release your circle. Leave the apples near a wooded area for the animals to eat. Keep the wolf fur in a majick bag and carry it with you.

King Arthur

King Arthur is both a figure in our mythic history and a sacrificial god. His myth teaches us about the desire for peace and harmony between diverging worlds, although he didn't always go about it in the right way to fulfill his stated intentions. For a brief time, Camelot was considered a paradise, but his actions ultimately undid that paradise. The way we look at the Arthurian myth today, as a bridge time between the Pagan and Christian eras, could have functioned as a manifestation to bring harmony to both sides. Instead, we lost the kingdom and experienced the wasteland.

Today, in your majick, Arthur helps you get the life you want, in your relationships, surroundings, and homes, but in a way that doesn't require you to give up yourself for it. Many people, particularly women, give themselves up for a happy home, even though they are not truly happy. The sacrifice is not working, even though they are doing all the things they feel they should be doing to make it work. Since Arthur's sacrifice did not work, he can help you understand when you need to sacrifice, and when you do not. He can help you not make the mistakes he did in his relationships, friendships, and kingdom.

Guinevere

Guinevere is such a difficult character for us to understand. Many portray her as the failed human queen, giving in to her passion for Lancelot, and like Eve from the Old Testament, becoming a scapegoat for all the bad things that happened afterwards. Others see her as a priestess, mediating the blessings of the Goddess of the land to a failed king who could not provide a son. The most esoteric way to view Guinevere is that she was a Faery queen embodied in the world, and she appeared to not have a lot of concern for human issues because, she was in fact, not human. Her presence in the world was necessary, but she would often get kidnapped by other kings. To her, it did not matter which king she was wed to, as long as there was a union between the human worlds and the Faery worlds. She didn't care about human battles. While some say she went to a nunnery, we know they were not quite established then in this historic context, so we know she withdrew herself and went back to Faery, because the old ways were not honored and the majick was not being used properly. There were no nunneries in 500 AD, so we know many of the modern tales of her are simply not true.

Today Guinevere helps us with our choices, such as when to stay and when to go. She helps us not get caught up in someone else's drama or battles. It is their journey, not ours. We have our own journeys to attend. Anything green can be used to call upon her—green stones, green candles and the green Earth.

Lady of the Lake

The Lady of the Lake is the more overt Faery Woman of the Arthurian myths. She resides upon the Isle of Avalon, beyond the mists. Sometimes called Morgan, Viviane, or Nimue, her character was divided into several personas in later retellings of the story. We know her simply as the Lady of the Lake. She is an enchantress, a healer, and a teacher of majick. She was the original possessor, and perhaps even creator, of the sword Excalibur. She grants the light of Excalibur, a central part of the Cabot Tradition's mythos of initiation. We carry the light of Excalibur in our swords today. She can grant the power of light and truth to those willing to carry the power of the sword. Her symbols are water lilies, apples, and the crane.

Excalibur Incense

1 tablespoon of willow bark

1 tablespoon of meadowsweet

1 teaspoon of dried water lily

1 teaspoon of powdered cattail

Pinch of crushed snail shell
Small sword replica like a letter opener or picture of a sword

Use the small sword to charge the incense, projecting your light energy through the sword into the mixture.

Lady of the Lake Equality Spell

Burn the Excalibur Incense while reciting this spell to be a change-maker in your community.

Lady of the Lake, grant to me (name yourself) the courage to see the truth of my life and to understand the truth when it is told to me. Help me to lift the spirit sword to protect my rights and the rights of all Witches, for the good of all. So shall it be!

Morgan Le Fey Oil

3 drams of almond oil
20 drops of apple oil
20 drops of amber oil
10 drops of rose oil
1 black feather
1 jet stone, small
1 garnet, small
1 quartz crystal, small

Charge on the Waxing moon for five days and on the Waning Moon for five days. Tie the bottle with a black ribbon charged in the Sun and tie a black feather with the ribbon onto the bottle.

Morgan Le Fey Prosperity Spell

2 black candles
1 red candle
Morgan Le Fey Oil

Anoint yourself and the three candles with the Morgan Le Fey Oil. Light the candles. Recite this spell and let the candles burn down until they go out.

Morgan Le Fey, Queen of Faeries, Ancestor of Mine, Radiant Being, Goddess of the Moon.

You who are known for your majickal power, I ask of you to bring your power to help me to secure financial balance to sustain me and my family. We are ever in your service. I work hard to achieve my goals, and I shall work my majick along with yours.

Teach me wisdom, clarity, compassion, and healing arts. May your voice be heard in the world today and always.

I bring an apple and a black crow feather as gifts to honor you.

So shall it be!

Sir Gawain

One of the most famous of the Knights of the Round Table, Sir Gawain's initiatory adventure is told in the tale of *Sir Gawain the Green Knight.* He is the nephew of King Arthur, described as one of the most compassionate and aware of the knights. He is loyal and true, a defender of women, and in some tales, his strength waxes and wanes with the Sun, making him a solar figure. He is also knowledgeable about healing wounds with herbs.

We call upon Gawain as a protector and teacher. He can use the majick of his shield and sword to defend, but he also tells us where we are failing in our own life. His advice is not just in our majickal practice, but also in all areas of our lives—family, job, and personal development. He can guide you to the right actions to balance your life and help you to avoid the battles that are unnecessary. You don't always need to battle forces that are against you. You can often simply neutralize them and move around them. He teaches many of the same lessons as the warrior goddesses and gods, but often in a more gentle way. He'll warn you of harmful relationships, people harming your identity and image, as well as more direct danger. He can help you avoid all these things and confront them when necessary. He's a great ally for those in business, helping you navigate your boss and co-workers while developing your career. He can protect your ideas so no one in your office steals them and unfairly takes credit for them. Any associations with knights—armor, swords, shields and other weapons—can be used to call him or honor him on a altar.

Queen Medb

Queen Medb is the Queen of Connacht in the Ulster myth cycle of Irish mythology, a sworn enemy of the King of Ulster, her former husband Conchobar mac Nessa. She is most famous for starting the Cattle Raid of Cooley, stealing Ulster's prize bull. She wanted wealth equal to her husband and tried to buy or borrow the bull to increase her wealth. Her messengers successfully negotiated for the bull, but made a drunken mistake and said that if Conchobar had not agreed, Medb's forces would have taken the bull. Upon hearing this insult, Conchobar's vassals' refused her representative, starting the raid and subsequent battles. This allowed the curse of Macha to be fulfilled upon the men of Ulster, giving Medb an association with Macha and the Morrighan through it. When told by a Druid that her son named Maine would kill her enemy Conchobar, and she had no son named Maine, she renamed them all with Maine in their name. The prophecy was fulfilled when one of her sons killed Conchobar, but the wrong Conchobar. Medb had many husbands and many more lovers, and she required her husband to have no jealousy. Queen Mab is a faery in Shakespeare's Romeo & Juliet with loose associations to Queen Medb.

I call upon Medb for protection and glamour. She is all about the Queen's persona and personality, helping you with majick involving how others perceive you. She likes to be queen, to have the power and prestige, and in your work together, she can help you feel like a queen. She can help guide you to what to wear, what to do, and how to act to exert this influence and esteem in your life. I tend to call upon her on the night of Venus, or in the hour of Venus for people who use planetary timing. Medb is an excellent strategist, helping you understand and outwit your enemies. She can help you dredge up powerful emotions to fuel your majick. She can help fuel your persona as royalty. With her help, you might start a spell with "I am Queen. I demand..." and fill in the blank with your desire. The world will respond to the command of a queen who knows her power. Her symbols are the scepter, the crown, and the royal globe.

Boudica

Boudica is the legendary queen of the Celtic Iceni tribe. She led her people in an uprising against the Romans as they occupied the British Isles. Her husband was an ally of the Romans, and when he died, his kingdom was left to his daughters, but the Romans ignored his wishes and annexed his realm. Boudica herself was flogged by the Romans, while her daughters were raped. She then led a rebellion against the Romans so fierce that it gave Emperor Nero pause to rethink their occupation, though eventually the Romans overcame their concern, and Boudica committed suicide rather than be captured again. In her majick, she invoked the goddess Andraste, a goddess of victory, and used a hare before battle as a form of divination, releasing it and seeing where it went to guide her decisions. Hares in all their forms are good talismans for Witches. Rabbit fur, symbols, charms, and pictures are all helpful.

I feel a great kinship with Boudica, considering her an ancestor and ally. She had two daughters, just as I have two daughters. She did everything she could to protect them, and still they were hurt. If you have children, you have a strong desire to protect them, but you have to pick your battles with other people. Today, she is an excellent ally when experiencing divorce, to make sure the needs of the children are met by both parents. She will help you decide what is right for your children, even if it is not your first choice. She also teaches you different ways to overcome your enemies, often by silent majick rather than direct confrontation. Her direct confrontation did not work for her, so now she teaches new ways. The hare is her most powerful symbol. Pictures or carvings of the hare can be used in her honor.

Scathach

Scathach is the teacher of great warriors, including Cú Cuchulain . Though spelled Scathach, it is usually pronounced Scar, like a scar upon your face or body. Her home is in Scotland, and in particular, the Isle of Skye. She trains the Irish warrior, and later her daughter, Uathach, is wed to him. Before that, Scathach herself might have been a lover of Cú Cuchulain.

She is a martial arts master and a master of all weapons and strategy. Today, she can be called upon to give you not only martial ability, but mental weapons, the mental sword that uses communication to confront. She helps us with our intellectual battles as well as our physical ones. If you are in the military or law enforcement, she will help you. She will teach all things in the ways of war, metaphorical and literal, to be an honorable and effective warrior. To her, the silent battle within is the most important one, something understood by all true warriors. She helps you make decisions in your life as a warrior.

I envision her standing upon a mound of skulls with her red hair blowing in the breeze. A sword is in one hand and a spear in the other, a red cape upon her shoulder as she stands ready. If I call upon her, which is rare in my practice, she comes within an inch of my face. She can take over your space. Once you acknowledge her and ask for her help, she will back off and speak to you. Expect her to come fast and close to you. She can literally knock you back on your heels. Celtic weapons such as the sword and spear can be used to honor her, as well as the color red and the image of the skull.

Spell for Binding a Deity's Influence

While we strive to have strong relationships with our gods, we might find at certain times that we do not want their influence in a particular situation or relationship. This spell will essentially "bottle" or bind a god's or goddess' energy in a specific situation. Use it with care, as often the gods will have knowledge and influence beyond our own understanding, and sometimes the thing we do not want is exactly the thing we need. Such bindings can close a door to future blessings, but at other times, it can be quite necessary.

This spell is a variation of the traditional Bottle Spell, to bind the harm and influence from a specific individual.

2 tablespoons of frankincense

2 tablespoons of myrrh

4 tablespoons of iron powder

4 tablespoons of sea salt

4 tablespoons of orris root (or oak-moss)

1 white candle

1 bottle with a cork or lid to seal it

1 black pen or black ink and feather pen

Black thread

Parchment paper

A symbol, stone, or herb associated with the deity

Write upon your parchment paper in black ink:

I neutralize the power of (name deity) to do any harm to me or anyone in my life (if you have specific concerns, name the people you wish to protect). I ask this be correct and for the good of all. So mote it be.

Light the white candle. Ideally do this spell inside a majick circle when the moon is waning. Mix the dry ingredients (plants, iron, and salt) in a bowl. Recite the spell and roll the parchment up and tie it with the black thread. Place the parchment, along with the symbol of the deity, into the bottle. Fill the bottle with the dry ingredients. Seal the jar. Drip the white wax counterclockwise over the lid to seal it. Bury the bottle somewhere it will not be open, broken, or disturbed. If you feel you need to undo the spell, simply open or break the bottle to release the enchantment.

Libation for Thanking a Deity

Just as there are moments when we might want to remove a deity's influence, there are often times we wish to truly thank a deity for a blessing, even if we did not know it at the time. You might find that you got what you asked for, and other times you will find you received what you needed instead. Both are reasons to give thanks.

Fill a special chalice or cup with a drink you feel would be suitable for the deity you wish to thank—wine, ale, mead or even simply honey dissolved in spring water. If you can find something from the deity's culture or country, all the better. Go to a special place outside and create a libation altar to the deity. You can place three smaller stones of equal height in a triangle and then a flat stone on top, or use a wooden tree stump.

Cast a circle. Honor the four directions and the spirits of those directions. Charge the cup and the drink within the cup. Hold the cup at the level of your eye and say:

I drink this cup for love, health, and prosperity, and I honor the powers that watch over me.

Take a swallow. Thank the gods and goddesses specifically, naming what you are thanking them for doing in your life. Then say:

I offer this sacred drink to (name the deity).

Take a second swallow and say:

And to all the gods and goddesses of the universe.

Take a third swallow of the offering drink. Then pour the remainder out onto the altar or another special place where it will not be trampled upon by others. Take a few moments just being thankful. Then honor the spirits of the directions, release the circle, and bid all spirits farewell.

Dedication to the Goddesses and Gods

3 feet of black cord

1 black ink bottle

1 black crow feather quill

Herbal mixture of rose petals, lovage root, pine needles

Parchment paper

Altar potion

Bowl

1 black majick bag

One night before a Full Moon, place herbs in a bowl, pour the potion into the herbs, and write this spell in black ink on parchment paper using a quill pen:

I dedicate my life to Witchcraft and the Ancient Ones and the Celtic Gods and Goddesses. I shall never use my majick to harm anyone or anything. I will obey the Threefold Law. By my will, so Mote it Be!

Tie nine knots into the cord. Each knot you tie, call on the Goddess and God:

Goddess and God, hear my voice and hear my vow.

Recite the spell out loud to the Goddess and God. Raise your hands to the sky, then touch the ground. Carry the herbs and parchment in the majick bag continuously for nine days and nine nights. Have the cord of nine knots in a sacred place where you will see it every day.

While this spell is written to the Goddess and God overall, you can adapt it to dedicate yourself to a specific deity if you feel so called by that deity and are prepared to make a commitment.

Chapter Thirteen: Borrowed Majick

Once you know the laws of majick and understand your own path, you can start to explore other forms of majick in the world. With an understanding of what is appropriate and right, what you should and should not do in terms of intention, you can borrow majick from any other culture, as long as its nature is suitable to you and your ways. Good Witches should educate themselves on the majick and spells of other cultures as much as possible. We want to understand the world we live in better, and due to the lack of majick in our own culture, learn how other majickal cultures lived and used these powers. But you must be careful. Many ancient practices were devoid of the ethics and concerns of today's Witches. Some things you shouldn't borrow as they are too damaging or harmful, to other and to yourself. Once you have an understanding of your own ways and the laws of nature, and have learned to be careful in all that you do, you can then successfully borrow majick and enhance your own practice.

Part of working with borrowed majick is learning not only about the culture and time where the majick comes from, but learning about and honoring their gods. The gods of other cultures are intimately tied into their majick. Just like the deity spells in the previous chapter, you can work with the deities of other cultures and honor them, as long as you know what you are doing and are respectful.

You can often find gods in other cultures who are similar to gods you are already familiar with. While it is important not to confuse the gods as the same, as they developed relationships with different cultures and in different systems of majick, a comparison can help you understand them better, particularly if ancient people did comparisons with them. The Greeks were famous for translating their understanding of Egyptian deities into their more familiar Greek pantheon, creating the connection we commonly see between the Egyptian Tehuti, who is actually more well-known by his Greek name Thoth, and the Greek god Hermes, giving rise to the later figure Hermes Trismegistus. The Romans, when invading the Celtic territories of Gaul, did the same as the Greeks. They conflated many Celtic deities with what they believed were their Roman counterparts, not even using their Gaulish names. They described Mercury as the most popular Gaulish god, whom we today believe to be Lugus, the Gaulish counterpart to Lugh and Lleu, though the Gaulish god Teutates was also linked to Mercury.

Ancient majickal cultures have established a long-standing tradition of borrowing majick from each other. One of the best examples can be found in the later Egyptian period, in the Greco-Roman-Egyptian majick found in what today is known as the Greek Magical Papyri, or PGM amongst scholars. There, spells of all sort are found mixing Greek, Roman, Egyptian, Jewish, Babylonian, and Christian names, words, practices, and images. While the PGM is a collection of notes and shorthand spells, so we don't know who was practicing what exactly, it does go a long way to show we are not the first people to borrow majick and we'll not be the last.

EGYPTIAN MAJICK

The first majick outside of the Celtic traditions I learned about was Egyptian. I am fascinated by the majick of the Egyptians. There whole culture is so mystical and mysterious. I know I'm deeply connected to that time and place.

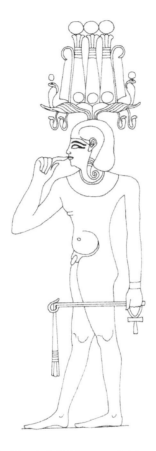

"Heka" by A.F. F. Mariette (1821-1881)

To the Egyptians majick was called Heka, and was both a force and a deity. Heka means to empower the part of the soul known as the Ka. The Ka makes majick. The hieroglyph of Heka is two flax stalks twisted together, which is often interpreted as two serpents, like the caduceus of the Greeks, with two outstretched arms. Heka as a deity worked with Hu, the divine spoken word, and Sia, the deity of omniscience, creating a divine triad.

Egyptian majick usually consisted of the power of spoken words and symbols, calling upon the deities, the use of rituals, and the powers of plants and stones. Majick was a part of life in ancient Egypt, with a wide variety of spells and charms for every possible facet of life, used from the Pharaoh's family to the commoners. To the Egyptians, the gods were known as the Neteru (singular Neter) or forces of nature. Many today interpret that as they were manifestations of a single force, what we today might call the Divine Mind. Neter is associated with the world of nature, for they were manifestations of the spirits of nature on both local and cosmic scales. Daily life—and all majick—was deeply entwined with the Neteru.

Isis was considered the master magician of the Egyptians and a powerful Neter. While in her story, she did not start as the most powerful goddess, she soon became one of the most powerful. As the creator god, Ra, Neter of the Sun, became older and more enfeebled, he would drool and spit as he talked. Though nothing but his own power could harm him, Isis took a bit of his spittle, and mixed it with the clay, forming a serpent. She breathed life into the serpent and set it free, so that it returned to Ra and bit him. He was hysterical with pain and could not heal the wound. Many tried to help him, but if the most powerful god could not heal himself, what chance did they have? Isis offered her services, but asked for his true name, the part of the soul known as the Ren. He gave her many of his titles and outer names, but she knew them not to be true. He hesitated to give his true name, because to have the true name of something is to have its power. He didn't want to lose his power. But she would not help without it. She covered him with her green cloak so no one else could hear, and he whispered his name, and it went into her being. With this name and power, she easily cured him from the snakebite. Soon after, he began to withdraw from the direct affairs of the world, going beyond to the celestial realm. Isis and Osiris, and then later their son Horus, took a more direct role over the Earth until they too withdrew, and the god was embodied in the Pharaoh. The story of Isis and Ra shows the importance of names and words in majick power.

Along with Isis, other popular Egyptian gods many Witches look to include Osiris, Horus, Thoth, Anubis, Bast, and Hathor. Osiris is the brother and husband of Isis, considered an Egyptian "Green Man" as he is the manifestation of vegetation after the flooding of the Nile. While considered a mythic first king or pharaoh bringing civilization to humanity in Egypt, esoterically, everyone is considered to become Osiris upon death. Their son, Horus, takes his place after Osiris is killed by Set, but only after a long dispute with Set.

Thoth is depicted with the head of an Ibis bird or a baboon. He is the scribe of the gods, the keeper of majick, knowledge, and wisdom. He is also the keeper of the Moon calendar. He is a great aid to those who are scholars, researchers, writers, or scientists. One version of the Egyptian creation myth starts with Thoth as the creator. Thoth is usually compared with Hermes in the Greek traditions, as they share many of the same attributes.

Anubis is the jackal-headed god of Egypt. Like the falcon-headed Horus, many Egyptian gods were depicted with animal heads to show their characteristics and essences better. Anubis deals with the pathways to the realm of the dead and back, though he is not specifically a god of the dead like his uncle Osiris. He is a god of journey and transformation. He can guide you and keep you safe when you are doing spiritual work between the worlds. If you are worried about your psychic abilities getting out of control, or bringing up the wrong information at the wrong time, call upon Anubis to help you. You will be helped. He is particularly helpful when doing any crossing over work with the dying, or mediumship work, helping people communicate with their ancestors.

Bast is the cat-headed goddess of Egypt, while Hathor is the cow-headed goddess. Today many of their attributes get mixed. The understanding of the Egyptian people regarding the gods changed over time, and at one point, Bast, or Bastet, was very strongly associated with the lion-headed goddess Sekhmet, though over time, the two became more and more separate. Sekhmet is considered to be a more destructive goddess. She was associated with protective ointments and perfumes. Call upon her to deepen your connection to a feline familiar, and to protect and heal cats of all kinds.

Bast

Hathor is sometimes depicted with cow horns or a cow's head. She is the goddess of all good things—happiness, joy, fertility, music, dance, drink, and femininity. She is associated with the dead in the Western lands, helping them on their journey. Various myths depict her as the mother or daughter of Ra, and she is considered to be his eye. Likewise she is either the wife of Horus or his mother, linking her to Isis. She is also linked with Sekhmet, and in one tale, transforms into the lion-headed goddess in a bloodthirsty rage. Otherwise she is generally considered a benign goddess to bring blessings and good things. She helps mothers with children and particularly blesses women giving birth.

Be careful when researching Egyptian majick, as many of the spells are curses and have ill intent. In a time and land where majick was so powerful, those who felt they did not have legal justice often resorted to majickal justice and punished those who had wronged them through spellcraft. Make sure you understand the spell you are borrowing fully, that the translation can be trusted. Don't do something you don't fully understand.

Egyptian Sun Incense
1 tablespoon of frankincense
1 tablespoon of calendula
1 tablespoon of chamomile
1 tablespoon of benzoin
1 teaspoon of cornmeal
9 drops of Isis Oil
Gold glitter

Burn this incense in Egyptian rituals to connect to the mystery and majick of any of the Egyptian gods and goddesses. It can be used during the wintertime for those of us in areas without a lot of sunlight. It helps stave off depression and makes you feel empowered.

Winged Sun Disk

Egyptian Sun Disk

The Egyptian Sun disk is a symbol of divinity and royalty, with variations found in Mesopotamia and Persia and later in Masonic and alchemical symbolism. The winged disk is often flanked with serpents. A variation, the horned sun disk, is found upon the crowns of many Egyptian gods. Isis has become greatly associated with the horned sun disk. A sun disk with a serpent was placed over Ra's head. Use this symbol to invoke divine power and royal authority.

Eye of Horus

The Eye of Horus

I love the Eye of Horus. It's a great protective talisman, as well as a symbol of royal power and good health. It was worn by many to manifest the power of the divine god Horus, as he is a solar god and avenging figure. In his myth, his eye is gouged out by his uncle Set, the dark god of destruction, and restored by either Hathor or Thoth. Due to his solar associations, the symbol was sometimes known as the Eye of Ra, though its other name—Wadjet—is associated with the snake goddess. Commercial charms of the eye in the form of jewelry are available and worn by many Witches for protection, like a pentacle. It can also be drawn on paper or traced in the air to activate its power and blessing.

Ankh

Ankh

The ankh, also known as the looped cross, is the symbol of life and reincarnation. Egyptian gods are seen carrying it like a key, as it is sometimes known as the Key of Life and is depicted on temple and tomb walls. I believe it is the symbol for return, as the cross is the human being and the loop shows that our soul comes back to a human life. It's been used in the Goth culture as a symbol of vampires, as in the same sense, a return to life, but I don't think that is how the ancient Egyptians saw it. Today many Witches wear it as a talisman to honor and invoke the wisdom and mystery of ancient Egypt and the Egyptian gods. We use the ankh in the symbol for the Cabot-Kent Hermetic Temple. It is a knot with the Ankh looped through it. You can use it in any spell to add life force to your work.

Cabot-Kent Hermetic Temple

Other ways you can use Egyptian symbols is to research hieroglyphs and their meanings and put together symbols based upon your intention. While the classic work of Sir Walter Budge is not always in favor with modern Egyptologists and Egyptian practitioners, I've found his work very helpful in researching Egyptian majick and symbols that I can use.

GREEK AND ROMAN MAJICK

Like the Egyptians, Greeks and Romans saw ritual as a part of their daily life. It was done both at home and in temple settings, by ordinary people and by professionals hired to perform rituals, sacrifices, and special spells. Respected philosophers studied it and practiced it, and beyond the orthodox rituals of the public, the Greco-Roman world supported various mystery schools, secret organizations to educate you on the nature of the soul, death, and reincarnation. Just like today, wands, herbs, symbols, and special words were a part of the practice of majick. It can be difficult to tell majick apart from religious worship and honoring the gods, and in many cases, there was no difference. Just like in other cultures, people would call upon the gods to aid them in their lives, asking the gods for things, making offerings, and through that process, often casting spells.

"Sulis Minerva" at the Roman Baths in Bath, England

One of my favorite Roman goddesses is Minerva. Known as Athena to the Greeks, she was adopted in Britain, linking her with the goddess Sulis at what later become the Roman Baths of England. Together, they became known as the goddess Sulis Minerva. Many sacred sites were devoted to her in England, after the Romans ruled. She is the controller of winds, guiding sailors and seamen, though she has the wisdom to do anything you ask. If I wanted to know if a spell had been successfully cast and granted, I called upon Minerva to tell me. I like verification of my work, and she would send a wind to confirm at that moment that my spell was successful.

Jupiter is the Roman father of the Gods. His Greek name is Zeus, and he is the sky father and lord of lightning and storms. To the ancients, storms also brought life, as the rains were thought to bring seeds to earth to make things grow; therefore storm gods are gods of life and light, not just darkness or potential destruction. They have two sides, just as we all do. As the All Father, Zeus can do anything, but his particular sphere of influence was the sky, as well as good health, wealth, and blessings. His planet, in astrological majick, is one of good luck and fortune. If you call upon Zeus to help you with a spell, you might expect to see a lightning bolt or two soon after, to let you know your wishes were heard. It doesn't necessarily mean he agrees and will do it, as Zeus has his own will, but it will let you know it was heard.

Hecate is the Greek dark goddess of Witchcraft. She is a guide to those who are lost and in the dark, and a mistress of majick, herbs, and spells. She is an ancient goddess, far older than the Olympian gods. While Zeus and his brothers Poseidon and Hades each split creation—getting the sky, sea and underworld respectively—she was so honored and feared that she was given a portion of each of the three realms, so that is one of the ways she is considered a triple goddess. She is often depicted with three faces, and sometimes those faces are of a snake, a horse, or a dog.

To me, Hecate is like the goddess Macha. She will go after wrong-doers, even without your prompting. When there is a chaotic situation, you might simply want her to take a look at the situation and help if she wills it. You can't ask her to do something specific. She must make up her own mind, just like Macha, and through her, the Morrighan, too. Hecate's symbol, her wheel, is an excellent symbol to use to call upon her. She can help teach you majick and the secrets of the underworld. When I've called upon her, I like to go to the crossroads. I go right out to the crossroads at the Salem common.

Hecate

One night, at midnight, I pulled up to the Common, not too far from the famous Hawthorne Hotel, and the ballroom lights were on. I brought an apple and some herbs for a spell with Hecate. I cast the spell and called upon Hecate. I put the spell down in the center of the crossroads with the apple on top of it, and I sprinkled the herbs over it all. I was in my full robe and cape, for it was cold. Everyone in the ballroom stopped and looked at me through the window. I didn't realize it. I thought for certain at midnight, there would not be people around. I didn't realize with the lights on that people were still in the ballroom enjoying a late night soiree. So when you visit with Hecate, you don't have to be so public about it. Any crossroads will do. You don't want to stand in a busy thoroughfare. Go someplace a little less conspicuous.

Hecate's Wheel

JUDEO-CHRISTIAN MAJICK

For several centuries, the majickal practices in Europe were continued by those Judeo-Christian magicians working with the grimoire traditions. While certainly folk majick traditions were being practiced among the townsfolk even while Paganism was being suppressed by the church, those who practiced majick in the Jewish and Christian traditions secretly thrived, documenting their workings in majickal books known as grimoires. The grimoire traditions went on to influence the majickal revivals of England, particularly the Golden Dawn and later, the work of Gerald Gardner, Alex Sanders, and many of the Wiccan founders that influence Witchcraft today.

Grimoires called the Keys of Solomon were highly influential in the more ceremonial styles of Wicca. Divided into *The Key of Solomon*, sometimes incorrectly referred to as the Greater Key, a book dating back to the 15th Century Renaissance, and *The Lesser Key of Solomon*, also known as *The Lemegeton*, dating back to the 17th century. Though both are attributed to the Hebrew King Solomon, famous for building the temple with the aid of spirits, djinn or demons, they most likely have nothing to do with the historic Solomon. At that time, it was quite common to attribute a book to a historic or mythic figure, such as all of the texts authored by Hermes or all the poetry attributed to Taliesin. Solomon is an interesting figure to Witches. While he was a Hebrew King, many myths surround his relationship with the Queen of Sheba, giving rise to the image of the two of them as ancient priest and priestess of a Middle Eastern Pagan goddess.

In the books are various symbols and sigils used in majick to draw the influence of the planets, angels, and what are called goetic spirits, sometimes thought to be demons. The symbols in the keys are very interesting to me. A friend made me a set of all the classic Key of Solomon "pentacles" in appropriate metals. He made them all at the right time, on the correct planetary day, in the correct planetary hour. He knew what he was doing, wearing the appropriate colors, in the correct ritual space, with the appropriate words of blessing. The set is extremely powerful, and all were well put together in terms of majickal correspondences, even though they are anchored in the letters, number sequences, and sigils of the Hebrew majickal tradition. Most of them have a strong "kick" to them, being used for so long by so many people, but there are only a few that I would personally use in my majick. Many have attributes that are hurtful and out of synch with my own sense of balance and goodness. Many have Hebrew writing, and it is good to only use the ones that you understand completely. Foreign words can have multiple meanings. I do like to use the seals of Venus. Venus is well aspected in my astrological birth chart. I often place the copper Pentacle of Venus on my altar to draw its blessings into my life. I put it upon the right side of my altar, to draw in the light of Venus, to give me more Venusian strength, power, and blessings.

The Third Pentacle of Venus
"This, if it be only shown unto any person, serveth to attract love."

If you are going to use the seals of Solomon, you must really study the entire grimoire and understand what forces you are calling upon before you use them. Today, many Witches choose the appropriate seal for their intention, and either retrace it on appropriate colored paper, or even photocopy the seals onto colored parchment paper. They can be rolled up and place in charm bags. Candles can be burned on top of them to activate their power with the candle spell. They can be placed behind frames or under mats to subtly bring their influence.

Another Solomon mythic influence that made its way into Masonic tradition, which in turn influenced the modern Witchcraft revival, is the use of the two pillars. Two pillars stood at the gate of Solomon's legendary temple, named Jachin on the right and Boaz on the left, which is how they are depicted in the Rider-Waite Tarot cards. In Biblical lore, they are bronze pillars decorated with the images of pomegranates and lilies at the top. Jachin means strengthen, while Boaz means strong, though modern magicians look at the two pillars much like pillars of the Tree of Life. The Tree of Life has three pillars—Severity in black on the left, Mercy in white on the right, and Equilibrium in gray in the center. The High Priestess depicts Boaz and Jachin in black and white, with the letters B and J, and the priestess guard a gate where the middle pillar might be found. Beyond her is a garden of pomegranates, not only a Biblical symbol, but also one found in the goddess traditions of ancient Greece. Some believe the gate is not an opening, but a printed tapestry of pomegranates, hiding the holy of holies, the inner mystery of the temple.

Today we look at them as balance, what is known in the east as Yin and Yang, the white and black polarity. We study this concept in the Hermetic Principle of Polarity. Together, they teach about balance. Many Witches put a black candle on the left side of their altar and a white candle on the right side. The black is for the Goddess, the Moon, the night, and this dark pillar of severity. The white is for the God, the Sun, the day, and for this white pillar of mercy. The dark candle draws in light for our majick, while the white candle transmits, sending out light for our majick. They create not only balance, but also a way station to receive and transmit our intentions. When you want to create balance in your life, charge a black and a white candle for this intention and let them burn. If one burns slower than the other, it can tell you which polarity is out of balance.

The High Priestess

The Jewish Tree of Life, the symbol summarizing the Jewish Kabalistic teachings, is another popular image that has been borrowed by many. It became a part of Christian teachings and was absorbed into alchemy and the grimoire traditions. The Golden Dawn, starting as an 18th century occult group in England, used the Tree of Life as its primary symbol and based all its teachings and systems around it. Today, many Witches look at the Tree of Life as another way to understand the universe and the various astrological and spiritual correspondences in Western majick.

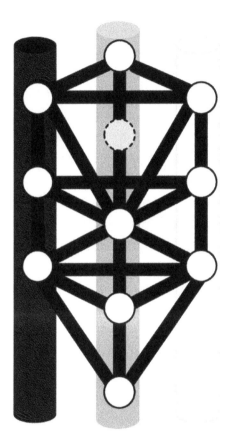

The Tree of Life

One of the most popular aspects of Judeo-Christian majick today is angelic majick. These very powerful entities are found in Judeo-Christian lore and philosophy and might have roots in other Middle Eastern cultural majick, but their dominant expressions as we understand them today come from the Judeo-Christian traditions. They are first mentioned under the names we are familiar with in the Old Testament. Despite popular ideas of very gentle, loving, and gender-neutral beings, Old Testament stories show a different side of angels. They are only human when they specifically take the form of a "man," but otherwise are often monstrous with many eyes, wings, hooves, and horns, mixing animal attributes. They are referenced in Christian myth and expanded upon in the Hebrew Kabalistic studies. Each of the ten spheres on the Tree of Life —properly called sephiroth, which means "emanation"—is ruled by an archangel and an order of angels under the command of the archangel. The seven archangels associated with seven planets are the most popular, but different texts list a different group of archangels, depending on the teaching.

The Golden Dawn focused upon four main archangels, for the four elements and four directions. They called their quarters using these angels, and they have later been referred to in Witchcraft and Wicca as the Watchtowers, borrowing another term from ceremonial magicians. Many Witches first learn to cast a circle with the archangels. In the Cabot Tradition, we orient the elements with earth in the north, fire in the east, air in the south, and water in the west, but angelic traditions usually switch air and fire, based upon the Golden Dawn's teachings.

Angels, unlike the gods, are traditionally commanded to do your will in the world. It's part of the majickal culture of this tradition. I personally don't agree with that. I don't like being a commanding magician. I like to have partnership with the gods. But if you choose to work with the angels, you can use their sigils much like the seals of Solomon in your spellcraft, putting the angels to work for you. It is very important to make sure the angel you choose matches the intention you have. Angels only have influence in their sphere of power. If you make the wrong choice, the majick won't work.

Archangel	Element	Planet	Influence
Raphael	Air	Mercury/Sun	Communication, Writing, Travel, Healing
Michael	Fire	Sun/Mercury	Strength, Healing, Protection, Light
Gabriel	Water	Moon	Psychic Messages, Childbirth, Dreams, Family
Uriel	Earth	Uranus	Manifestation, Death, Knowledge
Haniel/Anael	—	Venus	Love, Beauty, Herbs, Passion, Nature
Samael/Khamael	—	Mars	Protection, Destruction, Removal, Surgery
Tzadkiel/Sachiel	—	Jupiter	Good luck, Fortune, Prosperity, Guidance
Tzafkiel/Cassiel	—	Saturn	Mysteries, Binding, Spirituality, Meditation

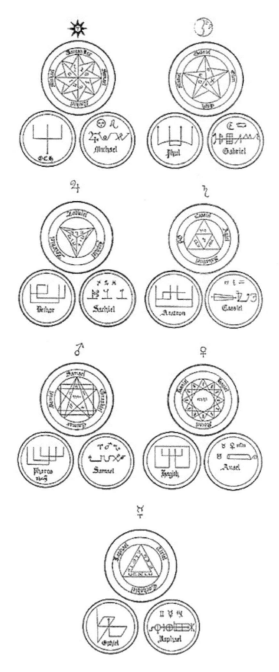

Seals of the Seven Archangels

While Uriel is considered an important archangel in the elemental circle, he is not considered one of the seven planetary archangels. Today we associate him with either Uranus or Pluto.

The very first time I used the four archangels in a circle, I had a very powerful experience. I had moved to Chestnut Street in Salem, Massachusetts, and created a majick circle on the floor of my home, "borrowing" the four archangels for the circle. In that circle I did a spell to "teach Witchcraft as a science to the world." With Uriel I could feel a wind coming from behind me, almost pushing me while I was in the circle. Two weeks later, I was in a club in Rhode Island, watching a friend perform and having no idea why I was there. I ended up meeting the director of continuing education at Welsley High School, and he invited me to teach Witchcraft as a Science in their continuing education program. That soon led to me teaching Witchcraft as a Science at Salem State College, and the rest is history!

NORSE MAJICK

Of all the borrowed majick in the world, I feel most comfortable with the Norse and variously related Teutonic traditions. They are most like my Celtic ancestors, being northern European tribes. With the Saxon invasions of England, similar traditions mixed with the British, influencing Witchcraft as we know it. Scholars today sometimes believe the Roman references to the Teutons were really referring to Celtic people rather than the Germanic, though it's hard to tell the differences between the people in these ancient sources. Today, Teutonic refers to the Germanic people, including those we know as the Norwegians, Swedes, Austrians, Dutch, Danes, Germans, and even English. In modern Paganism, we tend to think of the majickal traditions as Norse or Anglo-Saxon. While both are different, they have some similar practices, imagery, and gods. Modern practitioners reviving the traditions often identify themselves as Heathen, preferring a word more native to their traditions over the Latin word "Pagan." Those Heathens devoted to the sky gods known as the Aesir are known as Asatru, and those specifically dedicated to the god Odin are Odinist.

Odin

Norse majick is broadly divided into two main categories, seidr and galdur. In some ways, it's similar to the divide between the Norse gods. The gods fall into two tribes, the Vanir, who are considered more earthy and terrestrial, and the Aesir, the sky gods residing in the realm of Asgard.

We might compare it to the old gods and new gods of ancient Ireland, the Fomorians and the Tuatha De Dannan.

Freya

Seidr is the more feminine sorcery. Today, we associate it with shivering and shaking to enter into a shamanic trance, but it can include all manner of sorcery and nature majick and was associated with sex majick. While men could practice it, it was considered taboo. The Aesir god Odin learned Seidr, though Freya of the Vanir was considered its patron.

Freya is the "Lady" of the Vanir, with her brother, Freyr, the "Lord." She is a complex lady, for she can be both very kind and beneficial and also harsh and angry. You never know what you are going to get when you call upon her. She is associated with cats, much like the Egyptian goddess Bast, and cats are said to pull her chariot. She travels on her chariot through the sky, weeping for her lost husband. The tears that hit the ocean become amber, and the tears that strike the ground become gold. She is also associated with Venus, who is a goddess of love. Friday, the day of Venus, is Freya's day, though some say that day belongs to Frigga. Frigga is Odin's wife, and since Freya was his lover, they often get confused.

You can call upon Freya to help you with all forms of intuitive sorcery and sexuality. She is also a great protectress and will detect information for you that you need to know about. I also call upon her to help me when I'm traveling, particularly if I get lost driving around or wandering in the woods. She is the Lady of the Green Land.

Galdr is considered spoken or sung enchantments, including the runes. Runes are sounds as well as symbols, and together they each represent a mystery. According to Norse myth, Odin obtained the knowledge and power of the runes by hanging from the world tree, an ash tree called Yggdrasil, for nine days and nine nights. When he finished this sacrificial ritual, he gained their power and shared them with others.

Most popular among Witches and Pagans are the Elder Futhark set of Runes, made up of twenty-four symbolic powers. Runes can be put together in several different ways to create a spell. A single rune can be used in a spell to call upon its power. A series of runes can be written left to right to evoke all their power, and several runes can be combined into one shape, a bindrune, to unify their power. These symbols can be carried as a talisman or on a piece of jewelry, carved on candles or drawn on paper and placed beneath a candle spell, carved on wood, painted on stone, or even simply drawn in the air and visualized. Some Witches will empower commercial jewelry pieces with the runes upon them or have specific pieces custom made. Galdr teachings indicate it is also important to speak, chant, or sing the name of the rune to empower it.

Runes are also used in divination, like Tarot cards. Runes can be pulled out of a pack, arranged in a layout, or scattered upon a cloth and interpreted like cards or I-Ching, giving a general reading or answering a specific question. If you have a set of runes for divination, you can take out specific runes and place them upon your altar to evoke a majickal change in your life or use them in conjunction with other spellcraft.

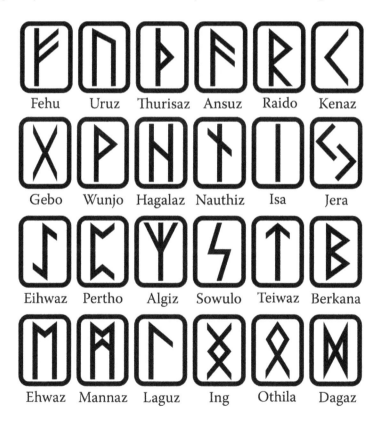

Runes

Rune Spells

Here are some effective combinations of runes that I use in majick:

Hagalaz – Othila = Protection, particularly protection of possessions.

Berkana – Wunjo = To increase the happiness and joy in your life

Fehu – Berkana – Kenaz = Increase prosperity

Fehu – Jera = Successful business or quick money

Laguz – Kenaz – Pertho – Algiz = Activate psychic abilities

Eihwaz – Raido – Ehwaz – Laguz = Psychic travel and astral projection

Algiz – Isa = Neutralize a situation

Ansuz – Teiwaz = Success in public speaking

Gebo – Wunjo – Ing = Blessings upon a relationship

Nauthiz – Raido – Mannaz = Connecting to the right person for the situation

Voodou Majick

One of the cultures I have a strong fascination with is the majick of Voodou and Santeria. A student once brought me back a piece of jewelry from Haiti depicting one of the *veves*, or symbols, of the *Lwa* (or Loa), the spirits of Voodou. That fueled my fascination for this very powerful and interesting tradition. It was syncretized with Catholicism, so many of the spirits are aligned with Catholic saints. Practices of Voodou and Santeria —popularized in American urban centers through shops known as botanicas, similar in many ways to early occult shops and our own Witchcraft shops—soon entered the practices of urban Witches and then became a part of modern American Witchcraft. New Orleans Voodoo and the folk majick tradition of Hoodoo continue to influence American majickal practices and are now making their way to Europe and Australia.

My other interest in African majick stems from my desire to honor the historical figure Tituba, slave and resident of Salem, and honor her African ways, though scholars today debate her ethnicity, questioning if she was part African and/or part Native American. I'm not sure we'll ever know for certain. It influenced me so much, I once dedicated a portion of my shop to Tituba. She had not been honored in our city at all, in any way, shape, or form. All the historic tourist displays write and talk about her, but none focus on her, how misunderstood she was, and how important she is. She teaches use how important it is to recognize and understand different cultures, from a time when people did not care about other cultures. So I decided to open a shop in her name. I painted a picture of her, drawing upon her spirit to guide me. I thought it was time for someone to give more attention to her story. We put the tale from her perspective down in the pamphlets in the store so tourists would know more than her name when they came to town.

Tituba

Voodou majick, or more properly African Diaspora majick, is from the traditions of both Haiti and New Orleans. There, two different but complementary strains of Voodou have emerged. Haitian Voodoo is more orthodox and hierarchical, while New Orleans style Voodoo, with a spelling that differentiates it from the more traditional spellings of Voodou, Vodou, and Vodoun, is more free-form and open. While Voodou is a mix of African and French Catholic practices centered through Haiti, Santeria is a mix of African and Spanish Catholic practices through Cuba. Rather than honor the Lwa, they honor similar spirits known as the Orisha. Similarities between the two have them often linked together, and while the religions are different, for the purposes of just the majick and spellcraft, they are brought together in this section of borrowed majick, as I've learned and practiced them myself.

The Lwa and Orisha are unique in our understanding of borrowed majick. Where most ancient Pagan religions recognized their spirits as gods, these African traditions have been syncretized with Catholicism, and therefore can't have any other gods beyond the Christian trinity of God the Father, God the Son and God the Holy Spirit. These spirits are not gods per se, but are unique to their tradition. Some describe them as gods archetypically, but most practitioners of the religions would be offended if these spirits were called gods. They are also compared to angels, saints, or ancestors, as they are often linked with saints, but that's not quite right either. Some humans can become Lwas, like the New Orleans Voodoo queen Marie Laveau, but not all Lwas were once human. Some Voodou practitioners recognize the iconography of other religions beyond Catholicism to represent their spirits. Some look at statues of Isis and see La Siren, a mermaid-like Lwa.

The Lwa and Orisha have very strong established traditions. Their lore includes what colors they prefer and what offerings of food, drink, and other trinkets are appropriate. They each have symbols, known as veves in Voodou, songs, and special days of the week. Some do not want to be placed next to each other as they don't get along. Often giving the wrong offering can be considered offensive, and difficult things can happen to the person making such an offering. Make sure to learn about the spirits you choose to work with, particularly if you plan on doing any long-term honoring of these particular groups of spirits.

Legba Spell

Tobacco

Corncob pipe

Red bag

Red ribbon

Coins

Legba's veve

Legba is the old man of the crossroads. His eyes are brighter than the stars. If you give him a gift of tobacco for his corncob pipe at the crossroads, he will work his majick for you. He can bring you good luck and good fortune, and send bad things elsewhere. He can raise you up from the depths to the heights. His other offerings include coins, rum, coffee, cane sugar, and cigars. He also appreciates a cane near his altar.

Place the veve of Legba in the red pouch, along with your offerings and tie it with the red ribbon. Go to the crossroads and say out loud:

Legba, Legba, Legba. I've brought you some money and a pipe. Please teach me and bless me.

He will always appreciate your gift. Though he works slowly, he works accurately. Give him the time to make changes in your life and teach you.

Legba's Veve

Coins to Oya

If you have an enemy and you are not sure who the enemy is, or you may have enemies but just don't know if you do, you can use this spell. You don't necessarily have to be under a curse, but the spell works to neutralize incorrect energies. You can tell when there are a lot of incorrect energies for you because things are just not going right. Oya is the Orisha who can stir things up, like a goddess of the storms. She stirs things up, sorts them out, and takes care of everything. She'll let you know who your enemies are.

I went to the Charter Street Cemetery in Salem, Massachusetts, where the old ancestors of Salem are. It was broad daylight, but I did not care. I felt the need to do this spell, and it had to be done in the graveyard. I got many stares that day by the tourists going by me. I took three pennies and tossed them into the graveyard chanting, "Oya, Oya, Oya. Let me know who my enemies are."

I got back into the car and people were still staring at me, mouths gaping open. Evidently they had never seen a Witch go into the graveyard to cast a spell. The very next day, a lightning storm grew and swept into Salem. A lightning bolt hit the Masonic Temple downtown, letting me know who was causing the imbalance in my life. The lightning was pink in color and was so bright and powerful that it caused all sorts of sirens and alarms to go off. With this knowledge of who was causing the problems, I could neutralize the energy, put up a stronger shield, and disassociate myself from this person. While I think we are perfectly capable of protecting ourselves and people really can't harm us, when your astrology is out of synch to your desires and intentions, as mine was at the time going through a tough Pluto transit, it can make you feel quite vulnerable.

Conclusion: Majick, Religion & Creation

All religion is about creation. Creation is never finalized. It is an eternal process. However, the Sun rises and sets without our assistance. Turning the Wheel of the Year is human as well as divine. We take an active part in the changing of the seasons. Witches are co-creators of the world. We transform energy into matter.

Witchcraft is becoming an integral part of the world-wide effort to make human life more responsive to the needs of the Earth. We are working spells of healing and cleansing to renew the world reserves. Let us touch the earth gently and heal nature. The Earth is a Witch's temple.

I have spent many many months in England gathering the power of my ancestors. I have brought to these shores that majick, both spiritual and physical. To stand on the Tor of Glastonbury, which is Avalon, and to cast a circle at Stonehenge have been both awakening and surprisingly natural. I am grateful to my Celtic Hwicce and Dobunni ancestors for keeping the Faery majick and Witchcraft alive and to all those "scholars" that fail to see that is not just the mist and the sound of the sea in a quiet country that leads one to believe in majick. It is all that and more, much more. It is a science, art, and a religion. Nothing in this world is supernatural; it is all natural. Witchcraft is a nature religion and path of life coming only from European tribes. As Witches we blend the energies of nature to promote healing, growth, and life. Our meditations and spells continue this practice. As followers of the old religion, art, and science, we use herbs, stones, metals, and the patterns of energy from the universe to keep the majick alive.

"It is only men who fear the curse of the Christians; the faery folk regard it not."
— *The Faery Faith in Celtic Countries* by TY Evanz Wentz. Citadel Press

About the Author

photo by Jean Renard

Laurie Cabot is a pioneer in the modern Witchcraft movement. As a teacher, author, and activist, she was one of the first to inform the public on who and what Witches are, and what they believe and practice, through many appearances on radio and television, including the *Oprah Winfrey Show*. She has championed the rights of Witches and Pagans through establishing the Witch's League for Public Awareness, and later Project Witches Protection, educating the media on inaccurate and demeaning portrayals of Witches and educating government representatives on the religious rights of Witches.

Residing in Salem, Massachusetts, Laurie has been a publicly active Witch, running several Witchcraft shops where she offered psychic readings, as well as hosting numerous classes and public rituals, including the first ever Salem Witch's Ball. She teaches "Witchcraft As A Science" to all, emphasizing meditation and psychic development, and established her own Cabot Tradition of Witchcraft. Former Governor of Massachusetts, Michael S. Dukakis, awarded her the Patriot Award for public service and declared her the "official Witch of Salem, Massachusetts." She later established the Cabot-Kent Hermetic Temple as a federally recognized religious organization for furthering the Witchcraft community and culture. She is the author of four other books, including the classic *Power of the Witch*. For more information, visit *www.lauriecabot.com*.

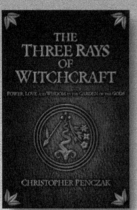

CPSIA information can be obtained
at www.ICGtesting.com
Printed in the USA
BVHW03s2325130518
515769BV00009B/104/P